Memory
of Trees

Memory of Trees

A DAUGHTER'S STORY OF
A FAMILY FARM

Gayla Marty

University of Minnesota Press
Minneapolis
London

The University of Minnesota Press gratefully acknowledges assistance provided for the publication of this book by the John K. and Elsie Lampert Fesler Fund.

Unless otherwise credited, illustrations are by Charles Edward Faxon and are from the Arnold Arboretum Library of Harvard University; copyright President and Fellows of Harvard College. Courtesy of Arnold Arboretum Archives.

Illustration of fig tree copyright Bobbi Angell

Published by the University of Minnesota Press
111 Third Avenue South, Suite 290
Minneapolis, MN 55401-2520
http://www.upress.umn.edu

Library of Congress Cataloging-in-Publication Data

Marty, Gayla.
    Memory of trees : a daughter's story of a family farm / Gayla Marty.
        p. cm.
    ISBN 978-0-8166-6689-8 (alk. paper) — ISBN 978-0-8166-6709-3 (pbk. : alk. paper)
1. Marty family. 2. Marty, Gayla—Homes and haunts. 3. Marty, Gayla—Childhood and youth. 4. Farmers—United States—Biography. 5. Farm life—Minnesota—Pine County—History—20th century. 6. Family farms—Minnesota—Pine County—History—20th century. 7. Journalists—United States—Biography. 8. Trees—Minnesota—Pine County. I. Title.
    S417.M355A3 2010
    630.9776′62—dc22
    [B]
                                                                    2009045646

Printed in the United States of America on acid-free paper

The University of Minnesota is an equal-opportunity educator and employer.

17 16 15 14 13 12 11 10   10 9 8 7 6 5 4 3 2 1

For Carolyn

Contents

As the Leaves Fell

The angel of the Lord encamps around
those who fear him, and rescues them.

—Psalm 34:7

The first of October is breezy, clouds scudding across the landscape southwest to northeast, broken by shafts of penetrating sun. The shadow of Gaylon's hat is deep in a stream of afternoon light as he drives a tractor in from the field, pulling two loaded box-wagons of chopped corn, the smell of wet greenness trailing behind. He sees the land now from the vantage point of Clyde's farmstead. Down the hill slightly to the east sits Jacob and Sam's fading red barn—his own fading red barn—now full of Clyde's hay. The burning colors of hardwoods and deep evergreens surround his house and his brother's, sketchy pastures lie north of the barns and south of the gravel road, and fields stretch to the railroad and highway and into the distance, broken by lines of hardwoods that follow the creek toward the St. Croix River.

Gaylon presses in the clutch, sets the brake, climbs down, and un-hitches the back wagon. He remounts and drives forward a hundred yards, sets the brake again, and climbs down to unhitch the front wagon, taking out the horizontal safety pin and pulling out the main pin. It lifts out easily, and the tongue drops to the side. He slips the pin back in the tractor hitch and inserts the safety.

As he stands up, the wagon, which has silently rolled down the grade, catches him sharply in the back. He feels something pop inside him. He is a man caught by surprise, though expecting it for years, caught by a piece of unfamiliar machinery on unfamiliar ground. It pins him by his torso against the hard rubber tread of the tractor tire. His arms fly forward to catch the lugs of the wheel; his cap falls to his shoulder. The box-wagon rebounds just as he is thinking the tractor will roll backward, that he must get out. In that second, he steps to the left and falls flat on the ground.

His face pressed to the earth, he thinks of the box-wagon, the green corn inside it, the weight of its corner against him, and the tread of the tire. Looking out over the surface of the earth, across the fields toward his house in the evergreens, he thinks of the wood smell of the house, its coolness inside. There is the last flash of a red-winged blackbird. Then he is blinded by a rupture of whiteness in his veins. He can't breathe and knows he will die. Soon he will be home to heaven.

Time passes. He doesn't want Clyde or Lorraine to find him here. There's a phone in Clyde's barn. He will call Lorraine, who is across the fields at home. He tries to push himself up but cannot. He pulls himself forward over the ground.

Slowly he drags himself up the grade to Clyde's barn, breathing in tiny sips of air. His head is bare in the sun and he is thirsty. Crossing the distance to the barn on his belly, he is met by the cool breath of the shadow of a speeding cloud.

At the milk house door, he looks up. The handle is so high. His forehead beads with sweat, and red blotches explode behind his eyelids.

Impossibly, he is entering the cool shade of the barn, entering the milk house, reaching for the black phone, dialing 358. Her voice comes low and lovely and professional: *Hello?*

For a moment he can't speak. She says hello again and he knows she will soon hang up.

"Lou," he breathes, his voice almost a whisper, a gasp.

"Gaylon?"

"Yes," he says with effort, a word for a sentence.

"Are you all right?"

There is a pause. She waits.

"Come quick," she hears him say. "I've been hurt bad."

"Are you still at Clyde's?"

"Yes."

"I'll come and get you."

"Yes."

He hangs up the phone and a veil of red heat falls over him, like water pouring over his scalp and down his neck. He puts his hands to his chest and feels nothing, an absence of sensation. Inside the cool milk house, breathless and watching, he waits.

Outside, the gravel is wide and warm. Across it, the shaded driveway is beckoning. There is a trail of dust as a car comes into view, turning, coming up the hill toward Clyde's driveway.

The accident happened almost as an anticlimax, after months—years for him—of the agony of selling the farm, of uncertainty, conflict, and heartache. The separation of our family from that particular body of land became manifest in his body, the body of my uncle.

I don't remember my mother's phone call but I must have been in the kitchen of my house in Minneapolis that Tuesday, the first of October. She spoke of his certain death. He had been at Clyde's, working on the farm that now included ours, and had been caught between a tractor and a wagonful of corn. He had been airlifted down to St. Paul Ramsey Hospital. He would probably not last the night.

It was pointless to go to the hospital, she said. Only immediate family could see him.

Aren't we immediate? I demanded.

No, my mother said, only spouse and children and siblings: my aunt Lorraine, my cousins Jonathan and Carolyn, and my uncle's younger brother—my father.

"Don't go," my mother finally said. "I just thought you should know, to prepare yourself."

I took in her words calmly, but she must have read the reason for my calm, correctly, as denial.

That night I couldn't sleep and lay listening to the sound of the trees, as I had so many nights that spring and summer. Their drying yellow leaves moved in the wind. The sound sharpened and masked the vibration of trains working in the rail yards across Monroe Street, masked the sound of Patrick breathing deeply beside me.

After a while, I sat up on the edge of the bed and opened the blinds to watch the branches of our elm tree sway in the light from the alley. Minutes passed, an hour passed. My shoulders ached. I lay back on my pillow and watched for glimpses of stars through the moving leaves.

Had Uncle died yet? Had his spirit departed this world he loved so much?

I felt myself disconnecting from all those things that keep you moored to daily existence: food, coffee, conversation. The world became only trees, wind, ground, and sky, the dome of turning stars that faded with the sliver of the old moon as the city turned toward the sun. Downriver, Uncle's still-living body was opened to assess the damage and begin the hours of repair as the stars reappeared and we faced again the outer universe.

The early October days and nights became a blur of impressions, vivid but unstrung: dazzling trees, a cool front of Canadian air passing through, days of highs in the sixties becoming days of highs in the fifties and then the forties, the golden daylight becoming sheer gray light and then black as I drive east from Minneapolis to St. Paul in darkness, heedless of the hospital's rules for visitors. Leaves fly across Interstate 94. I fling myself eastward and then off the freeway into a wide parking lot, into the round towers of modern medicine overlooking the city.

I enter the trauma center's well-lit hallways, a world without time. I am nearly running, blindly and on little sleep, a hard lump in my chest, overriding reason and regulation, sure they will stop me but determined nevertheless to close the gap between him and me, wondering if he might be conscious. Being there is all that matters, being within reach, being near him again at least once while he still breathes life, believing he will not rail against me or have the strength to question my faith but will accept my love despite the difference that has grown between us.

When I arrive at the station desk and say, "I'm here to see Gaylon Marty," the nurse asks only, "Your name?"

"I'm Gayla Marty," I say. She responds quickly and under her breath, "Oh, the daughter," as if embarrassed to have made a mistake, and points me to a room to the left. I walk where she points.

He lies semiconscious in a room with a dark window, his head and hands protruding from swaths of white, the respirator breathing for him in perfect rhythm, devices positioned around the bed and above him recording his functions.

"Uncle," I say softly, "it's Gayla."

His eyes flutter open briefly and then close, but the pupils move beneath his eyelids as in a dream, and the muscles around his mouth flicker a smile.

A nurse enters the room to check his monitors and IVs, speaking to him as she does.

"He can hear us," she says. She adjusts the valve on the IV bag.

"Can I touch him?"

"Sure," she says. "You can wash your hands and face there at the sink."

I take off my coat and roll up the sleeves of my flannel shirt, soap my face and hands with disinfectant, rinse, and then dry myself slowly. The nurse dims the light as she leaves, and suddenly the lights of the city outside become visible. I walk around the bed to the window and survey the landscape of St. Paul along the bend in the river. The sky is clear and a few stars manage to shine through the city glow.

Behind the silhouette of the farm the sky is the color of yellow roses — behind the black outline of the trees and the big barn, the pig and chicken houses, the empty corncrib, the arch-roofed brooder house, the gas tank under the oak tree in the middle of the farmstead. It's a Sunday evening in the middle of June. Daddy, Mama, and the baby twins and I have come home from church. I stand in the driveway facing the yellow sky. The windowpanes on the north side of the big house, Gramma's and Uncle and Auntie's house, reflect the sunlight and make it seem as if the house is blazing inside. Above the thick blackness of the woodshed and orchard is the white evening star; just south of it, the sliver of the new moon. The chilling air vibrates with a steady shriek of frogs and marsh life south of the road. As we stand beside the pearl-gray '57 Chev, mosquitoes rise up from the dewy grass and find our bare arms, my small bare legs. I hug myself in the cool air.

Uncle and Auntie's car approaches quietly. Its beams turn into the driveway beyond their house, emerge, and turn sharply across the lawn, illuminating us and the dancing insects. The yellow sky has lost its brilliance and the rest of the stars begin to assemble as I stand there. Daddy and Mama are lifting the sleeping twins out of the car, up the back steps, onto the porch. Uncle and Auntie get out of their car but Uncle stays outside, standing by his house, hands on the hips of his church pants, surveying the sky as I am while the others go inside the houses. A streak of purple-blue appears in the western sky.

"D'you see the dippers?" Uncle asks. His voice carries easily across the yard. I turn to face the north and search above the windmill and pump house where I know the dippers should be. I see the big one first, hanging low above the woods a quarter mile away, and then the little one, above it to the left and upside down.

"Yes," I answer.

"Can you find the North Star?" he asks.

I connect the dots on the outside of the big dipper's cup, as he has taught me, and extend my imaginary line to a bright star.

"Yes," I say. He has told me this is the star that sailors and travelers use, that the slaves looked for when escaping in the night.

I hear him say *Yuh* softly, sucking in his breath, as he does when he admires beautiful things. I sit down on the back steps of our house, pulling my hem down to my ankles to cover my legs, and admire the sky with Uncle Gaylon. We survey the Milky Way, arching over the fields of our farm east of the zenith, south toward the little lights of town. The yellow in the sky has turned to a deep green fading into inky blue-black. We are surrounded by sound and light: the sound of frogs and crickets and now and then the piercing cry of a killdeer or a snipe, and the light of stars.

I push the chair closer to his hospital bed. Sitting there, resting my head against the side rail, I reach through and stroke his familiar forehead, the olive skin, the creases from weather, the black hair, the familiar hairline and heavy brows. In spite of the awkwardness of the stretch, I begin to relax, and then to cry.

During those first days and nights he survived, I don't remember talking to anyone—Auntie or Daddy or my cousins, Jon and Carolyn. Carolyn is the real daughter; she looked enough like me that we could be confused. Of course they were all there. We must have sat together in one of those windowless rooms with incandescent lamps and couches, those rooms made for comfort and privacy in the midst of trauma for meetings of families forced together by tragedy, ours a farm accident, theirs a gunshot wound, theirs an uncanny fall. I can dimly see faces: Auntie Lou's heart-shaped face as she looks up from one of the couches; Carolyn's young face, pale and expressionless as we pass near the elevators; Jon's unshaven face and haunted look, his sloping shoulders; the vertical crease in my father's forehead; my mother's smooth whiteness of skin and hair blending into the whiteness of the walls and floors and shining countertops. And newspapers: news of the Twins beating

Chicago; Minnesota versus Toronto in the playoffs; Gorbachev outlining arms cuts; and places to view peak colors of the sugar maples and red oaks and birch before howling winds strip them bare.

But when I enter Uncle's room overlooking St. Paul, I leave the world of impressions. I enter a coherent, tangible space, sharp and condensed, like the beam of the North Star on a moonless night.

I

ATTACHMENT

1

Light

God said, "Let there be lights in the firmament
of the heaven to divide the day from the night,
and let them be for signs and for seasons and
for days and years."

—Genesis 1:14

Nrth, east, south, west. North is the barn, east are the fields,
south is our road, west is Gramma's house.

The barn is red with a dark green roof and three cupolas
on top.

The fields are green, brown, and yellow, different shades and tex-
tures, beginning in the spring with earth, which is light brown where it
is sandy, dark brown in the low flat places, almost black when it is wet.

The road is brown and straight and flat, except at the east end
where it rises up to the railroad tracks and highway.

Gramma's house is white with a dark green roof. Between our
house and Gramma's are the swing tree, the butternut tree, and beside
the path, two apple trees.

Milking morning and night in the barn. Cows, black and white, with
huge heads and beautiful names: Caroline, Debbie, Dixie, Dorothy,
Freckles, Speckles, Grace, Ginny, Jessica, Joan, Nellie, Millie, Molly,
Maude, Linda, Liza, Lizzie, Pam, Penny, Polly, Tina, Topsy.

The rhythm of milkers, hish-*hish*, hish-*hish*, hish-*hish*, the rhythm
of rubber cups pulling milk from the soft bags of the patient, chewing
cows, hish-*hish*, hish-*hish*. All their milk, fifteen, twenty, thirty pounds
of it, morning and night, going into a stainless steel milker, emptied
steaming into stainless steel milk cans, the cans set in cold waiting
water in the little milk house, cooling the milk until it's taken to town.

North, east, south, west. North is the pasture behind the barn and the
lane along the fence that leads the cows to the woods. East are the

railroad tracks and highway. South is town, three miles away. You can see the white towers of the mill across the swamp and fields. West is Gramma's house, which is also Uncle and Auntie's; just beyond it is the woodshed, then the orchard, then the creek flowing under the road into the swamp. In springtime the creek is swollen, the swamp turns into a lake a quarter-mile wide.

I sleep with the twins in the southeast bedroom. They have two cribs but they jerk them together across the hardwood floor to sleep together in one. In the summer, the marsh sounds come in the open windows all night under the shifting, sheer white curtains. In the middle of the night, the sound of the train comes across the fields from the east in a minor key, like a blast of harmonica.

The rhythm of milking, twice a day, morning and night, Daddy and Uncle milking twenty-six cows. They hunker down beside each cow, one by one, wash her teats and bag, throw a milking strap over her back, adjust the metal brace to hang free beneath her belly, hang the stainless steel milker on the metal brace, push the black rubber hose from the top of the milker onto the air line, open the valve. They lift four rubber-lined cups from the milker to the teats, and the rhythmic sucking begins. They squat beside adjacent cows, each with a hand on an udder, waiting to feel the milk let down and hear the first streams hitting the bottom of the empty milker. As they milk, they talk.

I stand in the middle aisle, petting the faces of cows, silent to avoid startling the wide-eyed nervous ones as I parade between their rows of long, strong faces. I stand still before Jessica and Caroline, my favorites. I dip a handful of yellow feed from the feedbox and hold it out to Jessica, feel her giant tongue wipe it clean from my palm.

With a stick, I clean hay out of the drinking cup beside each cow. Cats come out, waiting for milk: gray tiger-striped cats and cats the color of caramel, a black and white cat with long hair, a white cat called Summer.

Daddy and Uncle's voices rise and fall, Daddy's less clear and less often than Uncle's. Uncle's laugh is like a waterfall, Daddy's like a slow creek in summer. Behind their voices the rhythm of the milkers, hish-*hish*, hish-*hish*, hish-*hish*.

Winter, spring, summer, fall. Snow, mud, heat, dry leaves.

The barn in winter is a warm nest, a suitable place for baby Jesus, banked with hay and straw, close with the breath of twenty-six cows, huge oak beams low overhead supporting the haymow above. In spring, it is muddy and slick, cold with air coming in and going out as the cows do, eager to move after weeks inside. In summer, the air is heavy with the smell of milk, the steam from cows' heaving bodies, the heat of the day itself, even early in the morning. In fall, the barn smells of new hay and silage, strong and green, entire stalks and corncobs chopped to bits and blown into the silo at the east end of the barn.

Winter, spring, summer, fall. Silence, then birdsong, then crickets and frogs, then dry leaves falling, blowing, turning across the ground.

Waking in summer, we hear not only birds, robins, thrushes, red-wings, and larks, but the rhythm of the milkers, hish-*hish*, hish-*hish*, from the open doors of the barn. In the daytime, we sometimes hear a *moo* from the pasture. Before supper, we hear the sound of Uncle or Daddy calling the cows home, *C'm baaaaaaas!*

In winter, as I am carried by Daddy to the barn, the black night is silent except for his squeaking footsteps, left, right, left, right. Only when he opens the door to the silo room can we hear the rhythm of milking that leaks out with the line of light beneath the inner door. Then the inner door opens and we enter an envelope of warmth and light and sound, hish-*hish*, hish-*hish*, hish-*hish*. Twenty-six heads turn in unison to see who has arrived. Between two stanchions, I see the flash of Uncle Gaylon's smile.

Uncle is the oldest, has the middle name John, Grampa's name, and lives in the big house.

Daddy is the youngest, has the middle name Samuel, his uncle's name, and lives with us in the house that Samuel built, fifty steps straight east of the big house.

Uncle is joyful, Daddy is comfortable. Both can sing, and Daddy can whistle like a warbling bird, though it was Uncle who taught me how to whistle, riding to town in the truck with him one day, inspired by a red-winged blackbird.

Daddy doesn't talk much, just glances over at me once in awhile and smiles, lets me mind my own business if I stay where he can see me.

Uncle greets me in a large voice, asks questions, laughs out loud, explains tasks, tells stories and history.

In the spring, Uncle swings me into the wheelbarrow and bounces me off to plant the garden, narrating the whole time. He marks the rows with a string on a set of stakes, pulls a furrow the right depth with the V-hoe, sets in the seeds and then lets me do it, checking my work and diplomatically correcting me, praising when I get it right, then watering the row and covering it up and patting it down with the rectangle hoe, teaching me how to tamp it down with my feet.

Spring, summer, fall, winter.

In spring, leftover plowing, disking, dragging fields to be seeded; planting huge fields of corn, seeding two or three fields of oats, seeding alfalfa on fields tired from corn. A hundred-and-forty acres prepared. Clover blooming, fragrant with dew.

In summer, haying begins, the first green bales stacked onto the floor of the haymow. Young corn emerges from the brown and black fields. A pale green fur of oats springs up. Cultivating cornfields once, sometimes twice, coaxing the sprouts to knee-high by the fourth of July, we hear their leaves begin to make a rustling sound in the breeze. On very hot still days, we think we can hear their thousands of stalks and leaves growing.

The oats become tall and slender and gray-green, then their whispering stalks turn to yellow and are mowed down, gathered into bundles, shocked to stand like teepees drying in the fields.

The second crop of hay begins, tractors go back and forth between the barn and the fields—empty wagons out, full wagons in. I am riding held tight against Daddy's chest. It is hard or impossible to speak above the noise of the tractor, and the road is a blur beneath us. Tiger lilies blaze in the ditches. Daddy downshifts at the elm tree by our driveway but goes past it, the sound echoing off the houses as we pass. He brakes, we slow and turn at the big driveway of the big house. Daddy guides the tractor in and up the driveway, past Uncle and Auntie and Gramma's house. The exhaust pipe putts as we go down the slope again, under the oak tree by the gas barrel, past the chicken coop and granary and garages, around the curve past the milk house, behind the log barn, carefully into the wide-open doors of the big barn's driveway, between the haymows. The sound is deafening, then the tractor stops suddenly. There is a rustle and flapping of wings in the rafters, a pigeon or an owl.

Threshers come for the oats with their noisy machine, unbundling the shocks field by field, chaff flying. Oats pour into the bins of the granary north of our house, where hollyhocks bloom pink and red. The gold straw of the oats is baled and stacked in the old log barn, between the red barn and the milk house.

In the cornfields, the tall stalks tassel and the ears sprout long, sticky strands of silk. The smell of corn is strong in the hot air, day and night, mixing with the smell of warm milk around the barn. The clover and timothy keep blooming and the layers of hay bales mount under the rafters of the barn. The men's backs glisten as they stack bales onto racks in the fields and unload them in the hot barn. Mama and Auntie's arms turn brown from driving tractors. The corn dents— when you pull back the leaves of a cob, the yellow kernels have dimpled and hardened.

The first chill of September comes and chopping begins. Corn taller than men falls before the chopper, is pulled in wagons to a loud blower fitted with tubes that send it into the empty silo, thirty-two feet high, just higher than the peak of our barn. The fields lie shorn and clear as the silo fills, the noise of the blower going late into the night. The men wear jackets, gloves, and hats and use the single light on the tractor, plus the light of the moon if the timing is right.

The third crop of hay is baled on warm fall days until the first hard freeze kills it. The rest of the standing corn turns yellow and pale and begins to dry in the wind, rustling like paper. In October and November, the tractor goes out with the corn picker, plucking cobs from stalks and hauling them in boxed wagons to be unloaded by a noisy, narrow elevator into two slatted corncribs, bright yellow showing between the red boards. In the fields, pale stalks are left half-standing or crushed on the frozen ground.

The driveway through the barn is silent and cool, a restored home to the wilder cats, some nursing kittens conceived in summer. Standing on the stone floor under a single bare bulb thirty feet above, you can hear the milking rhythm on the east end, heifers and dry cows shifting in their stanchions on the west end, the giant sliding doors north and south shuddering in the wind, but all the sounds are muffled by banks of dark gray-green bales crammed to the roof.

All winter, hay is thrown down from the mows, bale by bale, separated and spread out loose in the mangers for the cows and heifers. Silage is thrown down twice a day from the silo, served to the cows before milking. Truckloads of ear corn, dried by the wind through the slats of the cribs, and sacks of oats from the granary are taken to town to be ground into dry feed for cows, pigs, and chickens. Straw bales are pulled from the log barn and spread out for bedding for the animals.

I am tiny on the driveway floor, but Daddy and Uncle do not seem much bigger. Toward the end of milking, Uncle comes out of the stanchion room, sets me on a hay bale in the far corner of the driveway, climbs up a ladder until he is even smaller, and then disappears into the mow.

I hear his voice exclaiming "Oh, oh! This hay smells so good!"

He goes on, "Smell that hay, oh my! Oh, I love that, yessir. Thank you God for this good hay!"

And then the bales come sailing down, tiny rectangles that loom overhead and suddenly bounce onto the straw-covered stone floor, bales longer than me and five times as fat. Two, five, ten bales, enough for the night and part of the next morning. Then Uncle's face reappears, he swings out around the ladder and descends, growing slowly to life-size again as he reaches the floor. Immediately, he opens the wooden panels in the wall to the west end of the barn — the old horse stable — rips the double strands of twine off a bale of hay, breaks it apart, and spreads the sections up and down the manger, fluffing them out as he goes.

"Yum yum! Eat that good hay, bossies!" Uncle says.

Spring, summer, fall, winter.

Spring. The apple trees between the houses bloom, and the plum tree blooms in the lane by the woods. Daddy brings some blooming branches in the house, Mama sets them in a vase, and the whole house is filled with perfume. Daddy and Mama take the storm windows off, put the screen windows back, and the wet outdoor smells fill the house. We are raking all the grass around the houses, burning the leaves, cultivating the garden, a rectangle of brown in the yard between our house and the milk house. Mama uncovers her strawberries. Uncle and Daddy help plant the garden: peas, lettuce, radishes, green beans, tomatoes, sweet corn, cucumbers, onions, dill, carrots, beets, squash.

Mama plants and weeds flowerbeds: gladiola bulbs stored in the garage all winter, pink and magenta cosmos, spidery cleomes, blue bachelor buttons, snapdragons every hot color, and spikes of holly-hocks by the granary. In the garden by our house, she prunes the yellow rosebush, divides the purple iris, plants flats of pansies and petunias. Against the red woodshed, Gramma plants zinnias. The trees bud: oak, elm, maple, ash, butternut, birch.

In June we eat salad and sit under the ash tree, shelling washtubs of peas until the skin by our thumbnails is tender. In July we pick beans almost every morning and snap off the stems. In August we pick sweet corn, tomatoes, and cucumbers. All summer Mama and Gramma freeze and can: peas and beans and corn, tomatoes and pickles, and store-bought plums, pears, and peaches. Gramma goes to the woods with sisters and friends to pick blackberries, black raspberries, and wild plums to make jam and jelly. The best jelly comes from sour crab apples off a tree in our yard by the road. In September we pick apples and make pies to feed the men who chop corn.

As the leaves fall, we pull up carrots and beets and onions and take in the squash. Mama washes the storm windows and the windows in the sashes, inside and out. Daddy puts them on, and we see clearly again the bare trees and edges of things outdoors.

All winter we eat and empty the boxes from the freezer and the jars from the shelves in the basement kept behind a soft, blue, cotton curtain.

Breakfast: cereal, milk, sugar, cream, eggs fried in butter, toast, more milk to drink.

Dinner: beef, potatoes, gravy, bread, vegetables, milk, and dessert.

Supper: pancakes, French toast, or macaroni in the winter; sweet corn, sandwiches, or macaroni in the summer; milk to drink.

God is great, God is good, let us thank him for our food, by his hand we must be fed, give us, Lord, our daily bread. Bless us. Amen.

Mama is always in motion. She moves quickly, focusing always on her task, several tasks at once, speaking directly, her mind ten steps ahead.

"In a minute," she says, "as soon as I'm finished with this."

"I'm busy right now, just a minute."

Time is measured in minutes, even seconds, on the kitchen clock on the chimney, a white and yellow clock with a sweeping, red second hand. Mama is busy.

Mama loves a clean house and having company. From the time before we get up until after we go to bed, she is baking bread, baking something for church, washing dirty clothes in the basement, hanging clean wet clothes on the line, cooking, washing dishes, sweeping, mopping, dusting, wiping cupboard doors and walls, scrubbing sinks, getting ready for company. In the evenings she practices songs for church, does the payroll for the school, irons, sews a dress for me. On Saturday nights she listens to the radio—the Grand Ole Opry or, in the summer, a baseball game.

Winter, spring, summer, fall. In winter, all the animals stay inside—cows, pigs, chickens, cats.

In spring, the pigs farrow and the wild birds build nests. Gramma hatches baby chicks under a huge umbrella lamp in the brooder house west of the chicken coop.

In summer, all the animals roam outside, chickens around their coop, pigs in their pen, cows in the pasture behind the barn and up the lane, through our acres of woods.

Gramma takes me into the chicken coop to help her gather eggs, even though I'm too short to reach the top shelves. Her hands have become too stiff to grasp them securely. It's warm, a golden place inside, with sun streaming through the many-paned windows to the south, yellow straw spread across the cement floor, overflowing from the chickens' roosting boxes.

The chickens are big white puffs with beaks, lurching and squawking suddenly. They scare me at first, but Gramma assures me while also warning not to reach toward any in their boxes or they might peck me. She points with her awkwardly bent hand toward the empty boxes I should check and I hoist myself up from a wooden stool to feel inside the highest ones, lifting out the white eggs.

"Careful not to break them," she says softly. "Only one at a time for now."

I place each one into a wire basket she's set on the floor.

Gramma spreads the chicken feed into the tiny wooden troughs to distract them as I gather eggs. Chickens in their boxes stand up and descend to the floor with a couple of big flaps of their wings.

Soon I am warm from the bright sun and from reaching, from the shock of grabbing an egg full of greasy manure, from the stress of being careful.

"Wipe it on the straw," Gramma instructs patiently. I wipe, steel myself against the texture and smell, climb back up on the stool to reach into the next box.

By the time I'm done, two eggs lie broken and oozing in the straw. I think the chickens must be angry at my clumsiness with their precious produce.

"That's all right," Gramma says. Although I know she thinks it's a shame, she's also grateful for my help. "Now it's just the water left. Here, toss this old water out, outside the door, and tip the pail to fill it again."

I empty the bowls and fill them with fresh water brought from the pump, splashing some on my hands to clean them.

When I see the look on Gramma's face, glancing at me, I realize I am grimacing.

At farrowing time, Daddy and Uncle take turns getting up to check the sows, sometimes staying out all night. They are tense because sows are unpredictable and can eat their whole priceless litter in a rage or lie on them in negligence. If a newborn pig doesn't suckle immediately, it can die of exposure and loss of rank. Horrible squeals emanate from the pig house. In the mornings, Daddy sits bone-tired and strong-smelling at the breakfast table, disappointed or relieved.

We are not allowed to go into the pig house alone in any season, in case we should fall over the side of a pen and be trampled. But if the litter is good, Daddy or Uncle takes the twins and me very quietly to see the rich-smelling baby pigs suckling from their mother, whose side heaves with her breathing. We must not make a sound or quick movement. The little pigs are perfectly pink and identical, with soft-looking ears and wrinkled noses. Sometimes there is a pig with black spots, and this is even more precious.

Even the tame cats often hide in the haymow to have their kittens. When they bring out their kittens, Uncle Gaylon shows us how to hold them, how to pick them up as their mother does very gently by the skin and fur on the backs of their necks, how to pet them softly while sitting on the hay so their mother can see them, how to set them down right next to their mother.

Some of our cats are so wild we rarely see them. The twins and I are forbidden to hunt for or touch newborn kittens until the mother brings them out from their birthplace and their eyes open, because newborn kittens handled by humans may be abandoned.

When robins build a nest on the ledge above the corn-crib door, Uncle Gaylon climbs up with the twins and me, one at a time, to show us the wonder of the sky-blue eggs. But we must not touch them under any circumstance. Wild birds are like wild cats: if they smell our smell on their young, even on their eggs, they may desert them. Also, they might attack us.

North, east, south, west.

North is the woods, where the cows pasture in the summer, making magical paths. We use the paths to find them and search for new calves.

East are the railroad tracks and highway, and beyond them, Gramma and Grampa Anderson's, Uncle Duane and Aunt Judy's, Aunt Doris and Uncle Bob's, Rock Creek, the Hendricksons', and church.

South is town, where feed is ground, milk cans are unloaded and returned sparkling clean, tools and groceries are bought, where Auntie works.

West is where the sun sets and floods the sky with brilliant colors, orange, red, and yellow, green just before blue, the color of Mama's ink.

At night, Mama sits at the dining room table and works for the school. She writes names and numbers in columns and rows in heavy books. She makes an adding machine go, clicking on numbers that her fingers know by heart, pulling a lever, making a scroll of white paper come out with rows and rows of blue and pink numbers, clicking and pulling as we lie in the dark. She writes with a fountain pen that she fills with blue ink, her gripping hand flying across the yellow page, leaving blue behind, the point making a hollow, scratching sound on the paper. She writes us to sleep.

Inside our house, outside our house, we are surrounded by people we love, people who love us. They are not too close and don't talk too much, just enough. Mama usually in or near the house; Daddy and Uncle usually outside, in the barn or the field; Gramma Marty in or near her house; and Auntie Lou in her house in the evenings, sometimes visiting ours.

Auntie works at the hospital switchboard, so she's gone during the day. She leaves and comes home in a mint-green uniform with a cardigan sweater slung over her shoulders, white shoes, lipstick and nail polish, chewing gum. She brings gifts of notepads and nurses' lotion, little packs of tissues and soaps.

North, east, south, west. North is where the ducks and geese fly in spring, toward Canada. East is the St. Croix River, the place the water goes after it joins Rock Creek. South is where the ducks and geese and almost all the other birds fly in fall, where it's warm all year, beyond the cities of St. Paul and Minneapolis. West is the Mississippi River, flowing south and east toward the cities, toward the place it meets the St. Croix, making a water road for ducks and geese and small birds to follow to the ocean.

Often in the summer I wake up when Daddy gets up for morning chores. As the light slowly comes, I hear the mourning dove in a white pine by Uncle and Auntie and Gramma's house, and then the chirrup birds, robins mostly, and then the red-winged blackbirds in the marsh and ditches with their long, melodic warble. The sun is coming up across our fields just south of the woods, behind the tracks and the highway and the Tillmans', shining directly on the shade in the east window of our room.

I get up quietly, dress without waking the twins, and slip through the kitchen and out the back door, where the sound of milking pulses from the barn along with the soft blare of a radio. The sun rising across the wet fields of clover and alfalfa and corn too small to whisper makes the grass in the yard and the plants in the garden glitter. It lights up the east side of the big house to a golden-white color, the color of milk. I see a flash of movement through the screen of Auntie's kitchen window, her glasses and watch and rings reflecting the light as she drinks a cup of coffee before leaving for work.

I walk on the gravel because it's warm and dry, looking for agates. Uncle is teaching me how to find them, training my eye to spot small blood-colored stones in the dusty tan gravel. I walk onto the road under the arching branches of the elm at the corner of our driveway, its new leaves draping down almost to my reach. I walk slowly east, toward the highway, between our fields on my left and the neighbor's marsh on my right.

As I reach down to pick up a tiny glint of reddish brown in the gravel, an agate half the size of my fingernail, a redwing flies over the road above my head and lights on the telephone wire, calling in quick succession, *Look at me, look at me!* I stop and look. The red on his wings is completely exposed above stripes of yellow on black. He is diverting me. I take a few more steps and he flies ahead of me, lighting a little farther down the line, calling, calling, calling, barely pausing between each trill in his throat.

One more agate and I will turn around.

I look down and begin searching but the redwing flies again, low to the ground and within my peripheral vision. He screams in alarm, then swoops back up to the wire.

I turn around. The redwing follows me, lighting along the wire as I go, chasing me and then calling less frequently, finally returning to a fencepost along the south side of the road.

Nearing the driveway, I see Uncle Gaylon standing in the east door of the barn, looking out over the fields, planning his day. He is deciding what needs attention this day, haying or cultivating or fencing or something else. He and Daddy have specialties. Uncle does more fieldwork, although there are some types of fieldwork Daddy is especially good at, such as cutting hay.

One morning Daddy comes in from mowing hay, shaken, his eyes watering, his forehead drawn into a knot between his brows, shaking his head *no* almost imperceptibly. He has hit a mother duck, a female mallard. He didn't see her until it was too late, she blended in so well. He always tries to look ahead of the sickle, suspended straight out past the right rear tire of the tractor, but this time he missed. In the face of danger, the deadening vibration of the tractor, its interminable approach, her instinct chose fight over flight and she stayed stubbornly with her nest. Suddenly there was a fierce flapping right above the sickle and as he hit the brakes, her brown body rose, lifting her up and then turning south, across the road to the water, but it was too late.

Beneath the sickle, her nest of spotted white eggs appeared in the grass, and her yellow feet, still there.

North, south, east, west.

The sun rises in the east, facing our house, and sets in the west, facing the big house. In spring and fall it rises and sets at the opposite ends of our road. But in winter it rises in the southeast, by Art Eiffler's, and sets in the southwest, by Art Anderson's. In the summer it rises in the northeast, on the east end of our woods, and sets past Clyde's.

In the northern sky are the North Star and the big and little dippers. In the south is Orion, marching east to west across the night.

At dark, the moon can appear anywhere. When it's big it rises in the east above the fields as the day ends, and sets in the west, over the woodshed in the morning. When it's half full, it appears at the top of the sky as darkness falls. When it's a sliver in the morning in the east, it's an old moon, about to disappear. If it's a sliver in the evening in the west, the moon is new.

Elm

Elm trees, I think you are a hundred feet high. You are like giant fountains — from far away, you look as if you are spouting from the earth and then spraying gracefully down. From underneath, in the summer, I stand in the cool pool of your shade with the rustle and sparkle of moving light like water all around. Your leaves are shaped like lopsided shadows of tiny fat canoes, with edges of tiny saw teeth. I think you each have a million leaves.

Our farm has many elms, but three stand out. First is the one that stands over the driveway to our house, welcoming visitors arriving from the highway. You make our small house as grand as the big house next door, which is surrounded by pine trees and oaks. Once, the highway was a dirt road along the railroad, and visitors came to the farm in wagons pulled by horses or oxen. Now they come in cars and trucks that stir your leaves as they pass by. In May, you spread a carpet of flat round seeds on the gravel, and then your leaves come out. Your roots go into the ditch, in a place where water stands every spring, near Mama's raspberry bushes. Your leaves drape down, but not far enough that I can touch them. You are a little reserved, your grooved gray bark a tower.

Second is the elm that stands behind the barn, over the entry to the lane. You stand at the southeast corner of the pasture and cascade almost to the ground — I can touch your sawtooth leaves and pull them down to me. You make an archway over the double row of tire tracks that head north along the pasture fence and then turn east to the woods.

Your roots are in a low spot, the last soft place behind the barn to dry out in the spring.

The third elm is not really on our farm. You are east and across the road to the south, along the curving creek that starts on the west end of our farm and wanders into a wide marsh before coming back on our east end. You stand alone in our neighbor Art Eiffler's pasture, taller than anything in that wide-open place, like a vase of flowers. I can see you from almost anywhere on our farm. In the summer, your shade forms a small dark spot in the wide pasture, where Art's cows meet for shelter from the sun and a drink from the creek.

"Why was that tree spared?" Uncle Gaylon wonders.

He thinks you are a survivor of fires that once swept through here. He thinks you may have been a council tree, because that's what elm trees were in the old days, before the settlers came. He has no memory of it himself, but his father and uncle told him about the Indians that passed through the east side of our farm, camped there, and traded with our family. Elm tree, were you a marker of theirs? Why didn't the railroad cut you down when it cut down everything else in a swath on either side?

Elm wood is not good for building. It was used for things like wagon wheels and machinery and work floors. Long ago, its bark made canoes. Elms grew along creeks where fields ended. They were spared because there was better wood for most things, because they weren't in the way, and because they were beautiful.

I will press you, little sawtooth elm leaf that once hung in a rippling strand low enough that I could reach you. You came from the tree that stands at the head of the path to the lane, the wide, generous, draping elm.

Underneath you, I feel enchanted, like a girl in a story. As I set off for the woods in the soft weedy ruts, you bless me. As I come back, you welcome me home and mark the border of safety.

2

Things of the Spirit

Shadrach, Meshach, and Abednego fell down bound into the midst
of the burning fiery furnace. Then Nebuchadnezzar the king was
astonished, and rose up in haste and said, "Did not we cast three
men bound into the midst of the fire? . . . Lo, I see four men loose,
walking in the midst of the fire, and they have no hurt, and the form
of the fourth is like the Son of God."

—Daniel 3:23–25

The smell of smoke is carried on the warmest drafts of air through
the dark shelves of the general store—shelves of flour, coffee,
beans, ribbon, soap, brown paper, jugs of yellow cider, bolts of
twine. The scales are still, the movement of air too subtle to detect. Cur-
rents of November cold pass through narrow spaces under the doors
and around the windowpanes. It is a Christian store, no tobacco, no
fermented beverages, and the dance hall upstairs has been converted
into homes for the storekeeper's family—nine children from ten months
to fifteen years—and three smaller families. All are now asleep, warm
in their beds, braced for the winter ahead. Husbands and wives and
children lie side by side in positions of care, care for a child, care for a
task left undone, care for a loved one far away, in St. Paul or Chicago or
somewhere in France, coming home now that the war is done, care lest
a last stray bullet has cheated justice.

Thin toes of warmed air rise through the ceiling of the sleeping
store, through the floorboards of the rooms above. They dance across
the floor, gliding silently from room to room beneath closed doors and
around the legs of beds and chairs and tables. Flames somewhere below
are now crackling. Fed by gentle but persistent drafts, the smoke grows
bolder.

In one of the rooms above a child cries out *Mama! Mama!* A woman
half wakens and soothes her. Then a boy wakens and sorts through
his dream of sun-warmth and fishing, of his mother cooking fish at a
hot stove, of the smoky fried taste of it, sorting that dream from the

darkness of his room, the coldest room, at the top of the stairs. Then he is fully awake, listening. Someone is down in the store, moving things.

No, it is not the sound of anything human.

The boy's reflexes snap, his body springs smoothly to action, feet filling his too-small shoes and then moving into room after room, waking his sisters, his parents, the Andersons, the Lindstroms, the French family at the end. They pull blankets off the beds around themselves and flee into the hallway, down the stairs, carrying babies and panicked small children out into the cold night. Across the street they begin to gather, counting, naming. Mama, the baby, Julia, Ethel, Viola, Amy, Della, Effie, Laura. The Andersons and their two children. The Lindstroms and theirs. The French husband and wife and two daughters. They huddle together watching as flames appear inside the windows of the store.

The boy and his father, the owner of the store, are still somewhere inside, trying to put out the flames, trying to save things, but it's too late. Goods light up like torches, then something explodes. Outside, the babies are crying and a girl cries out *Papa! Reynold! Reynold! Ray!*

Faces appear in the upper windows of neighboring stores along the main street. Lamps are lit and men and women hastily dressed emerge from their houses and shops to help. Ice is broken on the edge of the creek and a line is formed to pass water up by buckets. A team of horses is harnessed to pull water up more quickly in drums, joined quickly by another team, working in tandem. Men and boys, women and big girls, all hoist buckets and drums of icy water against the flames, then douse the roofs and buildings on either side.

The store is like a fiery furnace in the night, lighting the shocked faces of children and mothers, casting its heat across the gravel street, roaring like an unearthly beast from the Revelation of John. Black outlines of rafters and shelves, beds and ceilings appear through the flames like bones of a corpse. They buckle and collapse, and cinders fly into the night. One of the women begins to weep. The girl repeats her brother's name: *Ray, Ray, please Ray.* The children watch their father's store, all the precious unsold goods inside, their home with beds and simple clothes and toys, burning bright through the night.

My grandmother tells me this story, lying in the warm soft bed of her upstairs bedroom on our farm, two miles south of the village of Rock

Creek, where the fire happened. Not a soul among the families who lived above the store was lost, and for that they praised God, although they lost everything else.

"We didn't even have shoes," Gramma says, remembering her freezing bare feet as she stood in the street with her sisters, watching all their father's wealth and their own, food and clothing and dolls, burn before their eyes.

To my grandmother, the fire was an article of faith. She and her sisters and brother and parents and their renters had seen hell and been spared. They were Christians, no strangers to the image of fire: raining down on the evil cities of Sodom and Gomorrah; delivered from the sky to devour the sacrifice of Elijah before the prophets of Baal; in a furnace heated to seven times its limit, but Daniel's friends emerging, hair unsinged; and the lake of fire, where all those souls whose names are not written in the book will be cast on the last day.

After the store burned, when they sat in the little white clapboard church east of town, surrounded only by birdsong and a breeze, a sudden rush of wind alone could ignite the memory. The creek near the church became the link back to town, to the breaking of ice, the whinny of horses racing up the hill, the yell of shopkeepers and craftsmen straining as they worked the sharp line between cold and heat. Hearing the Bible story of Daniel's friends, they didn't have to imagine the blast of the fiery furnace. That miracle became their own. In my grandmother's testimony, the fire was lit and burned again and again, without mercy: only God, who had spared them, was merciful. Baptism became more than a symbol of death and rebirth of the spirit—it became a passing through water, a quenching of fire.

They sat in worship or prayer at East Rock Creek Baptist, reduced to nothing but each other, their own tender flesh and hair and smiles, and their Christian friends and extended family. They sang *Jesus saves! Jesus saves!* They sang *Praise God from whom all blessings flow* and were each other's blessings.

I sit in the same church forty-three years later, between Mama and Daddy, and stop swinging my legs. Our pastor, whose head is all I can see above the pulpit, is warning us. His glasses glint as he slowly surveys us, five pews on the right side, six on the left. His voice rises:

"Then the Son of Man shall send forth his angels, and they shall gather out of his kingdom all things that offend, and them which do iniquity, and shall cast them into a furnace of fire: there shall be wailing and gnashing of teeth!"

In the silence that follows, our skin prickles, our throats parch. I hear Daddy swallow and stop breathing. I glance across the aisle at Gramma, sitting beyond Auntie and Uncle. Her eyes are wide open, staring beyond the pastor.

Then the pastor's voice returns, softly now but rising:

"Then shall the righteous shine forth as the sun, in the kingdom of God."

Lying next to Gramma in the dark, each time she finishes the story I think of more questions.

"What did you *do?*" I ask. "Where did you live?"

"Well, people didn't have insurance in those days," she explains, thoughtfully. "It really tested our faith. We stayed with some people by the school for awhile, through the winter, until we moved to a farm east of town." Her voice perks up. "We liked that."

She does not tell me how, for the next seventeen years, their family moved from farm to farm, renting three different places east of town, one farm a mile west, another farm a mile south, spending two years with their grandparents on the Hendrickson home place while their two uncles were living somewhere else. The burning of the store was not only a glimpse of hell but a lesson. All earthly possessions could be gone in a night, in an hour.

"We were living east of Rock Creek then," she'll say, telling another story, blending three rented farms into one because it's easy, because those farms all connected by Rock Creek, the source of adventure. Full of brushy places and ravines filled with torrents in spring that subsided to a brook full of fish and swimming holes in summer, the creek was where she and Ray, who was two years older than she, went to fish, where they watched for wildlife and learned birdcalls. She tells stories of a boy and a girl running the countryside, fishing, picking mayflowers, and getting lost in the woods, of almost falling into the rushing creek in spring, of getting chased by a bull or a skunk or some bees, of finding honey, sweet gobs of it. True stories become made-up stories of bears getting honey, of foxes and birds that lead children home when they're lost.

"'Behold the birds of the air,'" Gramma recites from the Gospel of

Matthew, "'they sow not, neither do they reap, nor gather into barns; yet your heavenly Father feedeth them.' Jesus told us not to worry too much about food and clothes. 'Consider the lilies of the field, how they grow,' he said, 'they toil not, neither do they spin, yet I say unto you, that even Solomon in all his glory was not arrayed as one of these.'

"He didn't mean we don't have to work," she explains. "He said *'Seek ye first* the kingdom of God, and his righteousness, and all these things shall be added unto you.'"

Gramma's parents lived like that, some would say irresponsibly. After the fire, they had two more children, eleven in all, and took in a baby cousin whose mother died giving birth. They moved from farm to farm, working land they didn't own, living hand to mouth, learning not just to make do but to make more than the sum of the parts at hand. They lived the miracle of the oil and flour that never ran out, making hotdish and coffee and pie crust that not only kept the body alive but made it glad, sewing dresses that clothed but also mimicked the flowers of the field in shapes of the latest fashion: hats like caps of lilies, dropped waists and wide sunburst collars, bridal gowns and bridesmaid dresses festooned with ribbon saved and pressed and reused.

The center of their lives was the church at East Rock Creek, their own grandfather's church, across the field from his house. There they read the Bible, sang hymns, decorated the sanctuary in flowers of the seasons: plum blossoms in spring; wild roses, brown-eyed Susans, and tiger lilies in the summer; branches of colored leaves in the fall; bows of evergreen and dried bittersweet in winter. They sent money to missions and forswore liquor, tobacco, and unseemly behavior, things that weaken the temple of the spirit, things that offend. They tended first to the spirit, second to the body, and last to other earthly things.

Gramma was grown up and gone by the time her parents and youngest sisters and brothers moved back to the Hendrickson home place. Effie and Harold and Alvin still live there with their tiny mother, my great-grandmother. They have cows and pigs and sheep, cats and a dog, but most magically of all, they have honeybees. Harold and Alvin keep the bees in white, stacked boxes, collect the honey, pour it into glass jars shaped like honeycomb, and sell it in towns all around — Hendrickson Honey. It's gold and clear and tastes so good because of Effie's flower gardens. Behind the house, an arbor forms the entrance to a fairyland of flowers, with a windmill in which the smallest of us can stand and a round pond full of velvety-looking goldfish. In the house, Effie makes scrapbooks.

In the fall Gramma gives me an old, long, leather book with a red binding to paste pictures in, to make my own scrapbook. There is pencil-writing on the pages, but she tells me to ignore it, to paste right over. I can't read the writing anyway, and this is a practice book. After this I want to make a scrapbook like the one Effie gave me for my birthday, beautiful pictures, perfectly cut and pasted in a big book, held together by a silky string with tassels.

I sit in Gramma's living room on the blue carpet with a pattern of plumes, cutting out pictures she gives me. She sits on the edge of the couch, turning pages in a magazine with fingers frozen in the shape of a mitten. She pauses to look at a picture, marks the place, then turns to the next page, pushing the glossy page up, catching the edge with the nail of her thumb.

Arthritis has locked her joints into bizarre shapes, especially her hands, elbows, and feet, so scissors are beyond her. I hold the scissors, even though they are a challenge for me—she trusts I can do it.

The picture before me is horses, brown and white, running in a blur of sunlight across a green pasture by a gray barn. Sun shines through their flying tails and manes, outlines their outstretched legs. The picture is too wide to paste onto the first page of the book.

The Dutch clock chimes from the top of the china cabinet. Something inside it seems to open before it whirs and then sounds out the notes in groups of four.

"Half-past nine," Gramma says. She believes I am not too young to learn time, although I don't know why it matters.

Sunlight falls through the east window. From where I sit, I can look outside and see through the bare branches of the butternut tree in a straight line over the rise just east of the milk house to the woods. The woods make a gray border separating the plowed brown fields and a stand of pale dry corn from the blue sky.

Gramma first came to our farm as a working girl because the woman on the farm then, Mamie, was ill. Gramma loved the fields and the woods and all the animals, and Grampa's team of horses, hitched to a wagon of corn, blowing and swinging their heads in the cold air.

Grampa is dead now, and we no longer have horses. I don't remember him or our horses, although Gramma says I loved the horses and Grampa loved me. I was only one year old when, despite her protests, he allowed me to take pretty things from the china cabinet and play with them on the floor beside him, and I never broke a thing.

I cut the horse picture unevenly in two, and paste the first five running horses on page one of the scrapbook, and the last two, a mare and a colt, on page three.

Gramma has received special treatments for her arthritis, including bee stings, gold shots, and cortisone. The cortisone gave her a condition she calls moon face, which caused her to travel to University Hospitals and be packed in ice. Now she dips her hands in hot wax.

To do this, she heats paraffin in a coffee can on her kitchen stove until it turns to liquid, then dips her hands in it, lifts them out coated in hot wax, wraps them in a towel, and sits still until they cool. It's my job to turn off the stove and help her wrap the towel around her hands securely before she seats herself comfortably on the couch. Then I can sit at the table, dipping my fingers in the rest of the wax.

The wax fingers lie on the kitchen table, white but glowing from within. I touch the last one to make it straight and examine my row with satisfaction.

"Gramma, I got five," I call to her. She looks up from her Bible. I point to the row of five perfect wax fingers and she nods.

I feel hot suddenly in the bright morning light from the window. I walk through the arch into the blue-carpet room and sit down beside her, our arms touching gently so I don't disturb her hands in the pink-striped towel. It is cool on the couch where the fall air leaks through the plaster and wallpaper under the eaves.

Gramma sits beside me on the couch as I deftly lift page after heavy page of her scrapbooks and photo albums: the pink album full of her postcards from California and the rose parade, the brown album of photographs she's taken of the farm, and her long leather album of Hendrickson photographs. She's taken pictures of horses and cows, snowbanks taller than men, weddings of all her pretty sisters, snapshots of her parents and cousins.

There is also the small, heavy album with red and gold roses painted on a pale green lacquer cover. This is the Marty album, full of formal portraits set in pages stiff as wood — the album that belongs to the farm itself. Susanna Marty started it; she made one for each of her children's weddings. This one she left for Grampa, who had not married before she died. On the first page, Gramma placed her own wedding picture, standing with Grampa at the rented farm where her parents lived then, a mile north of our place. It's one of the few pictures of Grampa smiling, she tells me. He was so serious. She didn't have a wedding dress — times were hard in 1932, she says — but her dress was beautiful anyway. I've seen it in the trunk in her sewing room, pink silk that she says used to be beige.

On the pages that follow are Grampa Marty's parents, Jacob and Susanna, whom Gramma never knew because they died before she came to work on the farm. Then are wedding pictures of Susanna and Jacob's dark-haired children: Lizzie, Minnie, handsome Sam and beautiful Mamie, and Anna. Anna is the only one still alive and the only one I know, but Gramma knew them all.

The wedding pictures are followed by pictures of Grampa and his brother and sisters when they were children. There's a picture of four generations: strong Susanna, her tiny mother Salome, her beautiful daughter Lizzie, and her granddaughter, a girl named Susan, whose hair falls loose to her waist. The three women wear dresses to the floor, but Susan wears a knee-length dress with black tights beneath.

Finally there are pictures of Uncle Gaylon, first as a baby, then at my age with Daddy, who is a fat, round baby in white. Both of them have black Marty eyes like mine.

Every spring before Memorial Day, I go with Gramma to the cemetery to help her plant flowers. With her arthritis, she can't do it alone, bending and stooping, handling a shovel, carrying a heavy bucket of water. We plant geraniums on both sides of the Marty stone, east and west. She tells me where to dig the holes and how big, and I dig and carry water from the pump. She winces when she pulls the flowers from the pots and sets them in the watery holes, then we both fill in the gaps with dirt.

In the fall we go again. I cut away dirt and grass that's grown up over the edge of the name-stones in the ground, and match the names with faces in the photo album: Jacob with the gentle eyes and mouth. Square-faced Susanna, down-to-business but happy. Sam, who looked like Susanna but darker, and Mamie, with hair like honey. They all lie on the east side of the stone. On the west side, Susanna's mother is buried in the northwest corner — in the picture showing four generations, Salome was small and smiling in a velvet bonnet. Next to Salome is Susanna's half-brother, whose face we don't know. In the south corner, thin, sad-looking Grampa.

Three plots are yet empty: one beside Sam for his second wife, Margaret; and two on the west side, one for Gramma next to Grampa.

It is the Lutheran cemetery. There isn't a Baptist one, and anyway, the Martys were Lutheran in the beginning. Gramma says Grampa was raised that way, in the German Lutheran church, where services were in German and he loved the songs. He never made her stop going to her own church, though. In fact, they took turns going to each other's churches, and when Daddy and Uncle got old enough for Sunday school, Grampa let them go to the Baptist church every Sunday, getting rides from Gramma's sister Ethel, so they could get all their lessons in the same church. She knows Grampa is saved and in heaven with God.

"He suffered so," she says, rubbing her bent hands distractedly. "Now he's free of pain."

Gramma doesn't fear death. It's suffering she fears and hates. Hell reaches from its rightful place into the world. Because of sin it will always be like that, until Jesus returns, until a new heaven and earth are created.

"Gramma, I want you to be free of pain, but I don't want you to die."

"I don't want to leave you, either, honey," she says. She smiles. "But we all die. And I know then I'll be with Jesus and Grampa, and my dad, and all my grammas and grampas."

There are other families from East Rock Creek Baptist Church with headstones here. After we're done with the digging we walk slowly around the stones for awhile, she reading names to me, noticing new graves, and admiring the flowers, late-blooming asters and chrysanthemums.

Gramma gives me a project she can't do herself, but she supervises. On her kitchen table, she spreads an old newspaper, a tube of gold paint, a paintbrush, and a heavy oval picture frame. Sitting across from her, I paint the metal frame twice, once when I arrive, and once before I leave that afternoon.

The next time I come, she lays the frame on top of a piece of cardboard and I draw an oval, then cut it out slightly larger, which is hard because my hands are small, the scissors are small, and the cardboard is stiff. She places the cardboard behind the frame and has me trim it until it fits.

Then she directs me to take her wedding picture out of the Marty album, which requires cutting because it's been glued and lodged in the pocket so tightly. I can't believe she is going to ruin the Marty album, but she is certain, so I do as she says. She lays the oval cardboard over the photograph and has me draw an outline lightly with a pencil. Then, slowly and carefully as she hovers, I trim the photograph into an oval and place it upside down in the frame. She covers it with the cardboard, and I slide four wire clasps over it to hold everything in place. I open the little metal foot on the back of the frame and set it upright on the table.

She gazes at it and her mouth relaxes. Her young self and Grampa smile back at her, standing together on the lawn of the farm where they got married.

"That's nice," she breathes. "Thank you."

She carries it to her bedroom and sets it on the cedar chest beside her bed.

In December we put up Christmas trees. In our house, we have a short-needle tree with silver tinsel draped on the branches and lights shaped like candy drops. In the big house, Auntie and Uncle have a long-needle tree with huge lights, round with crushed glass like ice on the outside, that match the colors and furniture in their modern living room. In church, there is a huge spruce tree on the platform, where we will each stand to say our lines.

Upstairs in the old house, Gramma doesn't have room for a tree, but I help her decorate anyway. She has electric candles for the windows, a nice-smelling real candle inside a frosted jar, and three little choir boys that light up from inside. My favorite thing is a manger scene: a wooden barn with moss on the roof, mismatched animals and shepherds, kind Joseph, blue-dressed Mary, and round baby Jesus in a manger of molded hay, with donkey and cow, shepherd and sheep, a dozen gilded angels with different instruments, and silver wise men on silver camels. We set it all on a sheet of cotton sprinkled with gold and blue glitter so it looks like moonlit snow.

"This is the meaning of Christmas, whatever else you hear," Gramma tells me. The greatest gift of all is Jesus.

For God so loved the world that he gave his only begotten son, that whosoever believeth in him shall not perish, but have everlasting life.

I sit on the couch beside the manger scene, staring at the tiny adoring faces while the clock ticks, the chimes sound, and the hours bong.

On Sunday evening before Christmas, we have our Christmas program at church. All the children have memorized lines and say them, some with help. This year Bruce pulls down the giant tree and there is an uproar, then laughter because no one is hurt. A friend of Daddy's grabs Bruce, and Daddy and Uncle put the tree back up, and everyone sings. The ceiling lights are put out so only the lights of the trees shine on our faces. At the end, the children's names are called and we're each given a bag with a huge red apple, a salted nut roll, a chocolate Nut Goody, and a candy cane. As we leave, the church smells like apples.

That night during the opening of presents I hear the news — Auntie and Uncle will have a baby in the spring.

❧§❧

All winter we are waiting for Auntie Lou to have her baby. We are waiting, and she is becoming enormous. Auntie Lou is small, four feet, ten inches, and the baby makes her stomach huge right at my eye level. When I knock on Auntie and Uncle's door and walk through their house on my way to Gramma's, it's hard not to look at Auntie's stomach. She wears beautiful flowing clothes. One of her dresses has a pretty round collar that shows her collar bones; the print has big reddish-purple flowers with deep-green leaves. Even in winter, Auntie is warm and her cheeks are bright pink.

Uncle Gaylon is excited. The baby is due in April, maybe on his birthday. Uncle will be a father now, too — he's catching up with Daddy, his little brother, who has been a father four years, and Auntie Lou is catching up with Mama, her big sister. When Auntie and Uncle come to our house to divide the milk check and pay bills, they stay late and everyone laughs a lot.

To the horses in my scrapbook I add pictures of children and baby animals: a boy holding corncobs and squash, a girl planting seeds, a baby, a girl with a doll, a woman reading to a girl at Christmas, scenes from the nativity, a kitten on a pedestal, a newborn calf, a girl holding a lamb.

Gramma is nervous and hopes everything will go all right. Having babies is risky. Mamie, Sam's wife, was never the same after she had their son — she suffered with some unnamed illness for seventeen years until an operation, when she died. Gramma's cousin Betty came to them in a shoebox after her mother died in childbirth. Gramma herself was very sick after having Daddy; she lay in bed for weeks with a blood clot in her leg. It scared Grampa so much that he said no more children, two is enough, and even though she wanted more, she knew he was right.

Being born is also risky for babies. My brothers were so tiny at birth, no one thought they would live. Mama has told me how the first sight of them shocked her: no diaper would possibly fit. She couldn't even hold them. She and Daddy looked at them through the glass of the nursery in Rush City Hospital, where they lay like unfurled leaves on incubator pads, their legs and arms like spindles, each one no bigger than Daddy's hand. Because the firstborn was so weak, they gave the chosen name, with Daddy's middle name, to the younger one. And when they came home from the hospital after Christmas that year, the twins went almost immediately back, lungs full of mucus that made them bark in the night.

"It was terrible, terrible," says Gramma, who came to care for me during that time.

The twins often came down with croup, and still do, although they are now two. It's always at the same moment in the night, startling us awake. Daddy and Mama have become experts at treating them, one turning on the hot water, filling our little bathroom with steam, while the other scoops the twins out of their beds next to mine. Then, Daddy holds one twin and Mama holds the other, with receiving blankets like tents over their heads, dazed and barking, until their lungs open and they breathe freely again.

But, I reason, every living thing, every person around me, was born and survived.

When a cow is about to calf in the summer, she is let outside the barn to move freely. But in the winter, she stands stiff and straining in her stanchion, and when the calf is born, it slips out and falls heavily, nose and front feet first, onto the hay spread out for it in the shallow gutter. We are allowed to watch, without moving or speaking, sitting on a hay bale against the back wall, but not directly behind them.

Daddy or Uncle moves the wet calf, pulls it around by its front legs, and lets the cow out of her stanchion to turn around and lick her calf clean. She licks its nose hard until it shudders and blows and breathes, opens its eyes, and lurches to stand, to balance, to find its mother's full udder, and to bunt, curving its neck down and up like a bow to drink.

The miracle is how the calf knows to do this. It is knowledge from God in the calf's head and body.

Sometimes in the summer, a cow doesn't return from the woods with the rest of the herd, or she calves and returns alone. Then we go find the cow or her calf before dark. I run beside Uncle because he's happy and walking with big strides, swinging a length of twine in one hand as we walk up the lane, under the elm trees, turning east at the corner, past the plum tree, and under the fence into the woods. We follow the cow paths — grooves worn by hooves in the grazed grass — and the fresh cow pies they've left that day. He calls *C'm-boss!* because sometimes a missing cow will answer. If the calf has been left, he makes the sound of a cow deep in his throat, *Mmmoah!* He knows the private places and niches cows choose to calf, because he's been doing this since he was not much older than I, taught by his mother: a triangle of hardwoods, up against a stand of prickly ash, or in a mossy place in the birch near the boggy places called Applegate's.

When we find the calf it stands up immediately, tail wagging, and veers away. Uncle speaks softly to it, rubs its little horn ridge and ears and neck, talks baby talk very tenderly, and grins. He checks to see whether it's a bull or a heifer, loops the twine around its neck, and then we lead the calf home. Sometimes it bucks back, trips on ridges in the lane, and runs ahead so fast it makes us break out laughing.

From their place on the highway, east of our woods, Roy and Arleen Tillman saw the lights of Daddy and Mama's car leaving for the hospital the day I was born. It was a cold February morning before dawn, when farmers were going out to milk. The snow across the fields was a frozen white sea half as deep as the telephone poles, and the full moon hung above the dark outline of our farm, not long from setting. Inside the warm red barn, Uncle Gaylon milked the cows alone that morning. After chores in the bright morning light, he joined Gramma and Grampa in the old house where he still lived with them, across the yard from our smaller house.

All day they waited to hear some news. Gramma spilled coffee and dropped things. The last time a Marty baby had been born, it was hers, my father, in this house.

In labor all day, my nineteen-year-old mother called my father's name while he, nearly as young, sat in the waiting room of Rush City Hospital, praying and reading the Bible.

I was delivered during the evening milking, at suppertime, February 5, 1958, *on the 6:28 flight from heaven,* the pastor at East Rock Creek Baptist Church printed in the bulletin that Sunday. I was completely healthy, with black hair and eyes that promised to be brown like my dad's. They gave me a name my mother got off the radio, and I came home to sleep in the south bedroom, where the moon shone in the window all night long above the frozen swamp across the road, and the morning sun woke me.

Winter ended and the snow melted, flooding the ditches and creek, forming a lake where ducks and geese stop on their way north, where the marsh wrens and red-winged blackbirds nest as the water recedes. Next to the woodshed, Gramma's tulips bloomed, then the lilacs. Pink peonies and white bridal wreath cascaded around the front of our house, and apple trees blossomed between the two houses and in the orchard west of the big house. Daddy and Uncle plowed and planted corn, seeded alfalfa, and sowed oats in the fields from our house to the highway. Uncle Gaylon courted Auntie Lou.

Grampa hitched up his oldest gentle horse and turned over the dirt in Gramma's garden west of the big house. Next to our house, my father broke up a small plot for my mother.

Inside a shimmering pink baby book, my mother keeps a lock of my Marty-black baby hair and a copy of the church bulletin, which I ask her to read to me.

I imagine my dark head emerging from the dark night sky and the stars, even though that was not how it happened, I know that. I have seen a calf born more than once. But the pastor's version told the meaning: I came from God.

In church we sing *Praise God from whom all blessings flow!*
We sing this when the offering is taken.
Praise him, all creatures here below!
Praise him above, ye heav'nly host!
Praise father, son, and holy ghost!

We are born to praise God. We praise God for the world he created, we praise God that we are in it, we praise God for deliverance
from evil.

Each one of us is born for a purpose, with a gift and a calling from
God. We are born to do good and to learn and obey our calling.

Sons are needed for the farm to continue, to be stewards and husbands of the land, to make the family secure. The meaning of the birth
of a son is that the farm can continue, a calling of honor, perhaps the
highest calling except for ministry or missions.

On our farm, the order of things was mixed up. Sam's son should
have had the farm, but he left it for the navy and never came back,
except for short visits. So it was Grampa, the younger brother, whose
sons got the farm.

It should have been Uncle, Grampa's oldest son, who got the farm.
Gramma believed she had two sons for a reason, one for the farm and
one for God. She believed it was Daddy—the quiet one who loved to
read, highest student in his class, the thinker—who was called to seminary. But Uncle was drafted into the army, and while he was gone,
Grampa fell ill for the last time. Against Gramma's judgment, Grampa
insisted that Daddy be allowed to marry Mama and stay on the farm.

Daddy didn't believe getting married had to stop him from seminary. At church, he served as a trustee, a Sunday school teacher, and a
deacon. Uncle came home to the farm. Then, when a son might have
been a sign that Daddy should stay, I was born instead. Gramma believed Daddy should have no more children and prepare for seminary.

Grampa wanted Daddy to stay home with Uncle. He believed the
farm was best for brothers, working together. He believed that my
mother's second baby would be a boy, a boy for the farm to continue.
He was so sure that, before he died, he bought a toy riding tractor for
the new baby. It was under the tree on Christmas morning, waiting for
the twins to come home. For me he left a doll named Beth Ann, half as
big as I was, with brown curly hair. For Mama he left a garnet ring set
in four prongs. For Auntie Lou, another ring almost like Mama's.

In Daddy's Christmas slides a year later, the one-year-old twins were fat as small poultry, heirs to our farm.

In church, I try to sit between Mama and Daddy. I love the sound of their voices together, one on each side of me, and their arms making a circle, holding the book between them.

When morning gilds the skies, my heart awaking cries, May Jesus Christ be praised!

This is my favorite hymn because I love the sky in the morning, and I love the way they sing it: Daddy sings the melody and Mama harmonizes, five notes at the end are sustained, their voices blend together, voices so strong it seems as though they're holding me up. But usually when they sing, I am moved to one side. Daddy lifts me easily into his outside arm, outside the perfect circle of their harmony, where all the other voices in the room become audible, some of them distinct. I hear Uncle Gaylon's voice in the pew across the aisle, his voice strong and clear.

Be this, while life is mine, my canticle divine, May Jesus Christ be praised!

Be this, th'eternal song, through all the ages long, May Jesus Christ be praised!

I am glad Daddy stayed on the farm and didn't become a pastor. I am a girl, a gift from God to a family that had only sons in the generation before. I can be and do anything that God wants—a nurse or a missionary.

I am hoping Auntie has a girl I can play with.

Gramma tells me it was so much fun to grow up with all her sisters that she wanted to have a lot of children. But the stories she tells are always about Ray, and usually about fishing.

That was another thing she loved about the Martys—they fished. When she was still working for pay on the farm and Ray married a beauty queen from Wisconsin and moved to Seattle, she began to fish with Grampa and Sam on rainy days and late summer evenings, and then sometimes on Sunday afternoons. She and Grampa were a good match, even though he was so much older than she was, because they both believed in God and land and hard work and fishing.

In my scrapbook, I paste pictures of fishing: a fisherman with a net and a lobster box, a fly fisherman in a mountain stream. I lick and stick stamps from the National Wildlife Federation of bluefin tuna, blue cat-fish, Atlantic salmon. I paste in a pencil drawing by Gramma's oldest sister, Julia, of John Marty in a straw hat.

I also paste in pictures of birds: a blue jay and a bluebird, a red-winged blackbird and a red-headed woodpecker, a flock of Canadian geese, and ducks drinking from a hose.

Gramma teaches me bird sounds, as Uncle has. My favorite song, the throaty warble and sustained note of the redwing, is impossible to duplicate. Gramma admits it is hard; she can't do it either.

"It's like a yodel at the beginning."

A yodel, she tells me, is a kind of singing from Switzerland, and when Susanna's mother, Salome, came to visit, she called the cows that way. After awhile, all Salome had to do was stand behind the barn and yodel, and the cows came home from the woods.

Uncle Gaylon was born in 1934, so he is almost twenty-eight. I imag-ine he was like me, the only child on the farm for awhile, loved and instructed, fed and given things to do by Gramma, taught about birth and young animals, taught to cut out pictures, to recognize the songs of birds, to complete simple tasks. He was safe and warm in the house with his hard-working mother, quiet father, talkative uncle, and a grown-up cousin who visited from faraway places. He played with cats and the old dog, went to the barn during milking, helped feed the cows and horses. He learned the four directions, the seasons, the names of trees, and the names of his aunts and uncles, the Martys and the Hendrick-sons. Every Sunday he went to church, one week to St. John's Lutheran, the next to East Rock Creek Baptist.

Gramma's love for the farm was contagious. She loved the sun-rise east of the woods in the summer, the whishing sound of the pine trees over the porch, the porch swing for afternoon and evening naps, Grampa's devotion to his horses and the Bible, Sam's sense of humor, the fire in the stove and the kitchen filled with morning light, fresh milk and cream and butter and eggs, the order of everything. She loved the chicks and little pigs, kittens and cats, hunting for new calves in the woods.

God was in all of it, and she taught Uncle the meaning of every-thing she knew. She took pictures with her brownie camera and placed them in a scrapbook with his help: the cows by the barn, the border collie that herded the cows, the horses threshing oats, a rooster on the roof of a new car, Grampa with the mule they got by accident.

"What's that bird, do you know?" Gramma asks me, sitting in the house.

"A cardinal," I say.

"What bird is that?" Uncle asks an hour later, standing by the corncrib.

"A cardinal," I answer.

In the beginning, God created the heaven and the earth. And the earth was without form, and void, and darkness was upon the face of the deep. And the Spirit of God moved upon the waters.

And God said, Let us make man in our image, after our likeness, and let them have dominion over the fish of the sea, and over the fowl of the air, and over the cattle, and over all the earth.

The Lord God formed man of the dust of the ground, and breathed into his nostrils the breath of life, and man became a living soul.

❧

April comes, the snow is gone, and the baby is late.

One morning, I wake up and Auntie and Uncle have gone to the hospital. They have been there all night. My mother is nervous and excited; her stomach hurts in sympathy. The day wears on.

In the afternoon, Uncle calls and says, *The baby died. It was a boy.*

They don't know exactly why the baby died. Maybe it went too long without oxygen, maybe the cord was wrapped around its neck too tightly. Oxygen: the word for something we need to live, something carried in the mother's blood through the umbilical cord before we breathe on our own. The breath of God. Auntie and Uncle's baby never breathed.

My mother goes to the hospital and sees the baby. He was beautiful, she says, her voice breaking. She sits down on a chair by the kitchen table and cries out loud. He looked perfect, she says through a web of tears. He had dark Marty hair and skin. He looked like me when I was born. Auntie Lou didn't cry—she wouldn't even see him. Mama can't understand it. She is herself filled with grief. She cried in front of Auntie but Auntie didn't cry. Grief: a sadness so great you cannot be comforted.

My mother's grief and the thought of the baby never coming home are unbearable. I cry and my mother takes me onto her lap and holds me for a long time. That night she rocks me in Daddy's rocker and strokes my head, and then sits in our room in the dark. In their bunk beds next to me, the twins' small round shoulders protrude from their covers. Mama is looking at us, I know, thinking about how rich she is, how fortunate to have not one baby but three, all of us big, all of us breathing. I think about Auntie's baby and about Auntie and Uncle, how long they've waited. My throat constricts and burns and I start to cry again.

When I see Gramma, I run to her and hug her around her stiff waist. She cries with tears but almost no sound, and can hardly speak.

"The baby is in heaven now, with Jesus," she says, "and with Grampa," comforting me but also herself, her arm around me awkwardly because of her arthritis, her bent hand patting my leg.

Uncle, like Mama, cries out loud. His grief reaches from one side of the sky to the other. He doesn't understand why God has done this, kept this perfect boy from them. He and Daddy go to Olson's Funeral Chapel and buy a small coffin. They drive out to the Lutheran cemetery and side by side they dig the baby's grave on the south shoulder of the Marty headstone, dig through the still-frozen ground and roots of a bare maple tree into the mud that becomes muddier because it rains. They seem to dig forever, such a small hole but so deep, in the narrow space between the vaults of Grampa Marty on one side and Jacob and Susanna on the other. They dig all afternoon, and finally in the evening, in the rain, they place the baby's coffin in the grave. Slowly, their shoulders aching and their hands freezing, they cover it with cold earth. Uncle cannot be consoled, he grieves like King David, but God gives no reason for taking this baby. There is no explanation.

When Auntie comes home from the hospital, she goes into the house and puts all the baby things away and doesn't talk about any of it.

The baby has no name. There is no funeral. Not until fall is there a marker on the brown mound of earth, and then it is a metal marker, not stone like the rest of them. It says Baby Boy Marty, 1962–1962.

In my scrapbook, I paste pictures of flowers: mayflowers, dahlias red and pink and orange, pink bougainvillea, honeysuckle, blooming cactus, milkweed, water lilies.

I begin to draw pictures, of our farm, of children, of animals, of myself.

The twins are in the house playing, talking to each other, fighting, pounding, running, yelling. They have their own language—the rest of us are like foreigners. They don't understand our ways of doing things and get spankings almost every day. They accidentally spill milk at almost every meal and do things on purpose I cannot even imagine, such as pulling down our Christmas tree. When told not to do something, they immediately do it. They seem to love the ground and roll on it no matter what the weather is, dry or cold or wet. As soon as they get new clothes, they tear them. They throw blocks and toy tractors and trucks at each other. They break my dolls, pushing in the blue eye of Beth Ann and pulling out most of her hair.

Blaine gets nosebleeds, and Bruce sucks his thumb. One wash day, Bruce drinks Hi-Lex in the basement and has to have his stomach pumped; another day, he hangs over the basement railing and falls onto the washer and gets stitches on the top of his head; another time, crawling very fast behind the couch, he scrapes himself on a heating vent and gets stitches in his head again. But the twins are so cute, everybody forgives them.

They are a pair, a matching set. We in the family can tell Bruce from Blaine, but nobody else can, so most of the time Mama dresses Blaine in blue and Bruce in red. She sends them outside whenever she can. Daddy builds a fence for them on the west side of the house where they can play safely and Mama can see them from the kitchen.

On my bed, I spread out pictures of orphans from the war in Korea, which Daddy has received in the mail because he is a deacon. I study their faces to tell them apart. In mild weather and on all but the hottest days of summer, I take my play things onto our front porch and play there with the door closed, wrapping my battered dolls carefully and laying them in rows, wound neatly in receiving blankets left over from the twins. Beth Ann is the biggest, her hard plastic body scuffed with black marks as if the twins had stepped on her with Sunday shoes. There is the china-headed doll with the cloth body that once was Mama's— part of her face is gone, exposing a chalky porous substance inside, and her delicate hands are chipped. The littlest doll has an orange cast to her molded plastic skin, shocking blue eyes, and reddish-brown curly hair.

Beth Ann lies in a pink painted crib, and the other two lie shoulder to shoulder in a black rocking cradle with appliqués of Dutch boys and girls on each side.

I have decided I will be a missionary nurse. Auntie Lou brings me samples of supplies from the hospital: a clipboard and a note pad, Keri lotion, and empty bottles. I bandage my dolls, give them shots, feed and wrap them. They have been in war and have come to my hospital.

In the winter when the porch is too cold, I go to Gramma's house, pack an old cardboard suitcase with my dolls and pajamas, bundle up in snow pants and boots, mittens and scarf tied under my chin, and walk across the snowy yard to stay overnight.

In Gramma's soft springy bed, we turn off the pink, shell-shaped bed light attached to the headboard and crawl under the pink electric blanket. The bed smells like the drawers of her vanity, of loose face powder and cosmetics. I roll next to her gingerly, to avoid bumping her aching body.

"Tell me the story about the fire," I say, and she tells it again.

Then in the dark she says, *Listen,* and I hear the call of a bird outside, streaking past the house or roosting in the orchard or the pines, and she names it: a snowy owl.

She describes the woods, their bleak danger in winter, their dark dusty green in August, their fiery oranges and yellows and reds in the fall, their soft green buds in muddy spring, their darkness in evening, their terror and shelter at night. Danger is everywhere, but so is God.

The woods open up, and on paths worn by cows' hooves, I enter to sleep.

Maple

At the cemetery east of town, a young maple tree grows by the Marty family plot. When I go with Gramma Marty to take care of our plot, she tells me to water the tree too. Its bark is smooth gray and its leaves are yellow-green, like hands with three points, bigger than the pages of the book I use for pressing leaves. Its seeds are attached to a wing like a dragonfly's. There are millions of seeds every spring.

In the fall, maples make our woods dazzle. One Sunday, Mama and Daddy take the twins and me for a walk up the lane. Daddy takes pictures of us under the gold maples glowing in the sunlight. We walk through Applegate's, cross the highway, meet up with the creek, and follow it all the way to the farm where Mama grew up, where we surprise Grampa and Gramma Anderson.

Daddy sometimes calls the trees sugar maples, because their sap is sweet and some people tap them in the spring to get syrup.

Maple trees! Your colors in the fall are sugar to my eyes, orange and gold and red as candy.

3

Two Barns

Now the Lord said to Abram, "Get thee out of thy country, and
from thy kindred, and from thy father's house, unto a land that I will
show thee." So Abram departed, as the Lord had spoken unto him,
and took Sarai his wife, and Lot his brother's son, and they went
forth to go into the land of Canaan. And the Canaanite was then in
the land.

—Genesis 12:1, 4–6

The log barn is the oldest thing on our farm. It's so much smaller
than the big barn, right next to it, that it seems more like a shed.
Its roof is like the snow-covered wings of a giant bird spreading over the sheds attached to its sides, machinery under the north
wing, straw under the south. In the mow under the peak is hay. The
heifers, whose names I don't know, stay in the log barn for the winter,
snug inside all that hay.

From the south door of the log barn, Uncle Gaylon pitches straw
bales and I keep him company. It's a gray March day and I'm dressed
in two pairs of pants and a jacket, scarf, and mittens. Uncle is thin and
strong, dressed in jeans and a plaid flannel shirt under overalls and a
jacket, with brown leather high-top shoes, a blue cap above his always-tan face, and yellow flannel gloves to protect his hands from the sharp
hay. Since the baby died last year, he doesn't talk as much, but when I
visit with him awhile, eventually he thinks of something that makes
him smile.

He grabs each bale by its two strands of twine and hoists it easily
onto the wagon. Between taking a bale and pitching it up, he declares,
"Jacob and Susanna built this log barn."

I know Jacob and Susanna from the lacquer photo album on
Gramma's coffee table—Jacob with a mustache, Susanna with her hair
swept back—Uncle's grandparents, my great-grandparents. He invokes
their names as partners, like Abraham and Sarah.

I have never thought of them in work clothes. I turn to look at the log barn, a worn-out-looking thing. It's faded red on the outside, but inside, under those faded red boards, I can see logs, plain trees with the bark peeled off. I look at Uncle.

"The logs in this barn are trees Jacob and Susanna cut down as they cleared these fields," he says, nodding to the east as he keeps lifting and throwing bales. "This barn is solid as a rock. And there's hardly a nail in it!"

I think he's joking and wait to see him grin, but he doesn't.

"I've never been able to find one nail," he insists. "See?" He taps a yellow glove on the inside of the door frame. He makes way so I can step over the threshold and stand inside, under his elbow. I peer at the wall made of trees, trimmed and fitted together. I don't see any nails.

"How did they do it without nails?" I ask.

"They cut the wood so it fit together in grooves, and then they drove wooden pegs in certain places," he explains. He stops to look for a wooden peg but can't find one, so he forms a groove with one hand and places the edge of the other hand inside it to show me.

"The cabin was built the same way — over there." He gestures to the east, waving his arm past the milk house and windmill.

"The cabin was right there, on that high spot, across the path. Look, this is where Susanna walked every day to carry water to the cabin." He takes my hand and walks me along the rise to the little red milk house with the well inside. Then he counts out more paces, maybe fifteen or twenty through fresh snow, to the place where the cabin once was. There's not a trace of anything now. It's a hayfield, not even a bump in the cold earth beneath the snow.

"I like to stand right here on this spot," Uncle says, "and think of what Jacob and Susanna saw." He holds out his free hand and turns slowly. "Every morning they walked out the door of the little cabin and they saw the woods" — north — "and half-cleared fields to the railroad tracks" — east — "and a wagon track through the swamp" — south, along what is now the road — "and the creek" — west. I turn, too, following the sweep of his arm. "I wonder if they missed the mountains."

Uncle Gaylon has never seen Switzerland, where Jacob and Susanna grew up, but in the army he saw real mountains with snowy tops. Compared with Switzerland, this place is nearly flat. Jacob arrived in

Minnesota first, and bought a swamp and a high spot, with a cabin built by another Swiss. When Susanna came, they lived on cranberries from the bog, potatoes they planted, wild game, and coffee from the store in town.

"They lived here seventeen years before building the big house," Uncle continues. "Susanna had four babies in the cabin—Lizzie, Minnie, Sam, and your Grampa John. It was so cold in the cabin that once, when Susanna came in from chores, little Grampa had tried to get warm by rolling up tight under the bed. When she found him, his hair was full of frost! He caught pneumonia and almost died!"

I shiver, imagining a head full of frost.

The log barn was the first thing Jacob and Susanna built themselves. The trees from the cleared fields, dragged to the cabin by oxen, were trimmed from round logs to square beams and hewn out with Jacob's ax. The leftovers were sliced into wooden shingles for the roof.

"Every animal they had, they kept in the log barn," Uncle says, still amazed. "A team of oxen for work, cows for milk to drink, pigs for meat to eat, and chickens for eggs. And hay in the haymow!"

"Where were the horses?" I ask.

"They came later," he says. "Before they got the horses, they had to build the big barn. And before they could build the big barn, they had to build the house."

He nods, gazing at the big house that is his house now, imagining the time before it was built and the time when it was new, alone on a rise, when the trees around it must have been small.

"Sam was old enough to remember the day they moved from the cabin into the new house, and how their mama, Susanna, had waited for that! That's where she had her last baby, little Aunt Anna. Sam said they all felt like kings and queens sleeping in that new house."

Uncle turns west and surveys the big barn, hands on his hips.

"Yup. And then, after the house, they built the big barn. That was a real farm, with *two* barns. Then the Martys had a wonderful farm, just wonderful!"

Wonder. The farm is full of wonder.

When Uncle tells me stories like this, he takes off his cap and a glove and runs his hand through his dark hair, shakes his head with amazement, and replaces the cap. Then he looks back at me. His brown eyes sparkle. He smiles and I smile.

We walk back to the log barn door. He lifts yet another bale up onto the wagon. In a way, he is keeping an eye on me, and in a way, I'm helping. He likes my company. I'm interested in stories and don't interrupt.

The stories Uncle tells are really one story: how our farm got to be the way it is, so beautiful, so rich compared to the narrow valley in Switzerland. Dangers of cold and illness, the labor Jacob and Susanna suffered to make this farm—not just for their children, but for us, grandchildren and descendents they would never know—are all part of our story.

Fixing the fence north of the fields in the fall or spring, Uncle will tell how the woods once belonged to a fur trapper named Grant.

Hunting for a new calf in the summer on the east end of the woods, in the birches and swampy spot near the tracks, he looks for arrowheads and tells stories that Sam and Grampa told him about the 1800s, when Applegate still lived there in a house that is now a rock pile, a time when Indians who loved the land and hunted and fished with respect for creation still moved through and camped there and traded with settlers. He imagines what the Indians saw.

Walking home from the woods, Uncle points across the lane to land we don't own, once a place called Rosendale because of its wild roses.

West of our place where the creek starts, he says, beavers once made a lake so big that it had fish, and Sam and Grampa caught them.

Standing in a driveway, Uncle spies an agate, picks it up to show me, and tells how agates were brought here by glaciers.

Glaciers are the reason our farm is the way it is—not hilly but not flat either. It has rises and rounded ridges, like shapes under an enormous blanket. The woods along the north side grow on a ridge that resisted a glacier. From the edge of the woods, the fields gently slope down to the road, sagging through the wide, low spot we call the flat, which was scooped out by the glacier and still floods every spring.

Agates are not the only rocks brought by glaciers. Every spring, we pick rocks from the fields where the thawing ground has heaved them up. The twins and I ride in the pickup with Daddy or Uncle, picking up small ones while the men carry rocks too big for us to lift. At the end, we drive up the fence line to Applegate's and throw all the rocks onto a pile.

On the southwest corner of our land, where the barns and houses stand, the glacier left two low ridges at an angle, northwest to southeast. The old log barn, the big red barn, and all the other sheds are built along the ridges. Only the two houses facing the road are built square to the four directions.

Jacob and Susanna and Sam and Grampa carved our farm out of woods and wet places, clearing trees from a hundred acres between the homestead to the west, the railroad to the east, the woods to the north, and the county line to the south.

Visiting Gramma upstairs in the big house, I examine the faces in the gold-painted album of Marty photographs. Jacob with pale, gentle eyes and a full bottom lip under his mustache. Facing him, Susanna with a square jaw, firm mouth, and smile-wrinkles around her eyes.

In the attic of our house is a huge oval portrait of Sam and Grampa when they were boys. Sam looks like Susanna, and John looks like Jacob. Sam, the oldest, stands in front, with Grampa behind him. They wear wool dress jackets with silky looking ties, and their hair is parted on opposite sides. They look like pioneers we see on TV.

Bruce and Blaine watch Westerns on TV. It's not a new TV, but it's new to us, inherited from Uncle and Daddy's cousin Harold, years older than them. Harold Marty was Sam's only son, who left for the navy when he was eighteen, became an alcoholic, and returned to the farm only for visits. On Harold's little red portable television, the twins and I watch fuzzy Roy Rogers and Dale Evans, *Cheyenne, Gunsmoke, Bonanza,* and, on Wednesday nights if we don't go to church and Mama isn't watching *The Virginian,* we watch *Wagon Train*—all shows Gramma Marty doesn't watch on her TV.

Outside, even before the snow melts, the twins and I pretend we're in the old days or the Wild West, hunting for food, building shelters and cabins. We drag fallen branches into formations that we envision as taller than we are. In the grove of pine trees between the orchard and the road, we dig through the snow and the dry orange-colored needles, make a hole in the dirt and a circle with stones, and carry old kettles and holey blankets and pretend we're settlers. We are forbidden to start a real fire, but we pretend to be warmed by a pile of small sticks. Long sticks become the twins' rifles for shooting imaginary deer or rabbits, which are easy to track when new snow comes. I pretend to cook.

With the hay bales still left in the mow by springtime, we build barricades and forts and act out daring adventures, standoffs, and gunfights.

As the weather gets warmer, we become agate hunters. Wherever Bruce and Blaine and I go, if there's gravel, we look down and scan for a reddish glint, a chip or a chunk, and the telltale stripe of white or glitter of quartz.

Once, Uncle tells us, agates were hot bubbles in the lava of volcanoes, and gradually, when the lava cooled and became hard, the bubbles filled up in layers. Later, when the filled-up bubbles became rocks, enormous glaciers crushed and carried them from Lake Superior down to our land. When the ice melted, the rocks dropped into the ground in a new place, in a gravel pit or a river.

"Is this an agate?" Bruce asks Uncle, the expert.

Uncle can spot good places to look for agates, but agate hunting doesn't require going anywhere, really. The county road grader passes by every other day to turn over and rearrange the gravel on our roads, and once every year or two, a new load of gravel is spread from a dump truck—a fresh supply of hope to find a truly perfect agate. The perfect agate would be round or oval, with rings around a glassy-looking center. Once, on a trip up north, we stopped at an agate shop where we saw agates polished to a glassy finish. But most of the agates we find are no bigger than a fingernail. Sometimes we spot them through a layer of dust and give them a good spit to reveal their stripes.

Uncle says we can be the best agate hunters because we are smaller and close to the ground and have more time to look. But riding home from a field one day, he is the one with the eye of a hawk who stops the tractor, climbs down, and walks back to pick up an agate he spotted as we drove over it.

Even though he still sucks his thumb, Bruce is the most persistent agate hunger, spotting and saving even the tiniest chips, things you can hardly call an agate. Blaine is pickier in terms of size. I save only the ones with good stripes. We bring our handfuls and pocketfuls of agates home, where Mama finds them tucked into corners, on kitchen counters, in pant pockets, and by the bathroom sink. All the agates on the whole road, from the west corner to the highway, seem to end up in our house. Eventually, they end up in a jar, and we dream of having enough money to get them all polished someday.

If you were a hawk, you could look down on the land and see squares like a quilt, all white in the winter, different greens and yellows in spring, summer, and fall. Each square is one mile long and one mile wide, marked by the light brown gravel roads. But the oldest roads are exceptions, like the Government Road where Mama and Auntie grew up, because those roads were wagon trails once, and Indian trails before that, following the land instead of the sky. Old roads and creeks run through the squares like ragged rips.

I know this because of the plat book that Daddy keeps in one of our kitchen drawers. Some mornings, Uncle stops over after breakfast and they take it out and read the names of who owns what. I can't read the names, but one day Daddy shows me our farm and I see the square-mile blocks. I see that each square mile contains sixteen smaller blocks, a quarter mile by a quarter mile. The smaller blocks are what they call *forties*, because each one is forty acres. The Marty farm has five and a half small blocks: three and a half along the road called the Pine County line, and two just north of the first row. If you drive along Highway 61, a half mile of the highway forms the eastern edge of our farm.

On the next page of the plat book is the farm where Mama and Auntie grew up. The Anderson farm has five blocks, with two that touch the county line. By the time the little creek through the Marty farm gets to the Anderson farm, it is cutting through deep ravines on its way to Rock Creek.

On the plat maps, you see the squares and roads and creeks, but you can't see the trees. You can't see that the Marty woods are an island and the Anderson woods are the tip of a forest bigger than any farm.

Uncle and Daddy are talking about how to make the farm better. What is their task? They're telling each other Sam and Grampa's stories, remembering how and when all our farm buildings filled in the space between the barns and the house, and how some things disappeared, like the blades that blew off the windmill in a storm, never replaced because by then electric power had arrived.

This spring, Uncle turns twenty-nine and Daddy twenty-six. They themselves remember when some things were built. The cement silo, just taller than the peak of the barn, replaced a wooden silo toppled in a storm. A hole in the yard terrified them in 1940, when Uncle was six and Daddy three, before Sam's new house—now our house—emerged, complete with running water from a new well. At the end of the war, Sam built the unbelievable three-car garage. The year Daddy and Mama got married, Grampa and Daddy made scaffolding and climbed up to put a new roof on the big barn, beautiful green shingles over the weathered wood ones.

The farm has never had so many cows, but still doesn't sell enough milk to pay the bills. Mama makes money working at home as a bookkeeper for the school. Auntie's job at the hospital allows her and Uncle to have nice things now, but if she has a baby, she won't be able to keep working. There is no way to make more money for all of us without more cows, and there is no way to fit more cows into the two barns we have.

Cows fill the twenty-six stanchions in the east end of the big barn, and young cows with new calves fill the west end, where horses used to be. Behind their mothers, calves are tethered to the outer walls on beds of straw. Heifers fill the wooden stanchions in the log barn.

In the big barn, I pet my favorite cows, Caroline and Jessica. I like Caroline because she's almost all black, sleek and beautiful for such a big creature. I like Jessica because of the sound of her name and the way she watches me thoughtfully, unafraid but gentle, as if she'd like to talk. As Daddy and Uncle throw down silage and scoop it into the mangers, I clean out the big metal drinking cups between the stanchions. During milking, I pet the cats. After milking, after one of the men throws hay down and breaks open the bales, I walk back and forth, separating and spreading out the hay chunks in the mangers, breathing in the green smell.

Daddy and Uncle load up the milk cans, drive them to the milk house, and lift them into the stock tank of ice-cold water. The cans are as high as my chest but Daddy and Uncle are strong enough to lift them easily. Every other morning, one of the men backs the pickup next to the milk house, pulls all the heavy cans out of the cold tank, and loads them up again to drive them to town. At the Maple Island creamery, the cans are unloaded onto a moving metal track that carries them inside, where we pick up our butter and get empty cans to take home.

Every night, the men rinse the milkers and turn them upside down in the milk house; in the morning, they carry the two milkers into Uncle and Auntie's house to wash them.

The men also clean the barns. Every day they shovel the manure out of the gutters and throw it out the doors of the barn. In the summer, it lands in the manure spreader and heads straight out to the fields, but in winter, once the snow gets too deep in the fields, the manure collects in piles next to the barns to be brought to the fields when the snow melts.

This is the way it has been since Uncle and Daddy can remember, although Grampa used horses for some of the chores when the tractor wouldn't start or broke down or couldn't make it through the snow. It was Sam who made sure the farm was modern, first bringing electricity to the big barn, then the air-pressure line so they could use milkers instead of milking by hand.

Now, once again, there are two ways our farm can go, old-fashioned or modern. It can stay the same, or it can become a Grade A farm, a farm for the future, for the twins.

Last year at the state fair, Uncle and Daddy started looking carefully for ideas. Salesmen from a company in Lester Prairie come to visit and they even talk with the twins, despite the fact that Bruce and Blaine are only three. The salesmen show pictures of modern barns being built on other dairy farms. If we get a bulk tank, Uncle and Daddy won't have to haul milk cans to the creamery anymore, and our milk will be clean enough for Grade A instead of B, so it will be worth more money. New barns also have barn cleaners, which means Uncle and Daddy won't have to lift and shovel manure out of the new barn.

All winter, Uncle and Auntie and Daddy and Mama discuss the farm. If Jacob and Susanna could cross the ocean and make this farm, if Sam and Grampa could work so hard to make it better, if our family has been blessed—and it has—then they can do this. It's expected of them, to have faith, to act.

Upstairs in the big house with Gramma, I sit over the heating vent, embroidering dishtowels with a cat for every day of the week. I can hear Uncle and Auntie downstairs, eating supper and talking.

"It's a lot of money for a new barn," Gramma says, sitting beside me in her rocker. "I don't know how we're going to pay for it. Then we'll need a new silo too."

Once, Gramma tells me, we almost lost the farm. After Sam died, his widow—his second wife, Great-aunt Margaret—didn't want to live on the farm anymore. Grampa and Gramma had to pay her for Sam's half, and she moved to town.

"That almost killed your Grampa," Gramma says, her voice tight.

The snow has melted, the big barn and log barn are cleaned, and field work begins. We help rake the yard and burn leaves. Our trikes come out of the garage, and Bruce and Blaine and I hunt for agates and play with the dog Blackie and her puppies on the grass.

Decisions have to be made, and Daddy and Uncle and Mama and Auntie Lou make them.

The chicken house is empty, and we'll sell the pigs soon too. The Marty brothers will specialize in dairy. We'll build a new barn and it will be a hundred feet long, with stanchions for forty-six cows instead of twenty-six, a barn cleaner, and a bulk tank for Grade A milk. We'll milk more cows, and we'll rent land from Grampa Anderson to have more hay and corn to feed them. To do it all, Marty Brothers will take out a loan for $12,600 that will be paid off when we earn more milk money.

"It's a good thing Grampa Marty isn't alive to know," Gramma says.

But I think Sam would approve.

All our summer work goes on as usual, but now strangers are on the farm every day too. Men come to measure the space for the new barn, and mark it off with narrow sticks and orange tape that flies in the breeze. It's a long space south of the big barn, just as wide but much longer. The two barns will stand side by side, connected by a hallway.

Uncle leads the twins and me into the driveway and points, then helps us climb up to see the place where Sam carved his name when the big barn was new: *Sam Marty 1902*, in beautiful letters.

"Uncle Sam was fourteen years old when they built this barn," Uncle tells us. "They brought white pine up from the St. Croix River for all those big beams." He points and we turn, scanning the giant beams through the haymow, like giants holding up the roof of our barn. "Yessir, that was something! Thirty feet high—enormous!" He looks down at us happily. "And your Grampa was ten years old. He was the one who led the cows into this barn the first time."

In June, when we start to bale hay and put it in the mow, the space marked for the new barn blocks the tractor's way through what is now called the old barn. Instead of driving through, Daddy backs the tractor and hay wagons out of the haymow driveway.

Digging machines come, then machines that roll the ground flat. Then a truck full of cement that makes a gray border, like the edge of a puzzle, with blank spaces for doors. On top of the cement border, thin walls made of something like plywood are nailed up.

Everybody is excited, but especially Uncle. He smiles a lot and laughs.

When the men come to raise the rafters for the roof, I can't believe the new barn will be so low — I thought it would be tall. The old barn is thirty feet to the peak, but the new barn will be only twelve feet, with no haymow.

"You won't be able to go through the haymow driveway in the old barn anymore!" I protest to Daddy.

"We can back out," he says simply, and smiles at me.

After the roof is done, trucks come to pour the cement that fills in the long floor. As the trucks roar in and out all day, their huge drums turning, pouring out cement, the twins and I are forbidden to leave the circle of grass around the houses. After the trucks are gone for the day, we hunt for agates.

It is August 1963, and Mama starts writing in a diary every night before bed. Everything seems about to change.

For days, weeks, the cement dries. We're not allowed to go on it even after it's hard because the gutters are so deep — we might trip and bang our heads or knock our teeth out.

The new milk house is attached to the new barn, jutting out the south side, with windows facing Uncle and Auntie's house. The bulk tank, a huge stainless steel drum to cool and hold the milk, is delivered and anchored into the cement floor of the milk house before walls are built around it. A trench is dug from the milk house to the pump between our two houses — a long, inconvenient gash across the driveway and yard. Mama and Auntie's brother, Uncle Duane, comes to dig a septic tank behind the milk house.

The shingles of the new barn are light green. The walls are painted white, inside and out, which seems strange for a barn. Mama and Auntie and Uncle and Daddy all paint until late at night, listening to baseball on the transistor radio. One of the twins pounds a nail into the top of a paint can that is to be returned to the store, but he won't admit it, so we all get spanked.

Out in the field next to the houses, the corn is tall and green and everywhere it smells like tasseling. But inside the new barn, it still smells like cement. Metal plates are fitted across the gutters at the walkways in the middle and on the east end, and the twins and I immediately take our trikes and drive them around as fast as we can. Bruce takes a corner too sharp, tips the trike, and bangs his head, but he gets up and starts again, this time more precise about turning. The barn cleaner is installed and tested, making a deafening, scraping sound. Daddy grins.

Lying long and white beside the old barn, the new barn is perfectly clean, empty, and cool in the August heat. I'm disappointed — it's not beautiful to me, and it doesn't match anything on the farm. It's pale and flat, its windows wide and plain instead of tall with quarter-panes. The driveway through the old barn is now a dead end. Electric trainers hang above each cow's stanchion, upside-down T-bars made of wire that will give shocks when cows arch their backs, to keep them from spraying manure and pee all over the walk. Uncle assures me that the bars give only small shocks, like pinches.

"They'll learn after just a couple times," he says.

I am anxious about Jessica and Caroline. I visit them in their old-barn wooden stanchions, chewing new hay. I walk down the center aisle and pet all the cows' faces.

One late afternoon in September when Uncle calls *C'm baaaaaaaas!* the cows come from the pasture into the new barn instead of the old. They are completely confused. Nobody leads them — not me or the twins or even Uncle or Daddy. We don't want anyone to be hurt, especially on such an important day, but we are all there, plus the dogs, Princess and Blackie. The double doors at the west end are wide enough for two or even three cows, and they bunch up, peering into the bare cement room, hesitating. The dogs bark and circle but only seem to make the cows more nervous. Pretty soon there's manure and pee on the new walk and a cow slips. Bruce and Blaine and I are asked to stay outside because we make the cows nervous, but the twins can't stay out because they're sure they can help.

I sit down on the stone step outside the log barn and listen to the confusion and yelling inside the new barn. I look at the cement ramp of the big barn that the cows were used to walking up single file. It takes two-and-a-half hours to get all thirty-five of them into the new barn, with Mama, Auntie, Grampa Anderson, and a neighbor helping.

The second night, it takes an hour and a half, but the third night only half an hour. The cows are learning their stanchions, their faces to the walls now instead of each other, so when they walk in they must go a certain number of steps and then choose, left or right, step over a deep gutter, drink from a deeper cup. They are learning the smell of cement, the sting of the T-bars. But they are eating the same silage, the same feed and hay. Dorothy has the first calf in the new barn, a little heifer we name Daisy.

Caroline stands on the north side, next to the center walk. Jessica stands farther east, third from the end. They seem fine, but not as close to me.

The men have to throw silage down into the silo room on the east end of the old barn, and push the silage carts all the way through the old barn into the new barn, up and down the aisles, to feed all the cows. When the new barn is paid for, the men plan to build a new, bigger silo attached to the new barn.

In the old barn, the stanchions stand ready for the heifers to come in when the weather turns cold. The old stanchion room smells like silage, and the haymows are full. I imagine Grampa Marty leading the cows into it the first time, when it was bright and empty and smelled like wood. I walk into the log barn, which is empty now but ready to be filled up completely with third-crop hay instead of heifers and calves.

The old red milk house next to the windmill on the hill is deserted. Every other day, the bulk truck comes to pick up our milk from the cold tank in the new milk house. The driver pushes a giant hose through a trap door and attaches it to the bulk tank, and all the milk is sucked cleanly out into the tank of the truck.

People stop by to see our new barn. They comment on how nice our two barns look, the big red old barn and the long white new barn.

The log barn, no longer for animals, becomes the shed it always appeared to be.

My friend Beverly visits with her parents, who used to live on a farm nearby. Now her dad owns a hardware store twenty miles away. Beverly, a year older than me, is a town girl who loves farms.

"Show me the old barn," she says after she's seen the new barn. "I like it better." We walk into the old barn and climb up in the haymow and pet cats. I show her where the horses used to be, on the west end. We walk to the east end, down the aisle between the stanchions, through the silo room, and out by the log barn.

"This is the *really* old barn, the log barn," I tell her. "Jacob and Susanna Marty came from Switzerland and built this barn."

"Let's go in!" she exclaims.

I take her around to the sunny south side, to the lean-to with the stone step. Inside, there's a little space left for third crop. She pushes me inside ahead of her, and I clear away a spiderweb. She puts her hands on the worn doorposts and on the prickly straw bales. I point up to the beams under the shingles, not far above our heads.

"Let's play here," she says. "We're pioneers, and this is our cabin."

We play—peering into the well in the old milk house, poking into the dirt where Uncle thinks the real cabin used to stand, sitting in the north lean-to on machinery that horses used to pull, grinding imaginary grain between stones, pretending to sleep on the straw and looking up at the beams above us—until her parents yell that it's time to go.

The driveway past the big house is worn into ruts from all the construction, so we order a load of gravel. The morning after it's delivered, just as the men are finishing milking, Uncle sees me from the door of the new barn and calls me to hunt for agates with him. I spy one in the early light. It's so big I'm not sure what I'm seeing. I can't believe Uncle didn't see it first. I pick it up. It's still almost round, like the lava bubble it must have been, chipped wide open on one side, just a little on the other. The lines, white and reddish brown and clear, make an oval with two points, one sharp and one slightly more rounded.

"Uncle, is this an agate?" I ask him.

He glances over and flashes a smile, then takes it from me carefully and nods excitedly. He turns it over and sees the stripes coming through on the other side in a spot as big as his thumb.

"My, my!" he says, still nodding and then smiling wide. "Yes indeed, that's an agate! That's a beauty—my, oh my! You better show your Daddy!" He hands it back to me.

Inside the new barn, light floods straight through the open door on the east end. From between two cows, Daddy steps across the deep gutter. He stops to glance at the agate, and nods appreciatively.

"Make a fist," says Uncle. I grip the agate in my hand. "With your other hand!" he laughs. "When you make a fist, that shows you the size of your heart."

I make a fist with my left hand and compare it to the stone. My agate is as big as my fist, as big as my heart.

"Wait 'til your brothers see that!" Uncle exclaims with a big, ringing laugh.

The agate is kept on Mama's dresser because I'm afraid I'll lose it. Later, we take it to a polisher, where the big, oval, open side is made as smooth as glass. After it comes home, I can sit and close my eyes and hold it, feeling its weight, touching the dull side and the glassy side. I wonder how far it traveled, thinking of movement, of glaciers and agates and trees and people moving over the face of the earth as God moved over the face of the waters before there was earth, before there was time.

Oak

Oak trees fill our farm with friendly fatness, in the woods and pastures and around the yard. One stands in the middle of the open space between the barn and the houses, making shade over the gas barrel. Each corncrib has an oak tree for shade. A line of three oak trees marks the center of the lawn between the two houses.

The oak tree I know best is my swing tree, shading the pump house and sandbox. The huge trunk has rough gray bark with furrows as deep as my fingers, and the leaves are shaped like mittens with too many thumbs, dark and glossy on top and silvery underneath. They rustle like paper in the wind.

I sit for hours on the notched wooden seat of the swing, holding the ropes in my hands, facing northeast toward our fields and the woods beyond them. From early spring, when the snow melts enough that I can swing my legs underneath the seat, through summer, when the bare patch under my feet turns to soft dust, through August, when hard but furry acorns fall and force me to wear shoes, to fall, when the rusty gold leaves lay thick on the ground, I swing and tell myself stories, pumping myself higher to see the border of the woods above the growing cornfields.

Sometimes I turn and face the other way, toward the road and, three miles away, the mill and water tower of the town on the horizon. But the seat feels uneven.

Daddy has a Bible with four translations side by side. I notice in some versions that oak is the name used for trees called terebinth in other versions. Maybe it's because oak groves in England signify the same thing as groves of terebinth in Bible lands — sacredness.

Oak tree with a swing, you stand in the middle of my life: the big house on one side, my house on the other, the barns and sheds and fields and woods ahead of me, the road and town at my back, and your shelter above my head.

4

The Word

Thy word is a lamp unto my feet
and a light unto my path.

—Psalm 119:105

As we drive to Sunday school at East Rock Creek, everything white is bright in the morning light on the brown fields: white patches on black and white cows, white bundles of the Hendricksons' woolly sheep, white rectangle of our church. In the gardens, only asters and mums with their tough stems remain, leaves falling around them. Inside the church on the communion table, Gramma's sister Effie arranges a cornucopia, a wicker horn with corn and gourds spreading across a red and yellow cloth, a handful of oat stalks, two dark-orange pumpkins.

Our church will close. It's too small, not enough people to support a pastor, and we'll become one with the Baptist church in town.

Now thank we all our God, we sing, *with hearts and hands and voices.*

Sunlight through bare trees, through the windows, reflects off the white pages in the hymnal, off the thin white pages of tiny black words I can't read yet in Daddy's Bible.

At home, in Gramma's upstairs place, we all sit near the TV and watch the funeral of President Kennedy, Mrs. Kennedy all in black, Caroline the same age as me, John the same as the twins. Even though they are Catholic, no one mentions it now. Gramma cries when the black horse appears without a rider and rears up.

Daddy is on the pulpit committee to call a new pastor for the joining congregation, so our family invites a candidate over for dinner. He is very tall with a long name that sounds to me like Mackle-heron, and at the pulpit he is thoughtful and quiet. Later at our house, while the potatoes and vegetables cook and Mama cuts the roast, he takes the twins and me on his lap and reads us all the books we want: Woody

Woodpecker, Road Runner, and Mother Goose. He asks us questions like *What do you think of Jesus?* and listens to our answers. "He loved his sheep," Bruce says.

He asks if we know the story of Jesus and the children.

Yes, we tell him, people brought their children to Jesus, but his disciples tried to keep them away, told them not to bother.

"And what did Jesus think about that?"

"He said, 'Suffer the little children to come unto me,'" we recite.

"That's right," he smiles. "And he took them in his arms and blessed them."

The pastor's name is Lawrence McElheran, his voice is very gentle, and he pauses before answering. He listens and looks us in the eyes and smiles and even laughs in a gentle way. When I show him my doll, he asks her name.

"Beth Ann," I reply.

"That is a beautiful name!" he says. "In our family, we have a girl named Beth Ann, and I think she's just one year older than you."

In fact, he has five children, four girls and a boy, and Beth Ann is the youngest.

That week, the pulpit committee decides to call him to Rush City, and he accepts.

On the last Sunday of the year, we walk into our old church, the furnace burning for the last time. Facing the painting of Jesus the shepherd in the field with his sheep, we sing.

I heard the bells on Christmas Day, their old familiar carols play. Mama and Daddy's voices harmonize, different notes but close together. *And wild and sweet the words repeat, of peace on earth, good will to men.*

Inside my head, I hold the words: *wild and sweet the words repeat.*

We come again in the evening when the stars are up, to pray and sing again.

Standing at the portal of the opening year, words of comfort meet us . . .

The benches creak as people take turns praying.

. . . Till ringing, singing on its way, the world revolved from night to day . . .

The doors close on the green and pink walls, the shepherd and sheep, the communion table set with pine boughs and candles.

. . . Onward then, and fear not, children of the day, for his Word shall
never, never pass away!

Rush City Baptist is on the highway through town, painted white like
the country church, but it has a steeple and is square instead of long.
A big bare elm stands over the parking lot in back. Inside, under a soar-
ing ceiling, there are three sections of pews and two aisles. On the platform behind the pulpit, a life-sized wooden cross, polished smooth, is
fastened to the wall, with fluorescent lights glowing behind it. In front
of the platform is the communion table, a piano on the left and a little
orange organ on the right, whose quivery electric sound I don't like.
When the music stops, I hear the sound of the traffic outside on Highway 61. Our family sits on the right side, in the second-to-the-back row,
near the stairway to the basement, so Daddy can slip out easily with one
of the twins when they misbehave.

The town church was originally a daughter to the country church,
so we already know some of the people — Bergfalks, who live on our
road, and Whittakers, who own the locker plant where our meat is
butchered and stored in a huge freezer. There are lots of people we are
glad to get to know, including Alice Meissner, the only Baptist on the
school board; the family of a teacher named Swenson; and a woman
who wears a fur coat, her hair in a French roll, and who teaches Sunday
school in an unfamiliar accent.

The new Rush City Baptist is the third biggest church in town, after
First Lutheran by Rush Creek, and Sacred Heart Catholic on the main
street. There are smaller churches too, whose names I don't know.

Town is unfamiliar. The twins and I know the creamery on the
highway, where we hauled milk cans before the new barn was built. We
know the Mobil station with the red flying horse, kitty-corner from the
church, where Gramma's Uncle Julius Hendrickson and his Swedish
wife, Ruth, pump gas and wipe windshields and run the cash register.
On the main street through town, we know Peterson's Grocery, where
Mama gets crabby shopping, and Hilding behind the butcher counter
tries to cheer her up with his booming voice. We also know the bank
across from the park, where Daddy and Uncle go to deposit the milk
check, and the feed mill by the creek, where our corn and oats are
ground into feed.

The town is named after the creek, Rush Creek, which comes out of Rush Lake, a big lake west of town. The creek flows east to the St. Croix River. But the feed mill isn't connected to the creek anymore. In the feed mill office, the twins and I use pennies to get salted peanuts from a machine, and try to decipher the clock because we're scared of the big whistle that hoots at noon—it's so loud it makes the hair on our necks stand up. Out on the mill floor, back with the fertilizer and seeds, we find stacks of salt blocks and dare each other to lick them.

In the spring, I start going to town every day for six weeks of kindergarten. The class meets near the feed mill in the new tan-block municipal building, which also contains the fire station, library, and jail. Our teacher, Mrs. Moulton, is a member of the Baptist church and seems way too young to have been Mama's sixth-grade teacher once. She speaks very softly and clearly.

Six weeks seems like a long time. Mama takes turns with two other mothers on the west road driving children to town, including a new girl who just moved in around the corner from us—she has ringlets of long blond hair, beautiful drooping blue eyes, and a lisp. A lot of the town kids know each other already.

We sit at tables of six to draw and color and count, take naps, play farmer-in-the-dell and musical chairs, build with blocks, and plant seeds in cups of dirt. We learn each other's names, and we learn to write our own names on blue-lined paper, copying Mrs. Moulton's letters. The new neighbor girl writes her name, Kathryn Sybrant, and I show her mine. We notice that each of us has a *y* in both our first and last names.

At the end of the six weeks there will be a program for the parents in which we'll act out the story of the Little Red Hen. I am proud and yet embarrassed to be cast as the hen. Then chicken pox sweeps through the class and I break out, scalp to toes, and have to miss the program.

In Sunday school at the town church, I join a class with kids mostly older than me. Seven regulars are near the end of first grade and learning to read, so I sit next to the wall at the end of the table and try to follow along with help from the pictures. The stories are Elijah and Elisha, Isaiah and Jeremiah, Jonah and Daniel. I love the picture of Elijah going to heaven in a fiery chariot over the Jordan River, with Elisha looking after him, holding up his cloak in the wind to shield himself from the light.

Our teacher is the lady with the French roll and the accent. She doesn't ask me questions that require reading, but I have a good memory, so I often know the answers anyway. She leads a game, telling us the name of a book, chapter, and verse in the Bible, which we race to find in our Bibles. I feel the silky pages between my fingers and begin to remember by sound the names of the books in groups and sets: Genesis, Exodus, Leviticus, Numbers, Deuteronomy . . . Joshua, Judges . . . Job, Psalms, Proverbs . . . Isaiah, Jeremiah . . . Matthew, Mark, Luke, John, Acts . . . Galatians, Ephesians . . . first, second, and third John, Jude, Revelation.

Pastor and Mrs. McElheran's five kids are Miriam, June, Loren, Patty, and Beth. It's thrilling to have girls who are fun and friendly and pay attention to me. One afternoon in the spring when they come out to the farm, Patty grabs an electric fence by accident and can't let go. She starts to cry, but we pull her off and she's fine. She even laughs and wants to come back.

After school is out, we have vacation Bible school every morning for a week at church, and Patty and Beth invite me to come play at the parsonage. There's a weeping willow tree across the street, and I ask if we can play under it with our dolls. They say no because the lady who lives there is crabby, but later we see her leave, so we go over and play until she comes back and chases us out of her yard. We play sidewalk games and walk uptown to the dairy to get milk for their mother, but we also get sherbet push-ups and chocolate ice cream bars. We buy bananas and make chocolate-banana shakes at home in their kitchen.

In the summer, we sleep out on the porch because it's crowded and hot upstairs. They position the sleeping bags so we can look up and backward and see the sky between their house and the spruce trees of the house next door. They get me to stay awake and watch for falling stars, which I have never seen in my whole life, but lying there with them I see *three* falling stars shoot across the sky in one night. When I see the first star fall, I'm so surprised, I forget to wish, but the second time, I wish Uncle and Auntie's next baby will be fine, and the third time, I wish for a sister.

June McElheran is fourteen and comes to our house to be Mama's helper for a wage. She shells peas and snaps beans, hangs wash on the line, washes dishes, and does all kinds of things she wants to learn. She likes working on the farm because she's always lived in town, and here she gets to run around. She likes working for Mama because Mama is clean and organized and pretty and smart—she will show you how to do something, correcting you when you do it wrong and praising you when you do it right.

June is tall and skinny with freckles and reddish-brown hair that curves under or flips out, depending on how she sets her rollers. Her birthday isn't in June and her first name isn't even June, it's Audrey, but her family has always called her by her middle name.

June laughs a lot. Part of her job is watching the twins and me. The twins love June—she is the prettiest, most daring girl they've ever known. She likes Bruce and Blaine because they like to chase and be chased and are cute and funny. She likes me too, and talks to me sometimes when I'm hunting for agates on the road or playing with my dolls in the yard.

She's tall enough to drive the truck for the tow-rope when we put hay up in the mow, and she learns not to jerk the truck. She makes Uncle laugh. She also isn't afraid of heights—she climbs up in the hay-mow, up the windmill, up trees. One time, Patsy, another girl her age, comes out to the farm, and they both chase the twins. When it's the twins' turn to chase them, the girls climb up in a pine tree in front of Auntie and Uncle's house and don't come down. Bruce and Blaine yell up furiously, saying the girls have to come down or they'll get pine sap on their clothes. But June and Patsy aren't like girls they know—they don't care about clothes. They just laugh and babysit the twins from up in the pine tree for about an hour.

Mama is sewing dresses for me for first grade. She makes print dresses with double-breasted corduroy vests in solid colors and buys socks to match the vests. There are other things too, a black-and-brown plaid smock with white daisies around the neck, and a white blouse with a collar Mama calls Peter Pan. She buys me black corduroy pants and underwear in size 6x, and new leather shoes with ties.

June tells me the story of her first day of school, when the teacher kept calling her Audrey and she didn't answer until the teacher got angry, and how she went home crying and her dad had to go the next day to explain things to the teacher.

"You'll have a great day," she assures me. "Nothing like that will happen to you!"

With June, work is fun. We pick things from the garden, tomatoes in our wagon, sweet corn in our wagon. Sitting under the ash tree on the north side of the house, we husk corn.

Auntie's car comes in their driveway and parks behind their house. Auntie gets out of the car, slings her purse over her shoulder, waves to us, and lumbers into her house. All summer we haven't dared talk much about Auntie and Uncle's new baby coming, and Auntie's kept on working. I want to hug her but don't dare. I think she's brave.

I wonder what she's thinking, I wonder what Uncle is thinking, and I wonder what God thinks. I can't imagine what will happen if this baby dies too. Pastor and Mrs. Mac come out to the farm and help can vegetables and do chores and play music and pray with us. But thinking about the new baby has kept me from thinking too much about school. Starting school is such a little thing compared with a baby being born.

"The only thing we can do is trust God," June says, pulling the soft but tough green husk back from the yellow ear. "Trust when it's the one thing that seems impossible. Trust, and pray." She stops and looks at me. "Do you want to pray now?"

I nod but can't speak. June prays instead. She talks as if Jesus has walked under the tree with us and is standing there in the shade, listening. Then my voice asks him to please come into my heart. I inhale—breath of God that smells like corn silk—and feel calm.

The baby is born at the end of the summer, on Labor Day. Uncle calls and reports *It's a healthy boy!* Auntie is fine, and the baby is beautiful, his skin dark and his eyes shaped like almonds, so dark they're already almost brown. His name is Jonathan, the name of King David's best friend from the time they were boys playing in the woods. His middle name is Gaylon.

The bus comes in the morning when the shadows are still long. Everything, starting with the bus, smells like new shoes. I see Kathy and another girl from kindergarten named Heidi. We sit together behind the bus driver, who is friendly and calls us by name. There are big boys who act tough and sassy, including triplets who live a mile west of our farm, but they don't talk back to the driver.

All the children, first grade to twelfth, go to school at the same place, but the littlest of us go to classrooms in an addition connected by a tunnel. On the west side of the school, we sit in desks facing north. Across the street is a little white church with green trim and a steeple.

Kathy, Heidi, and I are all in Miss Gilbert's class. She is beautiful and tall with styled hair, red lipstick, and high heels. She smells like powder and perfume. It's peaceful in our room. The loudest girls and boys from kindergarten are in the other first-grade room with Mrs. Jarchow, who is older and looks kind but very stern.

I sit in the second row from the door, in the second to the last seat behind a very quiet boy with shiny black hair. I look at the letters above the board.

"What is this?" says Miss Gilbert, tapping the letters above her head with a long wooden pointer. "Who knows what this is? Carol?"

"The alphabet."

"That's right, the alphabet." Miss Gilbert smiles and looks from face to face. "There are twenty-six letters in the alphabet, and you are going to learn them all. In a few weeks you'll know them by heart! It may take some work, but you will learn them."

I'm stunned. I can't believe I will know all of them, in order, and so quickly. But I trust her: if she says we will, we must. All of us will learn to read.

She divides us into groups and names each group after a bird, then calls each group to a circle in the front, one circle at a time. I am in the cardinal group.

Above each letter is a picture of something that starts with the letter. A, apple. B, ball. C, cat. D, drum. E, the head of an elephant with a tusk and a curving trunk. F, flag. G, a fish. I know it must be a goldfish, I recognize the first letter of my name, but it's confusing. I think, what if somebody doesn't know about goldfish and just thinks it's a fish?

G is a confusing letter anyway. I know it can have two sounds, one as in Gayla and Gaylon and Gordon, and one as in Genesis, the same sound as J in June.

But I listen. After awhile we start talking about numbers and time. On the clock above the alphabet, the minutes go by, the long hand clicking from one tiny mark to the next.

Twice we go out to play: once in the middle of the morning, and once after lunch in the noisy lunchroom. We play on black tar, on swings, a merry-go-round, a jungle gym, and monkey bars made out of pipes. Some girls have brought jump ropes. Boys run and throw red rubber balls and orange basketballs. Baseballs aren't allowed because they're too hard. One girl falls on the tar after lunch and goes inside crying with a bloody knee.

In the afternoon, the sun shines into our room. Miss Gilbert opens the windows and door and pulls all the shades. When the small hand of the clock points to three and the long hand starts from twelve toward one, the orange buses begin to line up outside.

In school, we have Tom and Betty and Susan, Tip their dog, Mother and Father, and Zeke, the hired man. Tom and Betty and Susan play with a ball. Tip gets in trouble because he chases the ball into the garden. Zeke gets upset, but then he helps them get it out.

In Sunday school, we have Samuel, who heard God speak when he was a little boy; Josiah, who became king when he was eight and did what was right; Ahab and Jezebel, who sacrificed children to the god Baal; Nebuchadnezzar, who threw Daniel into the lions' den even though he didn't want to. We have Ezekiel, who saw visions in the sky, and John the Baptist, who ate grasshoppers and honey and baptized people in the Jordan River.

Genesis, *in the beginning;* Exodus, *going out,* as in the exit sign above the doors at school.

In the beginning was the Word, and the Word was God. John 1:1.

A is for apple. It's also for Adam, the first man, and Abraham, who left his home to follow God and would have killed his son for a sacrifice if an angel hadn't stopped him. A: agate, accordion, alfalfa.

B is for ball and Bruce and Blaine. Daddy takes them along to town one day and they come home with good-smelling leather baseball gloves from Nessel hardware, amazed by how much money they cost and that Daddy was willing to spend it. I wonder when I might get one, and think maybe we can't afford it.

C is for cow, corn, clover, collie, crappie, but also works with *h* to make the sound in cherry and chicken or the sound in Chevrolet, our car, and the sound of *k* in Christ.

D is for Deuteronomy. E is for Eve, Eden, Egypt, Exodus, exile, Esther, Ecclesiastes, Ezra, Ezekiel, Ephesians, and for Effie, elm tree, east, evening, and electric fence. F is for famine, as in the King of Egypt's dream of seven fat cows, and seven skinny cows that came up and ate the fat cows. It's also for fence—every spring we repair fences, drive the truck up to the woods and reattach barbed wire, repair the electric fence, straighten fence posts and replace a few. F is for faith—*Great is thy faithfulness, O God my father, there is no shadow of turning with thee.*

In town, the north–south streets are called avenues and have names from A to H.

The east–west streets are numbered, starting with First on the north side of town, and Fifth next to the creek. The school is between Eliot and Field.

Pastor Mac loves music. He says our church is rich in music and we better use it. There's always special music on Sunday morning — solo, duet, trio, quartet, or quintet—and sometimes Ellie Whittaker plays her marimba, holding sticks with yarn balls on the ends and accompanied by the little organ, which is the only time the organ sounds good. Sometimes somebody will play an autoharp, which Mama loves.

Guitars and other instruments are generally reserved for Sunday night, when there's more music than anytime else. Pastor Mac found out right away that Mama played guitar, Auntie Lou played accordion, and they sang quartet with Daddy and Uncle. It wasn't long before he brought a guitar over and then got other people to bring their instruments to church—more guitars, Roy Tillman's saw and harmonica, Rollie Whittaker's bass guitar that plugs in to a loudspeaker. There's a whole string band. They play and sing "There is Power in the Blood" and "The Old-Time Religion" and "When the Roll is Called Up Yonder."

On Saturday nights or sometimes Sunday afternoons, before playing in church, Auntie and Uncle come over to practice. I get to hold the baby while Auntie lifts her red-and-white pearly accordion out of its case with the furry red interior. She slips the leather straps over her shoulders, sits on the flat arm of our green chair, and begins to pull and push the bellows with her left arm, pushing buttons on the top with her left hand and playing the keys with her right hand. It's a dazzling miracle and she always looks so casual, lips pressed together in what Mama calls her sassy smile. She'd rather not sing, but Uncle and Mama get her to sing anyway. Mama suggests who should sing which part, but they all seem to do it easily. Mama lays the guitar on her lap with her knees together, ankles slightly apart, adjusts the tuning to Auntie's accordion, and then slides a metal bar over the frets with her left hand while she strums with a pick on her right thumb.

All together they sing loudly in four parts. Mama likes to sing fast gospel songs like "Will the Circle Be Unbroken?" Auntie's favorite is "The Great Speckled Bird," but they never sing that in church.

Mama has a typewriter she uses to address envelopes and type letters for the work she does for the school. The letters on the keys aren't in any order I can understand. She explains that the letters we have to use most make our fingers reach the least. She rolls in a piece of used paper with the back side up and shows me how to make capitals. I type my name.

"How do you spell Bruce?" I call to Mama in the kitchen.

"B, r, u, c, e," she spells, and I pound the letters.

"How do you spell Blaine?"

"B, l, a, i, n, e."

I type all our names from oldest to youngest: Viola, Gaylon, Gordon, Margaret, Lorraine, Gayla, Bruce, Blaine, Jonathan. Then I type them in alphabetical order.

I type my address: Gayla Sue Marty, Route 2, Rush City, Minnesota 55069.

From our classroom at school, we walk in a double line through the tunnel to the annex, then up creaking stairs to a wide wooden hallway. We wait outside the library, shifting our weight on the creaky floor. The library is so small that we have to take turns — only eight or ten of us can go in at a time. We're allowed to take books only from shelves in a space on the right, which we can borrow, two at a time, when we sign our name on a card.

It's impossible to know which books to take or why I would want to. They don't have many words on each page, so by the time I've looked to see if I want one, I'm done reading it. Once I check out two books without looking at them first and am disappointed. I'm not interested in picture books very much. It's words I want—I can't stop reading until I'm done.

Pastor Mac takes his time giving a sermon, but he doesn't go too slowly. He gives you time to think. His voice is interesting but he never yells or slams the pulpit. He looks up through the huge arched windows to the west and to the south, and then at us. He seems to be listening for God. On the first Sunday of the month, when he comes down to the communion table and sits with the deacons, he takes off his jacket and rolls up his sleeves, as if to serve us dinner. He describes Jesus's last supper with his friends.

In a Bible story he reads one Sunday morning, people bring a woman to be stoned because she has broken the commandment *Thou shalt not commit adultery.* Jesus writes on the ground with his finger. He says, "He that is without sin among you, let him first cast a stone at her." All of them go away. Then Jesus says to her, "Go, and sin no more."

Pastor Mac believes that Jesus is the example to live by, even giving up his body to be crucified without striking back. He respects Martin Luther King Jr. for teaching and following that example. The two black families who live in Rush City attend our church, or at least the children do—the Wilsons and the Longs. They live across the Government Road from each other, a little more than a mile east of our farm. Their parents drop them off for Sunday school and pick them up right afterward. But Pastor Mac goes out to visit them, and every once in awhile the parents come.

Pastor Mac also doesn't seem to believe in living apart from the world. He suggests joining the other churches for a Thanksgiving service together. When I'm invited to go to a movie in Pine City for Heidi's birthday, Mama and Daddy argue. Daddy thinks we shouldn't go to movies, but Mama says, "It's *Mary Poppins,* don't be ridiculous."

"It's *Mary Poppins* this time, but what will it be next?" Daddy says. "'Be ye not conformed to this world,'" he quotes from Paul's letter to the Romans.

"The Weichmans are perfectly respectable people who happen to be Lutheran," says Mama. "They've invited Gayla to be their guest at their daughter's birthday party, to see a musical starring Julie Andrews. Are we going to say no?"

"Would Jesus spend his time at a movie theater?" Daddy asks.

"Yes, I think he would!" Mama argues back. "He sat at the table with everybody!"

"Jesus could do what he did because he was God—we can't." Daddy shakes his head. "*I* can't."

"Well, we might as well just take her out of school," Mama says.

In the end, I go, and for weeks we're all saying *supercalifragilistickexpealidotious.*

Our family fishes. Sam and Grampa loved to fish, and Grampa and Gramma loved to fish, and Uncle and Daddy grew up fishing. We don't fish on Rush Lake, but prefer Goose and Fish and Horseshoe lakes south of town. Daddy takes Mama, Uncle takes Auntie Lou, or Daddy and Uncle go together if there's a miraculous day they can both afford to be away from the farm for a morning or afternoon. Usually Daddy will take one of us kids along to sit in the middle of the boat and learn how to be patient.

I am excited one cloudy morning to go with Daddy and Uncle, but after we park the car, rent the boat, row to the middle of the empty lake, and put down our lines, the afternoon stretches out in front of me with a wave of dread. Daddy and Uncle sit with rods and reels, I sit with my bamboo pole, and nothing happens.

Uncle notices my discomfort and tries a story.

"The disciples were fishermen," he says. "Peter and Andrew and James and John. Jesus came along by the lake while they were mending their nets and called them. He said, 'I will make you fishers of *men.*' And he did. They followed Jesus and became fishers of men."

I know this story, and I think that to Uncle and Daddy, it proves how persuasive Jesus must have been. But to me, it proves that real fishing is work, just as I feel now. But it gives me the idea to pray. I know I'm not supposed to test God, but Gideon did, and I pray silently, concentrating. I pick my favorite number and pray to catch eight fish.

The clouds overhead have broken apart and a ray of sun glints on the lake. My bobber goes down, but I'm like Thomas and don't believe it's anything until I feel it and Daddy says, "I think you've got a bite there." I wait, and it draws down again.

"Up," Uncle says, smiling. "Lift up."

I lift up my pole and a wiggling fish breaks the surface. Daddy smiles too.

"It's a little sunfish!" Uncle says. "You got a sunny!"

I catch eight fish, and then I stop and we row in, because I also know the story of the empty-handed disciples, back to fishing after Jesus died, whose nets came in so full at sunrise that they broke, just because the risen Jesus came by. I also feel too much for the little sunfish caught on my hook, separated from their watery home forever.

During church if I think too hard about Jesus dying, I feel pressure on my chest. I know I'm supposed to love the cross, but I hate the giant cross in front of us. I feel sorry for the tree cut down to crucify Jesus, and I feel sorry for the tree cut down and polished to hang on that wall. I distract myself by copying the names of the books of the Bible, in order, on the back of the bulletin, seeing how many I can remember. I lean against Daddy's arm and lift his Bible up to my face and breathe in the smell of the leaves — *leaves.* I have learned that paper is made from trees, that trees give up their lives to be books and Bibles, telling the stories I love.

Bruce and Blaine cannot sit still in church. They squirm and bother each other and sometimes are downright mean, pinching each other, bumping each other, poking elbows. When Mama or Daddy hushes them, they make faces and laugh.

The first time Daddy takes one of them out, Mama gets angry because Daddy spanked him on the church steps in full view of all the traffic going by on Highway 61. Daddy says it's nothing to be embarrassed about — are we going to change just because people can see us now that we're in town?

"You say *I* worry too much what people think," he says disgustedly. "You care about pleasing complete strangers."

Pastor and Mrs. Mac have different ideas about disciplining children than most of us are used to. Generally, they do not believe in spanking. Pastor Mac makes his own kids know they've done wrong by talking to them, giving them time to sit in a room alone so they can hear God, and sometimes taking away privileges.

Pastor and Mrs. Mac also believe that very small children shouldn't be forced to sit still in church, and parents shouldn't be forced to make them *be* still. They have a nursery space created for Sunday morning worship, where parents can leave their children if they want. But Bruce and Blaine are too big for the nursery.

Most of the people in our church, though, and probably in our town believe in Proverbs 23:13 and 14—*Withhold not correction from the child: for if thou beatest him with the rod, he shall not die. Thou shalt beat him with the rod, and shalt deliver his soul from hell.* Most of my friends have been spanked, some more than others. Daddy thinks he learned a lot from getting spanked with a switch once in a while, especially since he had to go out and make his own switch.

Mama spanks us more often than Daddy does, because we're with her the most, because Daddy doesn't notice things as much, because usually what the twins destroy or get dirty is something Mama has made or cleaned. What I disobey is her word. For grievous things, she'll invoke Daddy's help, which is the worst thing, waiting for him to come in from milking. It's true that when he spanks it hurts a lot worse, even though he uses his bare hand instead of the strap—his hand is harder than leather. But he never hits more than ten times, and by the time he gets to five, Mama begs him to stop because the twins scream so loud. Bruce and Blaine think screaming makes Mama or Daddy stop sooner, but I think it just keeps them thinking that spanking works, so I refuse to cry, and they've just about stopped spanking me entirely.

Mama wants to agree with Pastor Mac. She hates spanking. She remembers her father not just spanking but striking her older brother and sister until they hated him. "Provoke not your children to wrath," she quotes, "but bring them up in the *nurture and admonition* of the Lord, Ephesians 6:4." She just doesn't know what else to do than spank. Maybe there's a difference between spanking and beating—spanking *might* qualify as admonition. At any rate, Bruce and Blaine need a lot of admonition.

The first big fight Mama and Uncle have is about spanking. Uncle specifically told Bruce and Blaine not to hunt for Summer Kitty's kittens—they knew the rule, and he reminded them, but they did it anyway. They found her kittens, took them out of their nest in the haymow, and petted them before she brought them out herself, and Uncle found them doing it. They not only knew the kittens could be abandoned and die, but they willfully disobeyed, and he spanked them for it in the driveway of the barn.

Bruce and Blaine ran crying at the top of their lungs to our house, "Uncle spanked us!" Mama flew to the barn—she surprised Uncle by yelling at the top of her lungs: "Don't you dare spank my children, ever again! Don't you dare!"

Still, she goes right on spanking the twins whenever she thinks they need it. It isn't about spanking or not spanking—it's about who has the authority to spank whom. It's the first time we learn that Uncle has less authority than we thought.

Something is wrong with the boy who sits in front of me in school. He doesn't speak. Even when Miss Gilbert calls on him, standing right next to him, he looks straight ahead or down at the top of his desk and doesn't say anything.

"Ozzie?" she asks. "Ozzie?"

Why doesn't he answer?

One day she loses her temper. She stands beside him, looks at his paper, reaches down and writes across it, then pulls it off his desk. Her voice rises as it never has and she says his name as if spitting it, her face toward me but speaking to him. He is cowering in front of me. I feel shocked, my cheeks burn, I can't understand why she is yelling at him in front of all of us, and why he never speaks, never answers.

"Zero!" she yells. "O is for Ozzie and O—is also—zero!"

We are all paralyzed now. Her arm with the red fingernails and chalk make a slash above the head of a girl in front, striking out onto the blackboard: O, a giant O. She writes it hard, so hard that the chalk crumbles beneath her grip and sprays through the air. She holds up his paper for all of us to see and shakes it. Whatever is there, maybe nothing, she has covered with a dark black O.

O and Z become confused. O is for ostrich above the blackboard, for Ozzie in front of me, and for Obadiah the prophet, the shortest book in the Old Testament. The letter O is shaped like the number zero.

Z is for zebra and zoo, but also zero. Z is for Zacchaeus, the man who climbed up in a tree like a boy, to see Jesus. Z is for Zion. *By the rivers of Babylon, there we sat down and wept when we remembered Zion.* Susanna Marty was *Suzannah* when she came to America. I have seen it spelled in the trunk she brought with her, still upstairs in Gramma's house.

A to Z. In a language of the Bible, O is like Z, is called Omega and comes at the end. *I am Alpha and Omega, the beginning and the ending, saith the Lord, which is, and which was, and which is to come.*

Ozzie: outside on the playground I've seen him smile and play, but I can't think of his voice, I've never heard it. For Ozzie, I want first grade to end, I want summer.

❦

June comes to the farm again when school is out. Kathy Sybrant and I get to walk to the corner to meet each other and go to each other's houses to play. We jump rope. She tries to teach me cartwheels but I'm hopeless.

At vacation Bible school this year, I can easily read the easel with the words to the songs, and I go into the group that memorizes all the books of the Bible — law, history, poetry, prophecy; gospels, history, letters, prophecy.

We do Bible drills, racing to find verses and read them out loud.

Ephesians 6:1!

"Children, obey your parents in the Lord, for this is right."

Luke 6:31!

"And as ye would that men should do to you, do ye also to them likewise."

Psalm 34:1!

"I will bless the Lord at all times, his praise shall continually be in my mouth!"

We have a contest of who can memorize the most verses: you have to be able to say them exactly and also know the reference. I don't like contests but I decide to count all the verses I know by heart. I know twenty-one, but Joy Bergfalk probably knows a hundred without even trying. We practice in Pastor Mac's office because he's not there that early.

Pastor Mac finds me in his office, practicing verses.

"How are you doing?" he asks.

"I'm trying to learn verses."

"Well, that's good," he says. "But more important than how many you know is do you understand what they mean?"

"I think I do. I can't learn anything I don't understand very well."

"You'd be surprised," he says, smiling. "What's your favorite verse?"

"John 3:16. For God so loved the world that he gave his only begotten son, that whosoever believeth in him shall not perish, but have everlasting life."

"That's a good one," he agrees. "What does it mean to you?"

"That God, and Jesus, love all the people in the world."

He sits down in his office chair, a wooden armchair that rolls, tips back, and swivels, and picks up his Bible.

"Have you heard of Nicodemus?"

"I don't think so."

"He's the person Jesus was talking to when he said this." He reads to me very slowly the passage of Nicodemus coming to Jesus at night, of Jesus saying he must be born again.

"You see," he finishes, "Nicodemus was a very educated and thoughtful man, but even he had a hard time understanding. What do you think?"

"We start learning when we're born," I say, thinking of baby Jonathan making sounds, crawling, trying to pull himself up. "I think God wants us to keep learning." Pastor Mac considers this, nodding thoughtfully.

When Bible school ends, there's a baptism. It's the first baptism I can remember, although in Gramma's photo album I've seen a picture of a baptism in a lake. Now we bring a huge tank inside the sanctuary, a stock tank like the kind we use for watering our cows. The tall wooden doors on the east side are folded open and the tank is set up there with a white skirt around it.

Pastor Mac stands inside the tank in his white shirt. One at a time, people dressed in white robes go up the steps and he helps them step over the side. They then go down more steps into the water. Each one gives a testimony of faith, and then the pastor covers their face with a clean, folded white cloth and very carefully lowers them back into the water. He lifts them out again, streaming, in the name of the Father and the Son and the Holy Spirit.

All summer as Daddy and Pastor Mac and Roy Tillman work to raise the roof on our house, making rooms upstairs for the twins and me, we have fun with McElherans. Sometimes I go to town to play, sometimes June and I take care of Jonathan, and sometimes she helps Gramma take us fishing at Rock Creek. After dark, June helps us catch lightning bugs, and on very hot nights she secretly asks Mama's permission and then starts a water fight. Other nights we eat ice cream, and sometimes, after the work is done and Jonathan's asleep, everybody takes out their instruments—Auntie's accordion, Mama and Pastor Mac's guitars, and Roy's saw—and plays gospel songs.

They talk about the freeway going through next year, a mile west of our farm—all the farms will be split up, but it will be easy to get to the Cities. Everybody talks about places they've been and places they'd like to go. Mama says she wants to go to the Appalachian Mountains to see where her favorite music comes from. She and Auntie talk about growing up, listening to the Grand Ole Opry, longing to play the piano and sing.

Sometimes June and I sleep on the fold-out metal couch on Auntie and Uncle's front porch, if we promise not to make noise or wake Jonathan in the morning. We hear the night birds. Long before dawn, I wake in the cold dewy air, hear the mourning dove, and lift myself up onto an elbow. June feels me move and opens her eyes. We look together for the moon, and she spots a clear white piece of it, like a fingerprint of milk in the blue-black sky, and directs my eyes to find it through the pine boughs.

I'm thinking about second grade, wondering which teacher I'll get, Mrs. Selleck with the blue-gray hair, or Mrs. Edin with the face like an apple. Beth is going to third grade, where she'll learn times tables. Patty will go into fifth. Loren is thirteen, June will get her driver's license this year, and Miriam will be a junior.

Patty and Beth and I go to the dairy at Fifth and Dana and sit at the counter to split a chocolate shake made by Bernadette, who is skinny with hair like an orange crayon. We're the only customers.

"Did you hear about the cheerleading?" Patty asks. Beth stares at her.

"What's cheerleading?" I ask.

They explain that cheerleaders get the crowds at football and basketball games to cheer for their team.

"They do cheers," Patty explains. She jumps off her stool and directs her arms and legs in different directions as she spells Tigers, T, I, G, E, R, S, Tigers! Tigers!

She sits back down.

"Mim went out for cheerleading and somebody in church complained to the deacons," Patty says. Beth turns pink and stares at Patty as if to silence her. "He said no Baptist should be dancing in the streets."

"Patteee!" hisses Beth, glancing toward Bernadette, busy behind the counter.

Patty slurps the last of her shake, jumps up, and grabs Beth's arm as they run out. I have to leave some of my shake and run to catch up with them.

Heidi and I get Mrs. Selleck and Kathy gets Mrs. Edin but we still all ride the bus together and go to each other's birthday parties. Ozzie is gone. Now I know that the little church across the street from the school is St. John's Lutheran, where Susanna, Jacob, and their children attended services in the German language and Grampa Marty was a member all his life.

I get to start picking books from different shelves in the library. Mrs. Selleck lets me take out fat ones, like the Little House books, and I sit reading in my room at home, sometimes for hours, as if I'm gulping down food. Whatever work Mama has for me to do, I do it as fast as I can so I have more time to read. For Christmas, she and Daddy give me a whole set of books, a disappointment until I find out I like them — they're full of short stories and good pictures, mostly about real people. They announce that we're going on a summer trip in a camper to visit Washington, D.C., and other historical places, and also to the Appalachian Mountains.

Mama is happy because she has a piano in our remodeled living room. She sits down every chance she gets with a hymnal or songbook of some sort and works out how to play it. She never had piano lessons but keeps asking me if I want to learn. I think Mama plays just fine and I like to listen to her, especially when I'm falling asleep in my new room upstairs, but I start lessons with Mrs. Gaustad, the piano teacher who takes students when they can read. I go to her house by the park for dull lessons that remind me of the beginning-reader books at school—Tom and Betty and Susan and Tip.

All the piano keys have letters from A to G, but C is the simplest, the starting point. Fingers have numbers from one to five, beginning with the thumb. Sharps are scary notes, but interesting—I like the way they sound. I also like thirds and fifths, although I don't know why they're called that. Still, I'd rather be reading. Or writing.

On Mama's typewriter, I begin to make up poems, sometimes prayers, mostly about the baby sister I wish I could have.

That winter, Mama takes me to the high school play, *The Diary of Anne Frank,* starring a girl from our church, and I cry in the car all the way home. I decide to write a play. I invent characters that must move to a new country because they're starving, but they have to learn a new language and how to farm on rocky land. When I'm done, I type it on paper with no lines.

Pastor Mac is called to a church in Park Rapids. I can't believe God would call him away from us so fast—the McElherans have been in Rush City less than three years, and Park Rapids is so far away, a five-hour drive. Daddy says we can visit, but not easily.

After school is out, the McElherans pack for their move, but June will go with us on our trip out east. I ask Pastor Mac if he will baptize me before they go, but he says that when we bring June to Park Rapids, if I'm ready, he'll baptize me in his new church.

❧❀

June has brought a notebook and as we drive away from the farm in the camper, she begins to write in it: *We said our goodbyes to Gaylon, Lou, Jon, Grandma Marty, and Lassie. And at 10:05 A.M., Wednesday, July 13, 1966, we left our humble abode for our trip out east.*

The words are so beautiful that I ask Daddy to buy me my own notebook the next time we stop, and June lets me copy her first sentence into mine. For the next seventeen days, June and I take out our notebooks together and write about what we see.

Most of the time, Daddy drives. Mama and June take turns reading maps with one of us kids in the cab, and watching the other two in the camper. We drive through Waterloo, Iowa, one of the places June lived before coming to Rush City. In Illinois, we see Lincoln's birthplace; in Tennessee, the Hermitage Home of Andrew Jackson. We drive through the Great Smoky and Blue Ridge mountains for days and never get sick of it.

Mama turns the radio station to Nashville and listens to bluegrass and gospel. In Mammoth Cave, at Lookout Mountain, Cumberland Gap, and the Natural Bridge, Daddy takes pictures. We visit Jamestown, Williamsburg, and a plantation; the homes of George Washington, Thomas Jefferson, and Edgar Allen Poe; the cities of Washington, D.C., and Philadelphia; and an Amish town where Daddy says the horses make him remember Grampa. We visit relatives and family friends I didn't know we had, and swim in the Atlantic Ocean.

One night after dark we see an outdoor play, *The Book of Job*, with actors painted like figures in stained glass windows, and bats circling high above the lights, eating mosquitoes.

There was a man in the land of Uz, whose name was Job, and that man was perfect and upright, and one that feared God, and eschewed evil. And there were born unto him seven sons and three daughters.

When June stays in the camper, she turns the radio to rock and roll, and the twins and I hear Beatles songs. At the same time, she talks to us about the love of God. She hugs us and says she will miss us so much. She talks to me about what it means to follow Jesus as savior — to commit myself to seek his path all the days of my life, and to pray when I am afraid or discouraged. I realize God sent me a sister after all, not a baby sister but a big sister, just for awhile.

It's the first time I learn about the other side of the call — the driving out. Later I will hear Mama's angry voice at night, venting about people who drive out pastors God has called.

I am baptized in front of mostly strangers at Park Rapids Baptist Church, in a real baptistery with a painting of the Jordan River on the wall behind it. I can barely see the congregation over the rim, so I stand up on one of Pastor Mac's feet to give my testimony and say John 3:16 before he lowers me, floating, into the water, and then lifts me back up, heavy and streaming, onto the steps, where I take the hand of the woman helping him. She smiles and dries my hair with a blue-green towel.

A lot of people leave Rush City Baptist when the McElherans do, most of them from East Rock, and most go to the Evangelical Free Church in Pine City. Effie and Harold and Alvin Hendrickson leave. So do Uncle and Auntie and Jonathan. Gramma Marty and Mama and Daddy agree with Uncle and Auntie — they feel like leaving — but they decide to stay. They do not want to divide themselves between two towns, one for church and one for their children's school.

After Uncle and Auntie go to Pine City and we have different pastors, it's as if we are parts of two different flocks of sheep, heading in the same direction but on different paths. In Rush City, we get a fiery pastor this time, not afraid to raise his voice and yell, inspired to lead us in building a new church out near the freeway coming someday.

Gradually, Uncle and Auntie and Mama and Daddy also stop playing music together. Once in awhile they're asked to play and sing a quartet at an old people's home or a special service, but those times get rarer and then stop altogether. Mama lends her guitar to somebody who wants to learn, and that's the end. On Sunday mornings, we get into our cars and, at Highway 61, they turn north and we turn south.

Birch

Little birch trees, I love your whispering voices. Three of you stand east of our house and make dancing shadows on the walls of Mama and Daddy's bedroom in the morning light. In spring, you drop flowers that look like clusters of furry golden caterpillars. You look pretty in winter snow too, with your white bark and black lines like ink.

The other place birch trees grow on our farm is at the east end of our woods along the tracks, named Applegate's for the owner of that tract before us. Birch grow on the marshy ground like a congregation, because a path of bigger trees was cut down for the railroad. This is also where Uncle Gaylon tells us the Indians camped when Sam and Grampa were boys, so we always look for arrowheads there.

Grazing in the birch trees, our black-and-white cows blend in and seem to disappear, playing tricks on my eyes.

When we go on vacation at Mille Lacs Lake, a lot of the Indian crafts for sale are made of birch bark—little teepees and canoes, lamp-shades and picture frames. In their little house with no electricity, Grampa and Gramma Anderson have a picture made entirely of birch bark—a scene by a lake at dusk, with a cabin and a campfire by the shore. Everything in the picture is made of bark—the logs and furry shingles of the cabin, the miniature birch trees, the mountains in the distance, the wood on the campfire. Light from Gramma's kerosene lamp flickers on the picture and makes the campfire in the picture look as though it's really burning.

We are not allowed to peel birch bark, even though it's tempting, but sometimes I find a piece that a tree has shed by itself, and I pretend it's paper. With a ballpoint pen, I write a message or a name, and the smooth silky bark yields to my pen. On my desk, it lies like part of a beautiful, ancient scroll.

5

Houses

Who can find a virtuous woman?
For her price is far above rubies.
She girdeth her loins with strength, and strengtheneth her arms.

— Proverbs 31:10, 17

Mama remembers the first time she saw the Marty farm. She and Auntie Lou were in grade school, riding the school bus down a road that was new on the route that September. Mama sat with her shoulder pressed to the window and watched for farms across the flat fields, as the bus slowed and stopped for children. Her green eyes surveyed the lines and color of each house, barn, and shed, the borders of the grassy yards and gravel driveways, the kinds of trees and the freshness of paint, the names on the mailboxes.

Our farm took her breath away. Everything was built at an angle from the road so that as the bus approached, her line of sight came square to the southeast end of the barn, and then the broad south side appeared and widened into view. It was beautiful: a dark red barn with white trim, a straight roof and three cupolas, a cement silo slightly taller than the barn's peak, matching red sheds and corncribs, chicken coop and pig house. Clean black-and-white cows just out from milking, neat fences, white puffs of chickens in the driveway — and then in the September light she saw not one but *two* dazzling white houses under the spreading oaks and evergreens.

The first house looked new: one story with red trim, closed-in porch, Swiss gables north and south, two young spruce standing straight on the sloping yard in front. The second house was bigger: two stories with green trim, a screen porch across the front, and gables on all four sides. The two houses stood about a hundred feet apart, separated by a patch of high grass and connected by a footpath. A gravel driveway encircled the houses on an island of shady green grass. And the trees — not only oaks and evergreens but elms and fruit trees.

Mama turned her head as the bus pulled away, past a windbreak of pines. A creek ran out of the sunny pasture and under the road.

Each morning she waited for that farm with the two white houses, west of the highway. She examined details she'd missed: a three-story birdhouse on a tall pole, laundry on the clotheslines—bright white sheets and shirts, blue denim pants—a calm-looking sandy dog. She glanced at the children who boarded there, two dark-eyed boys, one a little older than she, round-faced with upward curves at the corners of his mouth, and an older boy with lighter hair. They wore neat, modest, clean clothes—they seemed confident but not loud. Once she caught a glimpse of their mother's shape inside the screen porch: dark hair, a glint of glasses, the pink of her full apron.

Through the seasons, Mama watched the farm with two houses, watched as leaves fell and revealed the shape of the big house and the lay of the lawn, watched the pinecones, butternuts, and apples that fell and were gathered up, watched as snow covered everything. She saw a bundled-up man plow the curving driveway on a red tractor, and electric lamps glowing in the windows on dark winter mornings. She saw another man drive a team of horses through the snowy barnyard and she heard the team's bells shake. She watched lilacs and bridal wreath bloom in springtime, and on the field next to the smaller house, she saw horses at work, with a thin man in a wide-brimmed hat riding behind them, leather straps thrown over his shoulders. One year, a new white garage with *three* doors appeared near the barn.

The two boys who got on the bus at the beautiful farm were Daddy and Uncle Gaylon. They shared a bedroom in the big house, built by grand-parents who died before they were born. It was a four-square house, with four rooms up, four rooms down, and a stairway leading straight up from the front door. They lived with their parents and their fun, loud Uncle Sam, whose son was in the navy and whose wife had died before their own parents had married. Sam lived with them until he remarried and built the smaller house across the yard for him and his new wife, Margaret.

Daddy and Uncle both remember when Sam built the house, because Uncle was six and Daddy three. They tell the story together, when they're sitting in our house with Mama and Auntie after dividing the milk check, or at the picnic table on Memorial Day or Labor Day. Uncle looks at our house close-up, as if he is six again.

"First, there was the hole," he begins. "My goodness, what a hole in the ground! It was absolutely huge. We couldn't believe it. Mom — Gramma"—I know he's telling this story for me—"she was scared to death we were going to fall in. But we just couldn't stay away, *couldn't* stay away."

"It was like a magnet," Daddy agrees.

"*Did* you fall in?" I ask.

"I can't believe that we didn't!" Uncle laughs. "No, we never did. Mother was so relieved when they finished the basement and that hole was closed up. But *then* — then came the lumber, the hammering, the nails! Mom was *sure* we were going to step on a nail."

"They worked on that house all through the busiest part of the summer, while Dad worked out in the fields," Daddy says, serious now. "That was the other thing Dad couldn't understand — why Sam had to build the house in the busiest time of the year, with all the hay coming in, and then the threshing. . . . When Dad got sick that fall, Mom blamed it on the new house."

"Sam just had to have that house done, 'for Margaret!'" Uncle says with force and a grin. I can tell he's mimicking Sam's voice, and that Sam was teasing his new wife and yet pleasing her when he said it. "And my goodness," Uncle continues, "if it wasn't the prettiest house when he finished it. Sam was so proud of that house with the Swiss roof."

"Sam said if he wasn't going to Switzerland before he died, at least he was going to live in a Swiss house," Daddy explains.

"He should have gone to Switzerland!" Uncle hoots, and a laugh bubbles out of Daddy too.

It isn't really a Swiss house. I know because I've seen another house exactly like it on Highway 61, north of Pine City.

"But the greatest thing — the greatest thing," says Uncle, "was the water. When they moved in, Aunt Margaret invited the two of us boys over and showed us the sink in the kitchen. She turned on the knob, and . . ." he pauses ". . . water!"

"It was miraculous." Daddy shakes his head, smiling. "We couldn't believe it."

"Then she took us to the bathroom, and there was not only a sink but a bathtub — huge! And a toilet that flushed!"

"That little bathroom," Daddy says, "seemed plenty big to us!"

"Oh, we couldn't stop talking about it. We talked about it for weeks. It drove Mom crazy!" Uncle exclaims. "We tried to think of excuses to go over to Margaret and Sam's, just so we could wash our hands."

"That was before the war," Daddy says. "All those years, Margaret had running water and Mom didn't. It was Dad that held out, until Marg and I got married — seventeen years!"

"Did he really not see the need, or was he just too stubborn to give in to Sam?" Uncle says, shaking his head.

"Just stubborn, I think," Daddy concludes. "It was the principle of the thing. Why Sam had to get married again and needed another house at all. Dad thought it was unnecessary, more of Sam's foolishness."

Grampa believed that marriage was for the farm first, and for any other reason after that.

Sam's house is where I live now, and part of what makes our farm so unusual. Sam and Grampa have both died but their widows are alive, Margaret in town, and Gramma still on the farm with her two sons, who are married to sisters. Two houses, two families, two barns, two silos.

But Sam's house is bigger than when he built it. The attic has been transformed into a sewing room and two bedrooms. Facing the south, Bruce and Blaine's room is paneled. Facing the big house, my room is sheetrocked, painted pink, and carpeted with a magenta remnant found by Mama. She is the one who realized Sam Marty's little writing desk would fit perfectly in my room. With a matching chair, the desk had come back to the farm after Sam's son Harold died. Now the dark wood desk with curving legs, tiny drawers, and six mail slots is where I sit in the nook next to the chimney in my room. At Sam's desk, in the house that he built, I write homework assignments and letters and poems.

I know Aunt Margaret, who's really my *great*-aunt, and it's hard to imagine her living in our house, even though it was built for her. She lives in town now, in a two-story stucco house the color of vanilla ice cream shrouded in evergreens. It used to be the house of Dr. Holmes, whom she cared for until he died. When one of us goes to town, especially if Daddy or Uncle has to stop at the bank or if Mama has to drop off the payroll at the school, we stop in to say hello. Often, Gramma goes along to trade news with Margaret while the rest of us run errands.

Aunt Margaret's front porch faces the park and the railroad tracks, which, if you follow them three miles north of town, run through our farm. Always at Aunt Margaret's there is the background noise of the rail yard, with loud crashes as cars couple and horn blasts as an express rushes through. Conversation is polite but seems a little strained, as if we're waiting for the crash of two rail cars or the blast of a train whistle. In nice weather, we all just stand or we sit in the wicker furniture on the porch. Sometimes the twins and I go to the park to swing or slide or climb on the bandstand while the grown-ups talk.

Aunt Margaret stands with arms folded, in a cardigan sweater and nice leather shoes, a wave pressed perfectly in her steel-gray hair. She seems to appraise not only us but the town and the farms around it, swapping news, looking down her sharp nose through jeweled cat-eye glasses. Mostly she keeps her lips closed around her big teeth. On a good day, she'll smile a slow, toothy smile at Uncle's or Daddy's jokes, and even tell a funny story of her own in a hoarse voice, usually about somebody from town, living or dead. Sometimes, she'll invite us inside.

For a long time, I thought the stiffness between our family and Aunt Margaret was because of the trains, but I've decided it has more to do with her house. It's a spooky house to the twins and me, starting with the dense trees outside and the minor-key notes of the doorbell as we stand on the porch. It's always dark inside, and she makes a bony silhouette in the dim light as she smiles weakly and says, "Oh hello, hello."

The rooms have high ceilings, heavy drapes with sheer curtains behind them, carpet that hushes every word, dark wood furniture, cloth-covered chairs and couches, and wallpaper. There's a room called a den, a word we associate with wild animals, where she talks on the telephone and takes naps. Glass cabinets are filled mostly with books and glass dishes. Crystal bowls are filled with ribbon candy and coconut bonbons too hard to bite—probably bought on clearance, Gramma Marty says later at home. A fat dachshund named Pepper sleeps in a wicker basket.

The house always smells of cigar smoke, which comes from Dr. Holmes, even though he is dead. We remember him in his old age, when he no longer practiced medicine, sitting in a high-backed chair in the living room, motionless and white-haired, with glasses that glinted so his eyes were invisible to us. He seemed so small we would forget he was there, and then he would startle us with a tiny gesture, a turn of his wrist or a sucking sound as he drew on his cigar. When Dr. Holmes died, his wife was already dead and he had no children, so Aunt Margaret, his housekeeper, inherited the cigar-smelling house and everything in it, plus an old Cadillac in the garage that she doesn't know how to drive.

If we're invited to stay for cookies or ice cream and pop, Aunt Margaret sends us with nickels to the Laundromat next to the bank to get root beer out of a machine. She serves Daddy and Uncle root beer too, as if they're still kids. They don't mind, since they don't like coffee. Aunt Margaret's is the only place besides Uncle Gaylon and Auntie Lou's where we drink pop. Under the chandelier in the dining room, she serves us root beer floats with glass straws in real glasses on crystal coasters or felt-backed place mats to protect the table's glossy red-black wood.

After eating, while the grown-ups stay at the table, the twins and I silently explore the house. The stairway turns at a landing and leads upstairs to darkened bedrooms with long mirrors and beds so high they have stepping stools, and to a bathroom with a claw-foot tub poised on cold white tile and glass cabinets filled with jars full of cotton balls, red rubber hot-water bottles, a stethoscope, a baby scale, and other implements we can't identify.

Aunt Margaret's house also has a doll, the most beautiful doll I've ever seen. It belonged to Mrs. Holmes and is now kept in a box like a tiny cardboard coffin in the back of the closet just inside the front door. On winter days, as we hang up our coats, I can see the doll's box in the closet. I don't dare ask for it. I long for Aunt Margaret to say I can take her out. When the twins aren't along, she sometimes thinks of it. "Do you want to play with the dolly?" she asks, and I have to control my happiness and take the box out carefully.

The doll is about three feet long, with a china head and hands that feel cold when I lift her from the box. She was made to decorate a bed with her skirt spread in a glorious circle around her delicate body. Her legs are soft cotton spindles with tiny satin slippers sewed onto the ends. Her face is shaped and painted, lifelike and lovely, but it is the dress that makes her magnificent—pale green satin with a matching crescent-shaped hat attached to wavy blond hair. Her dress and hat are both trimmed with crocheted lace and tiny pink roses. The satin is wrinkled from lying in the box but it looks lovely anyway.

I am completely happy playing with the doll, holding her until she is warm, laying out some playthings in a corner behind the furniture so I can talk to myself while the grown-ups are distracted, or, if I've been left there while Daddy or Mama or Uncle does business and Aunt Margaret watches *All-Star Wrestling* on the big television set. I don't feel sorry about the doll when I leave because Aunt Margaret's house seems like the safest possible place for such a beautiful object.

Aunt Margaret has many valuable objects, some of them said to be Marty-family things, which the grown-ups talk about from time to time. A vase that Gramma thinks was Susanna's, a plate a certain shade of green, a cherrywood bed, photographs. Aunt Margaret took Marty things from the farm when Sam died.

"It's not like she needs a thing," Auntie says, sipping her coffee and looking out the window toward her house. "Since the doctor died, that woman's loaded."

"The Marty heirlooms can't have any sentimental value to her," Mama says.

"Didn't she love Sam?" I ask, because everybody loved Sam.

"Aunt Margaret?" Auntie shakes her head. "It's just spite!"

Aunt Margaret is stingy, Mama and Auntie Lou and Gramma Marty agree. She makes coffee so weak they can hardly drink it, it's insulting, and she never sets a butter dish on the table—she butters the bread in the kitchen, so thinly it's nearly invisible. The chief reason to have a nice house is for hospitality, but Aunt Margaret manages to make every guest feel like they're costing her money.

I wonder what could make Aunt Margaret jealous of us. I wonder if it's because we live in the house built for her, or because she wanted children, or because she thinks, with our farm, we have enough. I wonder if she's angry because Sam died before he was old, or because she thinks the Martys treated her badly.

Mama loves Aunt Margaret's house in town.

"I would strip all the paint off the woodwork!" Mama says, imagining. "I'm sure that woodwork is beautiful—imagine the books on all those shelves. And reupholster all those beautiful chairs. And new drapes! I love sheers, but those curtains are too dark. And I'd take out that spruce tree in front of the living room window...."

Mama is unimpressed by houses that are too big, like the two mansions in town—a brick one across the creek from the feed mill, and the fancy three-story white house with porches near the creek on Highway 61. Instead she likes two-story houses with nice lawns: the insurance man's stucco house on main street, the Lutheran organist's formal house a few blocks farther down. Outside town along the highway, Mama loves Alberta Kirchberg's stucco house and gardens, and the Werners' farm straight east of our place, a pale green house with a wide porch, huge shade trees, and the creek running by. From the east windows of our house we can see the blue roof of the Werners' barn across the fields.

In fact, Gramma Marty tells me, the Werner place used to be the Hansen place. It's the farm where Aunt Margaret and her sister Mamie grew up.

Upstairs in the big house, staying awhile with Gramma Marty, I look out the window across the yard to our house. I can see that before Sam built our house, Gramma could look out the east windows of her house and watch the sun rise and track the men's progress in the fields. In the new house, Aunt Margaret got the view that Gramma had.

I look through Gramma Marty's photo albums for pictures of Aunt Margaret. There is no wedding portrait because she was a second wife, so I find her in snapshots with Sam and groups of people, dressed fashionably for summer and winter outings. I learn to recognize Hansen traits, the sharp nose and big teeth and heavy eyelids—in Sam and Mamie's son Harold as he grows older, and in the five brothers and three sisters of Mamie and Margaret. I forget all their names. I find a picture of their father on the steps of what is now the Werners' house.

"Old C. N. Hansen, he was a mean one," Gramma comments, gazing at the photo. "All the Hansens had a kind of sour temperament, and Sam thought it came from C. N.—the way he tormented his children."

Gramma usually saves criticism for things and behavior, like alcohol and cigarettes and swearing, rather than particular people.

"Is Aunt Margaret mean?"

"Not intentionally, I don't think," Gramma says. "At least, she wasn't when she lived at the farm."

"Daddy and Uncle say she played games with them in the yard sometimes."

"Oh, she could be fun, especially when Sam was around," Gramma says. She gets up from the couch painfully and rummages around in a basket for her embroidery. "Playing was one thing, but she never did a lick of farmwork unless she had to. She couldn't stand to get her hair mussy. In the middle of haying, or threshing, or canning—whatever it was—she would say, 'I have to take my nap.'"

Even though Gramma has arthritis now, I know she was never lazy. Almost every picture of her is outdoors and she looks happy. Daddy says Gramma wore pants to shock oats and kept up with the men, laughing the whole time.

"But didn't Aunt Margaret work for Dr. Holmes?"

"Yes, she did, before she married Sam, and then again after Sam died, but she didn't have to get her hands dirty," Gramma explains. "Sam, he could get away with saying things nobody else would say. Sam said the only reason she could tolerate working for Dr. Holmes was because she'd lived with C. N. so long."

"Did you go to Dr. Holmes?"

"Yes, the Marty family's doctor was Dr. Holmes," she says, which tells me he wasn't the doctor for her own family, the Hendricksons.

Gramma sits down in her rocker holding a hoop of embroidery, and I turn on the lamp above her shoulder. Even with bent fingers, she threads a needle against the light, peering through her bifocals, but I pull the knot for her, and then she takes up where she left off, on the pink- and red-flowered field at the edge of a white pillowcase.

She pushes the needle through, draws the thread.

"And when Sam died, then she went to live with Dr. Holmes?"

Gramma grips the hoop awkwardly while twisting the needle and thread, forming a knot that will make a stamen at the center of a flower.

"Dr. Holmes had a wife who was sick, and Margaret couldn't drive, so she wanted to move to town to live with them and take care of Mrs. Holmes," she explains. "So we had to buy out her half of the farm."

"What does that mean?" I ask.

"We had to have an appraisal, to see how much the farm was worth, and then pay Margaret half of what the farm was worth in 1951. It was thousands of dollars."

I am shocked.

"How did you do it?"

Gramma is intent on the embroidery. "We had to choose between selling the land or taking out a loan from the bank, which your Grampa would not do. That's when he had a nervous breakdown."

"But you didn't sell the land!"

"Well, finally Margaret agreed we could make monthly payments," she says bitterly, as if it's a taste in her mouth. "It took many years to pay her, and we couldn't afford anything else, especially after your Uncle Gaylon was called into the service."

My head spins. I thought the reason Daddy didn't go to college was that he married Mama, not that the Martys couldn't afford it.

Nervous breakdown.

"What happened when he, when Grampa had a nervous breakdown?"

"One morning after milking, on the way in from the barn," Gramma says slowly, "halfway to the house, he just turned the milk pail over . . . sat down on its bottom . . . and started to sing. I heard it from the house, strange singing, and looked out the window and saw him there by the oak tree, and I knew. He had to go to the state hospital in Moose Lake."

I know the name Moose Lake from jokes.

"So many others worked so hard on the farm for so many years," Gramma concludes, "but as far as the law was concerned, when Margaret married Sam, half was hers."

Widows, I know, are generally people to care for, but Margaret seems to be in a different category. She seems fine, living in town, keeping an eye on the park, walking to the post office, watching TV, talking on the telephone, caring for her dog, taking naps, serving coffee at weddings and funerals.

"We grew up in a shack," says Mama, and Auntie Lou adds, flashing her eyes, "on the wrong side of the tracks."

The Anderson house *is* a shack compared not just with the Martys' but with most houses. I know because Grampa and Gramma Anderson still live there and we visit. What you see when you drive by is a narrow gray house among ornery-looking box elders on one side of the Government Road, and on the other side, a jumble of buildings with peeling paint and leaky roofs surrounded by weeds and broken machinery used for parts. The house has three cramped rooms downstairs and two up, no running water, no electricity, a wood stove in the middle room downstairs, and a wood cook stove like a monster in the kitchen.

In the winters, Mama says, the cold always pierced straight through the mattress of the bed upstairs where she and Auntie slept. And year after year it stayed that way. She was ashamed to get on the bus in front of their house and avoided having friends over. The only modern convenience in the house was a telephone, which their dad needed to run his business. His business was machinery—a sawmill and custom work for farmers who didn't own hay balers or threshing machines.

By the time they were fifteen and thirteen, Mama and Auntie knew all the houses on the Government Road, and more than that, because after their big sister moved out, they took turns as their dad's tractor driver for custom work. They were good drivers with good manners— they said nothing when they ate in the houses of the farmers who hired their father. Dinner and the privilege of seeing the insides of other people's houses was the payment they got. They'd been fed in kitchens and dining rooms, large and small, dirty and immaculate, homely and beautiful. They took note of curtains and carpets, couches, chairs, tables, and drapes. In mirrors, they'd see themselves, blond hair in windblown braids, Auntie's blue eyes or Mama's green eyes, tanned cheeks and hands, sunburned noses and shoulders.

At night, lying in the big bed together in their house, windows thrown open and sweltering with summer heat, they compared notes, favorite colors they'd seen, favorite bathrooms, styles of faucets, toilets, floor tiles, and countertops. In the daytime, they'd sit side by side in the outhouse and leaf through catalogs—Sears, Montgomery Ward, Alden's, and Spiegel—choosing textiles and appliances for imaginary houses.

They made paper dolls to live in their imaginary houses. They learned to draw precisely, perfect miniatures of movie stars and pinups from Doris and Duane's magazines. They designed movie-star wardrobes and laid the colored cutouts in the sun, or at the table after supper, lifted them against the glass of the kerosene lamp to warm the wax and make it glossy.

Now, when Mama has an hour she can spare from housework, she calls her mother to put the coffee on. She loads the twins and me into the car and drives fast down the road to Gramma and Grampa Anderson's— our stomachs get butterflies as we go clappity-clap over the tracks and then over the quiet hump of the highway. Gramma Anderson pours coffee and gives us graham crackers and small glasses of milk from her gas-powered icebox. We stand on a chair next to the sink and drink water out of a pail with a stainless steel dipper, and then run outside.

"Don't cross the road!" Mama calls. "Stay on this side of the road! And watch out for bears!"

Compared with our farm, Gramma and Grampa Anderson's place seems to sit on the edge of wilderness, because bears, deer, foxes, woodchucks, and beavers live in the woods and fields. The Anderson woods are connected by forests to the St. Croix River. The creek running through the ravines is the same one that wanders out of our farm, but between the Marty farm and the Anderson farm is almost a mile of open fields and pastures, the highway, and the railroad—things bears and deer will rarely cross.

If we need a bathroom at the Anderson place, we have to use the outhouse. If we're there past dark, Gramma Anderson lights a kerosene lamp in the middle of the table and our shadows move like giants on the walls behind us.

If Grampa comes in, we get a whisker rub and a pat on the head, and we stay alert because we've heard stories about his temper. He once drove a preacher out of his yard who'd stopped to invite the kids to church. He wouldn't speak to his own mother because he said she was holier-than-thou and had called him the black sheep of the family because he drank. That was true, he did drink—and he hit his children, at least his two oldest, Doris and Duane, which scared Mama and Auntie so much they didn't dare misbehave. It was only because that hard discipline didn't make the first two children submit that Grampa finally relented and let his youngest girls go to Sunday school. When Mama got married, Grampa was still so mad at Aunt Doris that he said he wouldn't set foot in the church if Doris was there, so Mama gave up Doris as a bridesmaid so her father would walk her down the aisle. Grampa Anderson sounds a little like C. N. Hansen.

It was a miracle, Mama and Auntie agree, that they married good husbands. Grampa drove away Doris's boyfriends—nice ones who would have been good to her—before he let her marry a neighbor on the hill a half-mile north. But the Martys he accepted before Mama and Daddy even went on a date. The Martys struck a balance somehow. Even though they used horses, they also used tractors; even though they farmed dairy, John and Sam gave each other time off from milking; even though they wouldn't work on Sundays, they prospered. John Marty was serious, but Sam had a sense of humor, and neither one was above drinking a beer. Grampa Anderson decided that the Swiss were all right—coming from a small country that seemed to mind its own business instead of making wars all over the world—even though they were so dark-skinned and he thought *Marty* really sounded Italian. Maybe the immigrant Martys just *passed* as Swiss.

So Mama was the second bride named Margaret to live in the house that Sam Marty built. But she was a lot younger than the first bride, only eighteen in 1957. The day she and Daddy came home from their honeymoon, her parents stopped by after supper to visit. As Gramma walked into the kitchen, Mama snapped on a light. In the dining room, Mama snapped on another light. Then Gramma turned on a lamp in the living room and giggled. In the kitchen, Mama turned on the faucet and started giggling. Then the two of them, mother and daughter, raced from room to room, pushing up switches until every light blazed, opening handles until every faucet gushed, flushing the toilet, and laughing so hard they cried.

Ten years after Mama first saw the Marty farm from the bus window, she set to enlarging the yard herself. She asked Daddy to mow down the tall grass that separated the yards of the two houses, along with more grass that grew on the triangle north of our house, between the granary and garden and clotheslines, and another strip east of the house on which she looked out every morning. He cut those areas with the hay mower, and then she cut all of it smooth with the lawn mower, creating neat, clear green margins around her bright white house with the red trim and the bridal wreath. With an old scissor, she trimmed around the trees. She made a flowerbed west of the house with irises, pansies, and petunias, and by the rain gauge, a yellow rosebush. She planted borders of petunias around Sam's little red garage, which was now Daddy's. Against the east side of the gray granary she put hollyhocks, which grew into tall stalks of pink and white and red.

From the big house, Grampa Marty observed her.

"Don't you know you're just making more work for yourself, Margaret," he said, shaking his head but smiling. She knew he was pleased that she had the ambition and energy required to be a farm wife.

Gramma Marty said nothing, but set a hard course for Mama. It was a challenge to get sheets on the clothesline as early as Viola Hendrickson Marty did, but Mama rose to that challenge and everything else set before her — pies for family picnics, casseroles for church, weed-free gardens, streak-free storm windows, neatly patched jeans, everything clean and in order. Mama meant it when she called it a pleasure to see white sheets on the line against the background of fields and sky. It was the challenge of getting up when Daddy went to the barn at five, not lolling in bed, but getting her day under way, the essential work of a clean, well-fed, well-clothed family, of a life with beauty and hospitality, making coffee by ten and inviting her mother-in-law over, or walking the path past the apple trees to the big house for a cup at Grampa and Gramma Marty's table or on the big porch overlooking the road and the view to town.

To Grampa and Gramma, having Mama next door must have been a little like having Sam Marty back, the restless part of him that surveyed the world and detected the direction to go, the rewarding smile of one who believes in progress.

I hear Mama's stories in pieces. I hear them in conversations over coffee with aunties — Lou next door, Doris on the hill, and Uncle Duane's wife Judy on the highway — as I learn to drink coffee black, dipping cookies or rusks or Mama's cinnamon rolls.

"Daddy was always bringing you things," Mama says to Auntie Lou. "You were his favorite."

"Oh, I was not," Auntie retorts, but smirks just slightly, maybe for me. "What did he bring me?"

Mama begins to list things: a certain doll, a red jacket with real fur around the hood, shoes — her list of grievances; Auntie's triumphs.

"And then a brand-new accordion," Mama says. "And *lessons*."

"He got you a guitar," Auntie counters.

"He won that in a *bar*," Mama says, "on a *bet*. A *used guitar*. He didn't go out and get it for me — he was probably drunk."

Later, as I'm standing with hands in the soapy dishpan and she's working like a flurry around me, Mama confesses, "I was so jealous of Lorraine." It's like she's thinking out loud instead of telling me. "It was terrible," she says. "Once . . . once when I was supposed to pour hot water into a basin where she was washing her feet, I was so mad at her about *something* that I pretended I didn't know it was boiling and poured it straight onto her feet."

She stares at me.

"Isn't that terrible?" she demands. "I *still* feel terrible that I could do such a thing!"

Even now that Mama and Auntie have married brothers and live side by side on our farm with beautiful houses, despite loving each other and buying each other presents like lamps and blouses, they're still jealous of each other in the way they say sisters always are. Though Auntie has one child and Mama has three, the milk check is split in half. Auntie Lou has a job at the hospital and Mama has a part-time job for the school. Although Auntie has to share her house with Gramma, that means she has a babysitter for Jonathan right upstairs. Mama's job allows her to work at home where she can watch us while she works. Auntie Lou is always showing off in her exaggerated, sassy way — fashionable clothes with matching shoes, jewelry, and leather purses, shades of lipstick and coats with fur collars, stuffed animals on her bed and in the back window of a new car, and a real collie who's allowed to sleep in their house.

From traveling in the service, Uncle came to like Asian things, and now they drive to Minneapolis and Duluth to eat in Chinese restaurants and to shop. The things he chooses for their house have a simplicity of lines and colors that give their rooms an unusual openness. Our house is a crowded hodgepodge of furniture. Uncle and Auntie keep Shasta in their refrigerator and ice cream in their freezer. We get 7-Up only when we have the flu, and ice cream on birthdays.

Mama and Auntie talk constantly about how to improve their houses. Auntie's is bigger, with a huge porch and a swing big enough for Uncle to lie down for a nap. But some things about the big house are too much like the Anderson shack — a cellar for canned food and potatoes and onions with a stairway so steep it's almost a ladder; a wood stove on the main floor, and a woodbox on the back porch. Auntie has to do her laundry in the kitchen. Our house is smaller but newer. We have a basement with space for a washer, a winter clothesline, a coal bin, a lot of wood, and a furnace with ducts and vents that blow warm air into every room. The bathrooms in both houses are small, but ours is on the main floor and we don't have to share it with Gramma. Mama and Auntie seem to agree that we have the better house.

But, Mama points out, Auntie has a new kitchen—new cupboards and countertops, stainless-steel double sinks looking out through double windows, lazy Susans in the corner cupboards, and a vent with a light above the stove that sucks hot air out of the kitchen.

When Auntie came to the farm in 1960, less than a year after Grampa Marty died, Uncle Gaylon's gift to her was a modern kitchen. In fact the whole big house was rearranged, making the upstairs into Gramma's apartment. I'm just old enough to remember the day I was allowed in while the carpenters were still working. The kitchen was flooded with light and amazing color, the cabinets were made of wood they called *blond,* the counters topped with aqua Formica, and the floor sheathed in linoleum with huge haphazard snowflakes. Uncle had picked everything and designed it for Auntie, who was less than five feet tall. He made one section of the counter lower, which she called her baking center.

"It's ironic," I heard Mama say to Daddy as she scraped the beaters of her mixer and started scooping out mounds of dough onto a cookie sheet. "She doesn't even *like* to bake."

"Maybe now she will," Daddy said.

One Sunday after their kitchen was done, Uncle invited all of us over, dished big scoops of vanilla ice cream into Melmac bowls that matched the linoleum snowflakes, and poured strawberry Shasta on top. We ate slowly, feeling the fizz bite our tongues and the roofs of our mouths.

Mama had to figure out how to remodel our house for the simple reason that the twins and I couldn't share a room forever. She sketched plans and drew pictures, Daddy measured and found studdings, and Mama and Auntie Lou scanned catalogs for months to pick out colors, bedspreads, curtains, and linoleum. The work was done in a summer by Daddy, a neighbor, and Pastor Mac. They tore out Sam's Swiss gables, ripped off the roof and rebuilt it higher on the west side to make separate rooms for the twins and me, and built a dormer on the east side for another bathroom someday.

Downstairs they knocked out a wall and made our old bedroom part of the living room—one whole end of the house, with windows east, south, and west—so Mama could get a piano and built-in bookshelves and entertain more easily. The hall was closed off and made into part of the bathroom.

It's in the new, big living room, while I'm helping Daddy patch the place where the wall to our bedroom used to be, that Daddy tells me Sam died in our house, in this very spot—the room that used to be a bedroom. He did not die at the hospital, even though the paper said so—not Sam, not with Dr. Holmes.

I wait, ears buzzing, thinking he can't mean to tell me this. Like Mama, he's just thinking out loud with me in the room.

"What did he die from?" I finally ask, although I've heard the word *sunstroke* when Daddy and Uncle and Gramma caution us to drink plenty of water when it's hot outside.

Daddy stands on the ladder in the opened-up living room, working on the long, wide seam in the ceiling. I work on the wall as high as I can reach, scooping, pressing, pressing, pressing the way Daddy is.

"It was August, and the men were haying," he begins, as if repeating something he's heard or said many times. "Sam came in from the field because he didn't feel good."

It was a hot, hot day, but Sam was ice cold and dizzy, and Margaret put him to bed.

Sam lay in bed for more than a day, freezing and then hot—fevers so high he saw things that weren't there, he had convulsions—until Dr. Holmes came out to the house.

He was an old-fashioned doctor. But maybe he just knew there was no hope.

Sam's blood pressure got so high.

They bled him.

I am afraid to know, but I'm more afraid not to know. "What does that mean?"

"They opened his veins," Daddy says. My stomach quakes. "Blood went everywhere, on the ceiling. It was the worst thing I ever saw in my life."

"They let you see it?"

"Oh, yes," he says, his voice unusually steely. "Gaylon and I had to wash the walls, and the ceiling, this whole room, afterward."

I glance at his face, but it has no expression.

"How old were you?"

He pauses, seeming to calculate.

"Fourteen, I must have been," he says, "and Gaylon must have been seventeen."

"Why did *you* have to do it?"

"Dad got sick," he says, "and we didn't want Mom to have to do it."

I imagine Daddy on the ladder, fourteen years old. Young Daddy and Uncle wiping with rags, rinsing them out in buckets, turning the water red, pouring buckets of red water down the toilet, drawing new buckets from the faucet of the white bathtub. Their happy uncle has been taken away, Aunt Margaret is at the hospital and then the funeral home, their father is having a nervous breakdown, their mother is taking care of everything else. They are washing, washing until their arms ache, nauseated by the smell of sickness and blood, afraid to throw away the mattress but sure they will have to. They scrub, they stand down, they climb back up with new water.

I have slept under that ceiling since I can remember, made shapes of shadows in the dusk, but I have never seen a trace because Daddy and Uncle washed it clean. Like the hill without a trace of the log cabin—the cabin where Sam was born—the blood from his death has disappeared. Still, I realize now that to Daddy's eyes it has always been there. Daddy has not forgotten. It's only now that the bedroom is gone, made into a living room, now that his children no longer sleep there, that he can tell this story to one of us, so we know.

I begin to see that Aunt Margaret, like drought and heavy labor, like illness and death, is something that has been overcome to preserve and build up our farm.

And I begin to see a pattern, that Aunt Margaret has benefited in some material way from people's deaths—her sister's, Sam's, Mrs. Holmes', Dr. Holmes'. She is either very unlucky or she has made the best of things, depending on how you look at it.

We rake our yards in the spring. Everybody helps, working with the wind, which can come from any direction this time of year. The job seems enormous to everybody except Mama and Uncle. Mama's in charge and raking faster than anybody, and the men join in before supper or after chores because the evenings are longer now. The twins and I are recruited when we come home from school. Gramma watches the fire and supervises the hauling of leaves, or tends to perennial plants we uncover as we're raking.

We rake the west yard, from the chicken coop to the road; the back stretch, north of the path between our houses; Auntie and Uncle's front yard; our front yard; the narrow piece east of our house; and, finally, the north piece, the triangle of grass north of our house pointing to the old milk house. We all rake for two or three days, burning leaves, breathing in the smell of fire and the wet smell of uncovered earth. When we're done, the driveway around our houses is a light brown ring on a blanket of smooth, brightening green.

When we plant the garden, the men turn up the dirt and stake rows. Everybody plants seeds, covering them up, tamping them down. Mama and Gramma and Auntie and Uncle plant flowers. All summer the grass is mowed with the gasoline push-mower, mostly by Uncle and Mama. Trimming around the trees with clippers is mostly done by the twins and me, on our side of the yard. Weeding the vegetable and flower gardens is endless. Picking the strawberries and vegetables as they ripen, planning meals so we eat as much as we can, and then putting the rest up—freezing and canning, counting quarts and pints— is Mama and Auntie and Gramma Marty's job, and also Gramma Anderson when we get really busy. Boxes fill the freezer in our basement and another freezer on Auntie and Uncle's porch. Jars line the shelves in their cellar and our basement. In the fall, Mama pulls up gladiola bulbs and covers the rosebush and irises with leaves.

Cooking and dishes, three times a day. Sweeping the kitchen and shaking the rugs, twice a day. Once a week, dusting the floors with a soft mop like a slipper, dusting the furniture, watering plants, scrubbing sinks, tub, and toilet. Mama sorts laundry on the cement floor of the basement and soaks white things in Hi-Lex while I fill the washer with hot water and the rinse tubs with cold, then we wash loads from white things to dark—sheets first, barn clothes last—and they all dry on the clotheslines north of the house, white things early in the morning, sheets flapping if there's a wind.

There's also spring cleaning and fall cleaning: stripping things bare, washing down walls and baseboards, washing the bookshelves. Mama sweeps off the window screens and washes the storm windows, the sills, the inside panes. She's very particular, no streaks allowed. She begins to teach me how, too. Daddy lifts off one set of windows and hangs the other on the hooks, and Mama fastens them from inside. In spring, Mama cleans the basement, sweeps out the coal dust and wood-chips—we're not allowed to go down until after the dust has settled, when it all looks new and neat and bare. Upstairs, she or Daddy strips the floor wax and Mama puts new wax down. It's so slippery that we run and slide in our slippers for days.

Auntie Lou doesn't care so much about housework. She lets things go longer than Mama can believe, until Uncle has to nag her or do it himself.

Auntie loves cartoons, so Uncle buys her a color TV. She loves Bugs Bunny best, but all the Warner Brothers characters as well—Daffy Duck, Tweety Bird, Road Runner, and Wile E. Coyote. When we knock on the door and she opens, she says in her best nasal voice, "What's up, Doc?"

Daddy and Uncle both buy records for their hi-fis. Uncle likes Rachmaninoff and Beethoven; Daddy buys piano classics and Sibelius. Daddy also buys Mama records of her favorite country and gospel singers. On Saturday nights while the men are still in the barn, Mama listens to the Grand Ole Opry on the radio. Other nights, if there's no baseball, she listens to records of bluegrass and gospel singers. Listening to records, I dust all the furniture, fill the washing machine, and organize drawers.

I learn to sweep. I pick up the rugs and throw them on the back steps, then pull the broom along the edge of the cupboard.

"Not like that!" Mama exclaims and grabs the broom out of my hands. She drives the bristles into the space beneath the cupboard, brushes hard against the mopboard, presses the broom against the floor, bending the bristles. With fast strokes, she begins to produce a pile of dust and sand and crumbs. "Like this!"

She thrusts the broom back at me. I take it and begin again with force.

"That's better," she says.

Learning to wash dishes, I first used a chair and sat on my knees. Mama showed me how to rub each plate and glass and fork with the dishrag, feel it with my palm for sticking crumbs, rub it clean, rinse it, and set it in the dish rack on the washboard to the right. Now I stand at the sink. She says I take forever.

"You have to do it faster," she says.

I go faster for awhile, but then forget.

"Quit dawdling!" she exclaims.

"What's dawdling?"

"It's wasting time!"

"I can't help it."

"You have to help it. Here." She takes the cloth, washes all the silverware, rinses it, stashes it in the silverware holder quickly and easily. "There!" She puts two pans and their covers in the water.

"*Why* do you take so long?" she asks.

"I don't know," I say. "It's not interesting."

"Listen, you're going to do a lot of dishes in your life," she says, "so you might as well like it. But you better do them faster or that's *all* you're going to be doing."

I begin to concentrate: plates and bowls, glasses and cups, silverware, then middle-sized things, then the pots and pans last, stacked on top.

Every chance I get, when I catch up on housework, I escape — in the winter to my room to read, in the spring to hunt for agates on the road, in the summer to swing in the oak tree between the two houses or to walk up the lane, chewing on timothy, smelling the blooming things, telling stories to myself.

Bruce and Blaine and I brush the cows with a currycomb, a metal ring with teeth on one side. The cows don't seem to mind. We take the dog to go get the cows on summer afternoons, measure out feed on top of servings of silage, and sweep out the mangers when the cows are done eating. Bruce and Blaine begin to feed calves. They learn how to mix water with powdery milk-replacer in the milk house, work out the lumps, then feed the calves out of the pails, one by one. Some of the calves buck and spill, others are perfectly behaved.

Once in awhile Daddy and Uncle let us wash a gentle cow's udder, wring out the disinfectant-smelling water from the flat sponge-cloth, step in beside the cow, squat down, and wash her bag and teats gently, firmly, and completely of all the day's dust.

The pigs are gone now and we have more than forty cows, plus heifers and calves. With more cows, we need more feed, so we bought another forty acres north of the barns for a total of 240. The new forty is mostly swamp, good for pasture, but it also contains the ruin of a house from the very old days, when the forty was a farm called Rosendale. It's

still thick with wild roses with very sharp thorns, thick also with bur-
docks that stick to our clothes in clusters like prickly grapes.

For the additional crops we have a new silo, forty-five feet tall, but
we also need a pole barn, since the new barn doesn't have a mow. We
rent Grampa Anderson's fields, and plant all the corn and hay and
oats we can manage. Mama and Auntie drive the tractor for raking
and baling, not just on our farm but on the familiar farm where they
grew up.

To keep us busy, Gramma Marty takes the twins and me fishing at Rock
Creek. First we dig a coffee-can full of fat worms from the black dirt
behind the woodshed. Then she directs us to take the bamboo poles
down from the rafters inside the woodshed. With baling twine, we tie
the poles to the passenger-door handles of the car while she checks the
tackle box for hooks and bobbers. Then we all get in the car and go.

She avoids the highway, driving very slowly on the gravel roads
because her arthritis makes it hard to shift and brake—sometimes we
have to shift. She grips the wheel with her clawlike hands and we go
slowly enough to watch grasshoppers leaping from tall grass in the
ditches, slowly enough so birds on the fence posts don't fly as we look
them in the eye, slowly enough for bees to fly in one window and out
the other side. Buzzing frogs sound like trains as we pass them, a high
pitch that falls.

On the road a mile north of the county line we stop by the bridge
and Gramma parks on the side of the road, two tires in the ditch. I
help her down the steep slope and under the fence, which is her greatest challenge. The twins run the poles and tackle and bait down to
the water and begin to attach bobbers and bait to the hooks. Gramma
checks them all, sets each of us up with a pole, hushes us, and helps us
watch the bobbers in the water because we get distracted.

"Uh-oh, there, Blaine, you've got a nibble, don't you think?" she
says quietly. "Watch, now!"

She teaches us which to keep, which to throw back. Mostly they're
bullheads with stingers. When we get home, she teaches us how to skin
and clean them, feeding waste to the cats who come running from
the barn. We walk home with the little fillets, but Mama won't always
fry them—still too many bones, she says, or she's got something else
planned, or they don't taste very good.

Mama takes us shopping for clothes. She takes me to Cele's for white things and blouses and sometimes a dress or a hat for Easter. For shoes, she takes us to the Mercantile, which makes her nervous because she knows we'll all see shoes we like that cost too much. For coats, she drives us to the Cities—to Cambridge and then down Highway 65 through Isanti, Ham Lake, Blaine, and Fridley—to the Robert Hall on Central Avenue.

There is never enough money, even though our farm is a good farm. Field work, barn work, yard work, housework—but there is also town work.

Auntie Lou works at the switchboard at the hospital in a uniform, lipstick, and a headset and knows which cord to plug into which hole. She sits behind a window in the wall where she can also greet visitors in the lobby or talk to the manager in the office next door. The lobby is all the farther children under twelve can go. I have been past that line twice, once to get my tonsils out when I was six, and once to go to the lunchroom when I visited Auntie for two hours.

I admire the nurses all in white, wearing watches with second hands. One wears silver glasses with rhinestones. I want nursing to be my work. In the walk-in closet behind Auntie's desk, I examine the hats of the off-duty nurses and hold them to my head as I look in the mirror.

Mama is a bookkeeper and has been a secretary. For a whole year, from graduation to her wedding, she worked for Frandsen Lumber when the owner and his wife lived in an apartment over the furniture store. Now the lumberman has started a plastics company and he and his family live at Rush Lake. Since the twins were born, Mama has town work again, first working part-time at the school, and then working from home as the school's bookkeeper. She is very fast and neat and accurate because she was taught by Mrs. Froelke. Mama is honored now to write out Mrs. Froelke's payroll check. She treats it with respect just as she treats all the checks with care—checks for the teachers she had and the ones who are new, for the janitors and secretaries, for the principals and superintendent.

There is no comparison between what Mama and Auntie can earn from town work, without getting dirty, and the egg money Gramma Marty and Gramma Anderson once made. But the grammas never had anything but egg money, and they made enough of that for thread and fabric and buttons.

Mama and Auntie have always been proud they married for love. They say with superiority that Gramma and Grampa Marty married *for convenience,* although once when I was little I asked Gramma while we were working at the cemetery if she had loved Grampa, and she said yes and began to cry and couldn't stop. Auntie and Mama tell again and again how happy they were to move to their husbands' houses, to turn lights on with switches and water with faucets, and I think *What is convenience?*

Our baby brother Steven comes home from the hospital on a piano-lesson day in May, near the end of third grade for me and first grade for the twins. He lies asleep in a big new crib in Mama and Daddy's bedroom, fair and almost bald, with closed eyelids, blue-veined like a baby robin's.

While Mama feeds Steven and reads *Time* magazine, which she started getting for just that purpose, I wash dishes. I learn to hang diapers on the line, take them in when they're dry, and fold them perfectly to set on Steven's changing table. I fold laundry and more laundry. Later, I'm allowed to hold the baby. Sometimes, when Mama needs to do something else, I sit in the big chair and feed Steven his bottle and read *Time,* about the Arab-Israeli war and Apollos in space and the Beatles. I walk him to sleep, back and forth on the new living room carpet. Mama says I do excellent work—I am a marvelous helper.

All summer, Kathy and I ride our bikes and meet at the corner after supper dishes are done. The sun is still high, so we ride west down the county line to what is now a dead-end by the Ekstrand triplets' house. We watch the gravel trucks and Caterpillars building the freeway. Kathy has a one-year-old sister and works harder than I do. Her dad grades roads for Chisago County, so he leaves before dawn, comes home at four-thirty for supper, then goes out to do field work on their small farm. There's no grandma or aunt or uncle at her place, so Kathy does a lot more garden work than I do, and she has to dust every single day because her mother is even more particular than mine. She also has an older brother who tells her what to do. Kathy says I'm lucky that our baby is *not* a girl because her baby sister gets into all her things. Now her mother is expecting another baby before Christmas.

At night through the open windows, we hear not only the train from the east but freeway construction from the west, big cats and trucks working until the very last light, sometimes after dark. We hear freeway-building sounds all day. While I walk Steven to sleep in the afternoon, I hear it. Over the sound of the milkers in the evening, I hear it, especially on days when the breeze comes from the west-northwest.

In September we get a new trailer house for Gramma Marty, parked and secured next to the orchard fence, across the driveway from the big house. The stairs in the big house became so difficult for her that sometimes she was trapped upstairs for days.

The trailer house began as an idea for the Anderson place — Mama and Auntie went hunting for one after Gramma Anderson had gall-bladder surgery. They found a pink and black one, but Grampa wouldn't have it. Then they realized it might be perfect for Gramma Marty, and she agreed. Now she has only two shallow steps in and out of the trailer, a view from every room of birds on branches, and her own phone in case she needs to call for help. She can take care of Jonathan without keeping him in the house all day, and her sisters and friends and Gramma Anderson can come over easily to visit. Auntie and Uncle and Jonathan have the big house to themselves, and Mama knows Gramma can no longer see how many times our car goes in and out of the driveway.

To make ends meet at our house, Daddy goes to work at Plastech. He works the swing shift as an assistant foreman — two days, two evenings, two nights, then two days off before starting over. He also keeps doing farmwork, milking and barn chores and trips to town, but sometimes when we get home from school we find him asleep in bed.

Even without extra work, Daddy can sleep anytime, anywhere. He snores. His favorite thing is to take a nap on Sunday afternoon. Sometimes at the dinner or supper table, he falls asleep with his fork in his hand.

The twins start getting up in the morning to do chores, taking turns. Daddy wakes one of them to come out during milking to feed calves and clean the mangers and walks.

When school is out again, Mama starts giving me an allowance. It's true that I help a lot, but Kathy's mother has had twins and her summer is a lot busier than mine. She has a million more diapers to fold, and her little sister, who is two, is into everything and talks constantly. Kathy is almost too tired to ride her bike in the evenings.

Feeding Steven his bottle, I read about riots in hot cities all over the nation; the life of Martin Luther King Jr., now ended; more Apollos in space; Nixon and Humphrey and Robert Kennedy running for president. I see photos of war in Vietnam. When some nurses living together in Chicago are murdered, I see a map of their apartment showing the path of the killer.

On the night Robert Kennedy is killed, I am sleeping on our porch because it's so hot upstairs. The windows are wide open and the sounds of the swamp across the road come through the screens, the hum and shifting of road construction in the background, the screech of night birds all around me. I hear footsteps in the grass outside the windows, footsteps on the concrete stairs outside the front screen door, voices carrying across the night, the machinery on the freeway. I imagine men with guns and knives parking their cars on the side of the road and walking up to our house. I imagine a man alone with a gun. A bug hits the screen and drags across it like a hand. Nazis rush in to our house in the night, taking us all away—taking Steven, or taking the grown-ups and leaving us children alone.

In the daylight, I begin to play by the woodshed, behind the lilac bushes. I pull out weeds from the wild roses and clear a space to play unseen, wearing down the dirt until it's smooth and shiny. Gramma Marty gives me a scalloped wire border from the woodshed, and I stick it in along the dirt I've turned over. I transplant flowers that have multiplied behind the trailer, Johnny-jump-ups and wild violets.

When Gramma Anderson comes to do her laundry at Auntie Lou's or to have coffee at Gramma Marty's, she notices my work and admires it. When I go with Mama to Gramma Anderson's for coffee, Gramma walks me to her garden to show me where to take some lilies-of-the-valley. We dig out little sections and she sends them home with me to plant them in my garden.

I compare the grammas' gardens. Gramma Anderson plants in odd, natural shapes. She has a stone and marble bird bath and lets wild perennials have room—bushes of bleeding heart, columbine, clumps of daisylike relatives, the carpet of lilies-of-the-valley under her grove of lilacs—all these and more grow along the curved crest of the hill above the creek. Her flowers grow in profusion, one color lapping into the next. I can see her garden from the north window of her kitchen where she stands to wash dishes without running water. She keeps baby-food jars and little vases full of violets and lilies-of-the-valley in her windowsills.

Gramma Marty grows tulips, zinnias, dahlias, bachelor buttons, and other annuals and bulbs along borders—along the woodshed, the fences, the house, and her trailer. Her gardens make symmetrical shapes with spaces of weedless soil between each plant. Her lilac bush was planted to shade the path to the outhouse on the north end of the woodshed, flanked by a screen of wild roses. She lets wild flowers—mayflowers and trilliums and dogtooth—stay in the woods, a reward for spring walks.

Their handwork is like their gardens. Gramma Anderson keeps boxes and boxes of cloth, bags and bags of rags. She saves and considers. *Oh, a lot of blue here. Hmm, quite a bit of red and purple. Would that look all right?* She pieces bits together on her treadle sewing machine, sitting among the piles of boxes. She makes rugs and crazy quilts and other wild and colorful things.

Gramma Marty is not so wild, not always so colorful. She works in blocks of more orderly color. On her bed is a cream-colored, popcorn-stitch bedspread that she crocheted before her wedding, overwhelming for sheer size, weight, and degree of detail. She made a baby blanket of sixteen blocks, each block with a patchwork butterfly in four perfect rows with a border embroidered tightly in black.

When the two grammas sit together in Gramma Marty's trailer, Gramma Anderson brings her crocheting or knitting and her plain hands fly—a green border for a pillowcase, a pair of purple booties. Gramma Marty can't grip those kinds of needles anymore, but she still tries to embroider, awkwardly holding the hoop with one hand, pressing the needle through with the other.

Piano is my handwork—scales and gavottes and marches and hymns. Bartok and Debussy are my favorites. But when I need to be alone to think, I go to my lilac garden and dig in the dirt, grip weeds, and hum. After school starts, I go to my garden on Saturday or Sunday afternoons. When the leaves fall, I cover my mayflowers and lilies-of-the-valley and read: every Laura Ingalls Wilder book, every Childcraft book, biographies of Florence Nightingale and Clara Barton, *The Secret Garden*, Hardy Boys books, *Harriet the Spy*, and the Bible from beginning to end. I read so much I have to get glasses, but as I ride home in the car afterward, I am amazed by the leaves on the trees, suddenly sharp and distinct. I stare at every tree and drink it in with my new eyes — ruffled oaks, tender elms, fluttering birches, bristly spruce, brushy pines.

In town, Plastech is expanding into buildings downtown and on the edge of town. The office gets a computer, and Mama gets a call because they need good office staff. She takes the job so Daddy can quit working in the plant and put all his energy into the farm.

Twice a day, Daddy and Uncle milk forty-eight cows, almost twice as many as they milked in the old barn. Forty-eight cows to wash, to milk, to feed with forks full of heavy silage. More hay to bale, stack, unload, and pack into haymows. Daddy's and Uncle's backs hurt. They start going to chiropractors and doctors for slipped discs, and learn to do exercises morning and night.

Bruce and Blaine are strong and are good at everything physical — they like to do things people think they can't. When I got the training wheels off my bike, before they even had bikes, they grabbed my bike from me and rode around the barnyard faster than I could run, rode around me in circles until I gave up in frustration, went into the house, and waited for them to get sick of riding it, which was a long time.

Now the twins begin to lift milkers off the cows going dry, they throw down hay bales, feed silage, and relieve Daddy and Uncle. They start to time the milkings, to help the men go faster, to impress Mama and stop her from complaining about how late Daddy comes in from the barn. They work as fast as they can so they can play catch and pitch to each other.

They are playing ball with Jonathan too — Blaine is the pitcher, Bruce is the catcher — and they are always running, racing each other from the house to the barn, from the barn to the house, from anything to anything.

Splitting the milk check is getting more complicated because our house still gets only half, even though the twins are working and cost more to feed. Mama and Uncle argue about what is expected and fair.

Instead of allowance, Bruce and Blaine get a calf to raise. She's Daisy's daughter and they name her Dinah, dote on her, and ride her around like a pony. The plan is that, when she's big enough to be bred and start milking, they'll get the value of the milk she produces, and when she calves, if it's a heifer, it will be theirs.

At my desk in the back of the fifth-grade classroom, I'm done with my work. From the teacher, who is cleaning cupboards before Christmas, I take a stack of beautiful white paper with blue lines and a pink rule an inch from the top. On the bulletin board by the door is a poster of a bare tree with a pear swinging on its stem and a fat brown partridge sitting on a branch. I take up my pencil.

"The Twelve Days of Christmas," I write, and then I begin a story about a girl who lives in an orphanage, a Victorian house on a hill above a creek, like the Carlson house above Rush Creek, which has been vacant since the Hillcrest nursing home was built. But the house in my story is in a city. I give the orphanage nice grown-ups and children, and I give my main character a best friend like Kathy.

Every day of vacation, I write. I write at the little writing desk up in my room, warm next to the chimney, though I get restless because I can't see out the window. During the day, the air is clear and dry, the sky a piercing blue above the fields of dazzling snow. At night, I write the sky and the snow into my story. There are twelve days and twelve chapters. At the end, when the girl is adopted, she has to leave her friend, but I plan a sequel. All winter, I write.

In the spring when we pick mayflowers in the woods, I pull the little red wagon along and dig up clumps of them, carry them home, and put them in my garden under the lilac bush. The lilacs bloom, then the roses. I sit in my garden, weeding and digging, shaping the chapters of the story inside my head. I rewrite the story.

Carpenters come to tear the stanchions out of the west end of the old barn so we can stack hay from the stone floor to the rafters. More men come to put up a pole shed behind the barns to store more hay.

Mama has a long-range plan for our house too, and gradually we see her make it come true. After the sea-green carpet and piano in the living room comes tile to cover the hardwood floor of the dining room, a modern dinette set, and a hutch cupboard for the good dishes. Slipcovers, a stereo, a couch to match the carpet and built-in book-shelves above it, matching chairs, then drapes. In the bathroom, double sinks and a new bathtub with a shower. She takes out loans and pays them off.

Next, Mama imagines an addition across the whole north end of the house—a breakfast nook in the kitchen, a big mud room with washer and dryer and closets and sink for washing up after the barn, and a walk-in closet for her and Daddy's bedroom. On the outside, she'd like black shutters and trim to match. She can see it in her mind.

When summer comes, Mama begins to pay me, not an allowance, but a monthly wage to care for Steven, keep the house picked up, cook, and do dishes, so she can keep working. I'm only eleven, but she believes I am responsible. Besides, there are grown-ups close by, Gramma in the trailer, Daddy and Uncle outside.

This arrangement turns out fine. Steven is easy and naps in the afternoons. Dishes have become easy for me, and I start to cook simple things—fried eggs for Daddy in the morning, spaghetti or macaroni-and-cheese or goulash for lunch, tuna sandwiches and Jell-O on hot days. I take Steven to visit Gramma Marty in her trailer. It's hot in there, and she's usually watching Jonathan, who's five now, so we go outside and sit together while the little boys play in the sandbox, making sounds like the noise of the freeway construction. If the mosquitoes are bad, we sit on Auntie and Uncle's front porch while the boys play with blocks.

I learn how to make the house look neat so Mama feels relaxed when she comes home from work at five o'clock. I learn when to close the windows and draw the drapes if the day will be hot, close them on whatever side rain comes from, and open them up again when the rain is over or a cool front comes through. I figure out what to make for supper so that meat is thawed out and potatoes are prepared. My favorite is meat loaf because you can bake instead of peel the potatoes. Mama has me write a grocery list and then she buys things.

I organize my work to wear Steven out before dinner. Then I write at the dining room table while he naps in the afternoon. Sometimes I write in my room after supper.

The freeway construction ends and everyone is waiting for the freeway to open. When I go to my piano lesson at 115 South Dana, Gramma Marty comes along to visit Aunt Margaret at 135 South Dana. There's lots of news to exchange. Rush City not only has a new nursing home, but a new bank, a new post office, and a new clinic, and our congregation is going to build a new church on the freeway-end of town.

The Highway 61 traffic going north on Fridays and south on Sundays is so bad we take the west road to town. Daddy takes the twins and me to the overpass a mile south of our place and we look at the two ribbons of empty road stretching in each direction as far as we can see.

On a windy school day before Thanksgiving, the governor rides up the freeway, stopping in every town to speak, cutting a ribbon near Rush City, the halfway point between the Twin Cities and Moose Lake—though eventually the freeway will go to the twin ports of Duluth and Superior and the halfway point will be Hinckley. The governor's trip is called the Parting of the Pines.

The Sunday before the freeway opens, the Ekstrands' house burns down while they're away visiting their father in a hospital in the Twin Cities. It burns almost to the ground, and they never rebuild it.

Thanksgiving is at our house, with Auntie and Uncle and Jonathan, and Grampa and Gramma Anderson. It's a good dinner, but Gramma Marty misses it because she doesn't feel well—she has a headache. She walked to Auntie and Uncle's house but then decided not to walk across the yard.

After dinner, Uncle and I take her a plate of turkey, mashed potatoes, and cranberries. She's napping on the couch, sun streaming through the porch and the window above her. She opens her eyes and looks at us.

"How are you feeling, Mom?" Uncle asks. "Did the aspirin help at all?"

At first, she doesn't respond, as if shaking sleep from her mind. Then she opens her mouth slightly, and on her tongue we see the aspirin, half dissolved. She makes an indistinguishable sound, yet doesn't seem to be in pain.

"Mom, how are you feeling?" Uncle asks again. Again she makes a noise, now as if she's trying to speak. The sound emerges as though her mouth is covered instead of open. Suddenly, her eyes are afraid.

"Stay beside her," Uncle directs me. "Can you? Sit right here. Mom, I'm gonna call Lou."

I kneel beside the couch and lay my hand on Gramma's arm. She looks at me. Tears emerge from one of her brown eyes. Uncle dials the phone and asks Auntie and Daddy to come, and they cross the yard in their coats, entering through the door with a rush of cold air. I move away and Daddy squats beside the couch, Auntie bends over Gramma, and Gramma lies helpless, speechless, looking up at us with frightened eyes, opening her mouth to show the aspirin that can't be swallowed.

Carefully they dress her in her coat and hat, wrap her scarf around her neck, pull on her boots. I sit in the back seat of Uncle and Auntie's car and they put Gramma in beside me, leaning against me. I put my arm around her and stroke her shoulder. Uncle brings a blanket to cover us both and takes a seat in front, then Auntie drives down the west road to the hospital.

At the emergency entrance, Gramma is lifted to a wheelchair. Even though I'm not quite twelve, Auntie leads me through the halls of the hospital to stand in the lobby, across from Room 101, as Gramma is dressed in a hospital gown and helped into bed. Her glasses are laid on a table and she looks toward me at the door, but I know that I am blurry to her.

She dies nine days later of pneumonia, a complication from a stroke. Her funeral is held at the Lutheran church, the only church big enough to hold the crowd. Daddy tells me Grampa's funeral was held there too.

She was only sixty-one, the first of her eleven siblings to die. They all are there, weeping openly with shock.

"She was such a hard worker," they say. "She worked so *hard.*"

"They mean the Martys worked her to death," Daddy says under his breath. I'm surprised to see his chin set angrily and his eyes flash. "She loved to work! She died of *not* working."

Miraculously, her hands, made clawlike by arthritis, are now smooth in the casket. They appear normal and healthy, ready to thread a needle or bait a hook.

We drive to the cemetery and pray in the cold wind around her casket, standing on the graves of Jacob and Susanna, Susanna's mother and brother, Sam and Mamie and Harold, Grampa and the baby. We drive away before she's laid into the ground — that happens later, while we're eating lunch in the basement of the Lutheran church, hugging our relatives, while Bruce and Blaine and our cousins are out throwing rocks into the creek behind the dam. Her body finally rests inside the ground beside the bones of Grampa as snow covers the earth.

The trailer house is not empty for long. The next summer, Grampa and Gramma Anderson move in. Grampa assents only because it would be a waste of space otherwise and because Gramma needs modern plumbing, with her health the way it is.

"Finally!" Mama says, glad to prevail over her father's stubbornness. "Nobody deserves it more than Mother does."

"Grampa's such a case," Auntie says.

Grampa will rent the shack to a local man who doesn't care about plumbing or electricity.

In the old view—in Grampa Marty's view, and Gramma Marty's too—I can see that a family works for the land and the land supports the family. In the modern view—the view of Aunt Margaret and Mama and Auntie Lou—land provides security because it can be bought and sold.

When Auntie and Mama clean the old house out, there isn't room for everything in the trailer. Some things go to Auntie Lou, especially those she identifies as antiques. A gateleg table goes to Mama. There's a chest of drawers I can have if I want to refinish it. Auntie will teach me how, although she can't really help because she's expecting a new baby and it's dangerous to breathe the dust from sanding and the chemicals from the stripper. She is so sure the dresser will be beautiful and the job not too hard to accomplish that I agree.

For a month of summer mornings, while Gramma Anderson watches Steven, Auntie Lou and I go out to Sam's garage, spread newspapers on the grass, and pull the dresser out. She sits on a chair and drinks coffee while I strip and sand and stain and refinish. Auntie counts seven coats of paint I strip off, including blue, yellow, and brown. I uncover grooves and details lost under the paint. The wood itself is oak and more beautiful than Auntie expected. We go to the hardware store and buy six new handles, dark brass. At the end, she brings me a matching mirror from her attic to hang above it. She reports that there's a brass bed in her attic too, although it's pretty beat up.

"That was Gaylon's and mine when we were kids," says Daddy.

"Can I have it?" I ask, and it's mine. I cover it with Gramma Marty's crocheted spread.

I find old flowerpots and fill them with slips and cuttings. I'm sick of pink walls, so Mama and I paint them candlelight yellow. As I write at my little desk at night, the wind blows and acorns from the swing-tree fall on the roof.

Spruce

On the Marty farm, evergreens don't grow in the woods, only around the houses by the road. Pines shade the front lawn of the big house. Beyond it, a double row of tall, shaggy spruce curves around the southwest corner of the orchard. From a distance, it is that spiky grove that makes the profile of our farm.

Sam Marty, my great-uncle, planted different kinds of spruce trees around the house he built in 1940. It was a simple house except for the Swiss-looking roof, as if the pointed gables had been folded down. He painted the house the colors of the Swiss flag: white with red trim and red shingles. Sam died before his dream to visit his parents' birthplace came true, but the house was a sign of Switzerland, a cottage surrounded by spruce trees, like the evergreens on a mountain postcard.

The two blue spruce shading the porch grew up stout and straight as twins. To me, they seemed to stand for Marty brothers—Sam and Grampa John, then Daddy and Uncle, and someday Bruce and Blaine.

Seven years after Sam died, I, and then my brothers, arrived in the house that Sam built. For many winters, Daddy put Christmas lights on a narrow little spruce tree by the road that lit up the snowy lawn in the night. All the spruce trees were beautiful when covered with snow. When we remodeled the house and raised the roof in 1965, Mama chose green shingles and painted the trim to match.

I have mixed feelings about those spruce trees because their needles in the grass of our entire front lawn live up to the word *needle*—sharp and painful—even for my feet, which are tough as leather from running barefoot all summer on gravel roads and fields of cut hay. Compared to the short, four-sided needles of spruce, the needles of pine on the front lawn of the big house are long and silky and feel soft as moss. You would never know from spruce needles that their wood is soft and perfect for paper-making. Spruce trees also drop sticky cones and sap that make our front yard miserable to mow. And during the short days of winter, they block the sun we crave.

Still, I was upset when a tornado, or something very close to it, snapped off the top of one of the twin blue spruce. It was a hot summer day when towering white clouds filled the sky and darkened, and the air turned green and motionless. We heard the siren blow from town, three miles away, and ran to the basement. What seemed like stillness suddenly felt like a vacuum, like air rushing outward and away, everything emptying, and then a rolling wall of wind seized and thrashed every tree — we could see them through the narrow basement windows swaying wildly. Then came the rain that gradually washed the air from green to blue to clear again. When it was over, we came up and looked out at the lawn littered with bunches of leaves and small branches, and we saw the new flat top of one blue spruce, unsightly as a lost tooth. The little Christmas tree by the road lay tipped in the ditch.

II

SEPARATION

6

Husbands and Wives

Behold, thou art fair, my beloved, yea, pleasant, and our bed is
green. The beams of our house are cedar, and our rafters of fir.

— Song of Solomon 1:16–17

Mama was at war with manure. Her continual dread was that
one of us would carry the smell with us off the farm. Barn
work, even walking into the barn, made us smell like
manure and had to be followed by washing. Mama stopped going to
the barn for fear that the smell would cling to her hair, which she had
styled into a beehive once a week in town.

Enemy number two was mud. Every spring, Mama swore she
would get a sidewalk from the driveway to the door, and she lamented
that our driveway was gravel instead of tar. Finally, Daddy poured a
sidewalk, but there was no paving the driveway.

Mama came home from work at Plastech later and later in the afternoons. She was assigned to an executive nobody else wanted to work
for, a manager who advanced to production scheduler, a perfectionist who made her cry, but still, she was proud of her work. Her pay-
checks bought us eyeglasses, decent shoes and jackets, and the addition
to the house she'd been hoping for. Now we had a place to leave our
barn shoes and clothes, a mud sink, closets with louvered doors for
hanging barn clothes, plus a washer and dryer that we could hear from
the kitchen.

Mama quit gardening because she couldn't keep up with it and
because she made enough money to buy everything we needed at the
store. She came home from work and walked furiously behind the lawn
mower, burning off tension. She quit doing the farm books and carried them across the yard to Auntie Lou, saying she'd done them long
enough and nobody listened to her anyway. She got angry when Daddy
came in late for supper or when Uncle Gaylon took all the field work
and left Daddy with barn chores.

"Just set the milkers down and come in, even if he isn't there!" she pleaded.

"Right," Daddy said. "When did three cows ever finish milking at the same time?"

On other days: "Just tell him no, *you're* going to go to the field, *he* can do the chores!"

On Sundays: "Tell him you have plans! Why can't you tell Gaylon *you* have plans?"

But Daddy couldn't. Uncle's back was killing him, and he was Daddy's older brother. Daddy's back didn't feel so great either, but he was better at barn work because he was patient.

One night while Mama did taxes, with books and papers spread all over the dining room table, she told the twins and me, "If anyone asks you what your father does, *don't* say he's a farmer. You say he's a *dairy farm owner and operator.* That's what he is."

Rush City was growing. The view was the same from our place — white grain elevators, silver cone of the water tower, and lights of the ball field at night from spring to fall. But Plastech had a new, modern plant south of town, and on westerly winds we could hear the whine of the new freeway traffic day and night. Beyond the freeway, on the shores of Rush Lake, farms were sold and divided into lots where people from the Twin Cities built houses and moved in. New kids came to school.

My class had sixty-six kids, the twins' class had almost eighty. Most of us lived in the country — a third of us on dairy farms — but the class leaders were town kids. Half of us had been together since kindergarten, the other half we generally called *new,* with some from families that moved a lot, and some from families whose fathers commuted an hour to the Cities. All together, our parents were not only farmers and business owners now but machinists or die cutters, press operators or assembly workers. Some picked up a second job at Plastech on B or C shift or worked in secondary operations.

Plastech made parts for companies that produced toys and parts for vending machines, furniture, and snowmobiles. The Plastech president was interested in snowmobiles and bought them for his kids — lots of people bought them for themselves and their families, and everybody tried them out. The land around Rush Lake and down by the St. Croix River, east of us, was perfect for motorbikes and snowmobiles. Almost all the twins' friends in the country, farmers or not, had motorbikes and compared stories. Motorbikes had a practical use of getting one to and from the fields in a hurry. But the twins wanted a snowmobile too, so they tried to think of reasons the farm needed one.

Our farm was also growing. In 1970 it almost doubled in size. After Grampa and Gramma Anderson moved to the empty trailer house on the Marty farm, Grampa sold the Anderson land to the Marty brothers — 200 acres at a low price. For six years, he'd been leasing the fields to us to plant hay and corn, and now the monthly payments could earn equity. In addition, the Martys agreed to care for Grampa and Gramma for the rest of their lives, and Grampa could keep his sawmill, shop, and lumber rights to the woods.

Uncle Gaylon declared our farm plural — Marty Farms — a total of 460 acres. Bruce and Blaine would grow up and own a farm that was now two farms.

The twins loved the Anderson farm more than the Marty farm because half of it was woods and creek. With their milk checks, they saved up and bought little Kawasaki motorbikes, crossed the highway and headed east on the county line, and tore around the old Anderson cow paths and logging paths, buzzing up and down ravines, finding good places to jump, and looking for tracks of deer and bear the way they hunted for agates on gravel roads.

Grampa Anderson's woods consisted of hardwoods and evergreens and covered sixty acres. He'd carefully harvested from those woods all his life, cutting mature pines and oaks and hauling them out on logging paths north and south of the creek, sawing them into boards at his mill over a ravine. The saw was powered by a John Deere engine or the Minneapolis Moline he called Minnie. He knew every tree in his woods and, although he was almost seventy, still did jobs for other people as well.

Grampa Anderson loved machines but never liked animals, except dogs and cats. He called horses *hay burners,* sold the cows out of his pastures before I ever knew them up close, and sold off the chickens and pigs long ago too. For Grampa Anderson, the whole point of farming seemed to be about using his favorite machinery, and he chose crops accordingly — hay for hay balers and oats for threshing machines, crops he could sell like lumber. For years he baled and threshed for farmers — the Martys included — who couldn't keep up at busy times or who didn't own the needed equipment. Now he used his farm buildings to store machines, and he spent evenings in his shop repairing them.

When we took down the old log barn on the Marty farm, Grampa Anderson came to the rescue. The log barn at ninety years old was clearly a hazard, and we weren't allowed to go inside it anymore. The roof sagged badly and needed new shingles to keep it from rotting, which would have been a waste of money in Uncle's and Daddy's eyes. They hired our pastor's son David, who wanted summer work, to tear down the barn, a job they thought would take two or three weeks.

David pulled off all the wooden shingles and then didn't know what to do. The barn had not a nail in it, just solid logs with huge notches fitted together, now fused fast. The men looked it over and shook their heads — there was nothing David could have done any differently. They lent him a hand now and then, but they were busy with everything else. So week after week, David took the log barn apart piece by piece, growing as strong as the men who put it up. There came a point when nothing budged. Grampa Anderson surveyed the whole thing, not surprised by the power of the logs. Then he coached Daddy and Uncle through pulling the rest down with tractors.

The Martys drove International Harvester tractors, red and white instead of John Deere green and yellow. On our H tractor, Blaine learned to cultivate corn. Uncle Gaylon took him out the first time to cultivate the flat while Uncle raked a field of first-crop hay south of the woods driving the 400. Uncle showed Blaine how to lower the four curved teeth of the cultivator into the dirt between the rows of weedy young corn; how to watch and steer so that the tractor wheels — narrow in front, wide in the back — and the four teeth of the cultivator fell exactly between the rows of corn; and how to turn at the end of the row so not a single tender shoot was uprooted. First Uncle explained the process and rode along on the tractor, showing how things were done, turning expertly. Then he got off, hands on his hips under the cloudless blue sky, and watched Blaine do it. Finally, he got on the 400 and started raking, still watching Blaine.

At the end of Blaine's field, the turn came too fast for him. He braked, but the sharp metal teeth raked over the ends of four rows, exposing sunbursts of roots like tiny white hands reaching out of the black soil, pushing the green tops down into the dirt. Blaine straightened the wheel and began the return, hoping Uncle didn't notice but knowing no mistake is ever hidden when cultivating — the corn cannot be set back in. He had left a gap.

Uncle appeared on the hitch bar behind him. He didn't correct Blaine but repeated his directions, showing again how it is done, addressing exactly that thing he knew was untimed.

All morning as the sun reached for its peak, Blaine repeated the pattern — the slowing, the turn, the exact angle of directing the tractor's small front wheels between the plants, rotating the tractor neatly on its rear wheels so the cultivator teeth moved smoothly out of the way of the corn, then coming around to the next set of four rows. Each end became neater, tighter, the young corn remaining untouched.

"Beautiful!" Uncle exclaimed when he finished raking. "Beautiful work! You're the Martys' next expert cultivator!"

It was a good thing, because Uncle needed a better backup than Daddy. Cultivating seemed to hypnotize Daddy — whenever he had to do it, the fields were full of gaps where the tractor had veered slightly off course, enough to down four or eight or sixteen plants. Bruce didn't show promise either — he was distracted by birds and flowers and moving things, variations of color that caught his eye. It was only Blaine who had the concentration, and a drive for precision.

Bruce was good with the cows. Working around the barn one day, he noticed that a cow, left inside to labor, was taking too long. She stood as if dazed, every now and then banging her stanchion. Uncle and Daddy were gone — one in an Anderson field, one in town. As I walked through the barn, Bruce was anxious. He asked me what to do.

I looked at the little hooves protruding from the back of the cow.

"What would Daddy or Uncle do?" I asked.

Bruce pulled a length of baler twine from the hook on the wall, stood beside the cow, and talked to her and stroked her flank. He tied the twine around the calf's ankles, gently pulled, and ten minutes later delivered the calf.

It was a big calf. Bruce wiped the mucus off its mouth and pushed its chest to help it start to breathe. By the time Daddy got home, the calf was standing by the cow and sucking.

Besides housework and cooking, I washed milkers and drove the tractor for raking and baling hay. The first time Uncle and Auntie took me out to try the tractor, I was twelve, probably older than Mama and Auntie when they started driving tractor for their dad, but it was still too early for me. I dreamed about that first try so often—clutch, brake, shift, brake and clutch release, throttle, the rhythm of the baler, the bright sun, the smell of oil and gas, the smell of cut hay, Uncle's hand and voice signals—that I must have learned it all in my sleep. The next summer, without much trouble, I knew how to drive.

It was always early afternoon when we drove the tractor and wagon out to the field. As we began, Uncle released the power takeoff to start the baler, *ker-ker-ker-chunk*. He grabbed the draw hook from its loop on the side of the baler, hopped up on the hay wagon, and pulled on his haying gloves from his back pocket. I could start without lurching, keep the baler uptake perfectly in line with the windrow of hay, watch ahead and behind, and respond instantly to Uncle's signals—first finger up for faster, thumb down for slower, palm up and "Whoa!" for stop. As bales inched out of the chute toward the wagon, Uncle watched them, swung the draw hook into each bale, pulled it back onto the rack, and lifted it with one knee and carried it by both strings of twine toward the back of the rack, stacking it firmly in rows, back to front, up to six bales high. We moved steadily along the edges of the field in a slow spiral toward the middle, the baler eating the windrows and packing them into bales, the rack gradually filling.

I liked the windrow beneath the wheels, the *ker-ker-ker-chunk* of the baler, how strong it made my arms, how fast the sun cleared up my skin in June. Uncle was my baling partner, and I liked his look of intent, his grin when it was going well, the way he jumped off the rack to lift a handful of hay to feel the texture and weight of it, smelling it, biting off a stem and chewing to test its dryness. Hay too wet would clog the baler, break the twine or a shear pin, and get moldy in the mow if it made it that far. Hay too dry made the cows' milk thin.

I loved hay days—the pale blue sky, high flat-bottomed clouds if there were any at all, shimmering heat. Hay days were always beautiful or they wouldn't be hay days. Killdeers swooped and darted, called *Kill-deer! Kill-deer-deer!* and the tall corn rustled. When it was very hot, evening was even more welcome.

From the trailer house, Grampa Anderson looked out with approval. The Marty farm was a dairy operation he admired because we had enough hands to make vacations and days off from milking possible. It was forward-looking, and he was proud to be part of it.

He'd been through a change. A coronary had stopped him cold, put him in the hospital, opened his ears to the doctor and his heart to the pastor. He accepted salvation, quit drinking, exchanged his cigarettes for a pipe, and from the day he put his overalls back on and walked into the sunlight, he began taking Gramma to church whenever she wanted to go.

Uncle Gaylon and Auntie Lou's baby girl was born at noon on Christmas Day 1970. Just saying her name, Carolyn, invoked music. She was a brown-eyed beauty and stole Uncle's heart from me, which was as it should be. Now Uncle and Daddy each had his own girl. Everybody on the farm adored her. She was impossibly cute, as smart-alecky as Bruce and Blaine when she learned to talk, and she dressed in little cowgirl dresses and Western hats and boots to play outdoors, unafraid of dirt or danger.

Auntie left her job at the hospital. She took over the farm books from Mama, opened a garden north of her own house in the black soil where the pig yard used to be, and shared work with Gramma Anderson.

It's hard to know just when Uncle Gaylon began to change. I didn't know about his temper as early as the twins did because I spent time with him in the field, where he was happy. But in the barn, with Daddy and the twins, he yelled — the cows were too slow, they kicked too much, they were stupid. He yelled at the twins and Jonathan too. Maybe it was the tearing pain in his back.

He had back surgery in the Cities, lying in traction for days. He and his hospital roommate talked about everything from baseball to fishing, but mostly about God. His roommate gave him a book called *The Prophet*, which bothered Uncle, and when he came home, he began to read books by Francis Schaeffer, a Christian theologian and philosopher.

Uncle was freed from pain but scared of it ever returning. Maybe he was also worried about making ends meet without Auntie's income. Maybe he was worried about having not only a son but a daughter to raise and keep safe.

I felt like a big sister to Carolyn, so much older that we couldn't play together. Instead I sewed clothes for her and baked her birthday cakes on Christmas Day. But Uncle didn't really want me to be like a big sister to Carolyn. As much as he cared for my welfare, his first responsibility was to protect his own children, and that included protecting them from the twins and me. I could feel his wariness. Bruce and Blaine and I had crossed into the dangerous land of our teens, more dangerous because we were attracted to people and possessions and music and ideas that he was beginning to identify as secular. And Daddy and Mama weren't protecting us — Daddy didn't think he could, and Mama was too secular herself.

While Uncle was laid up, Daddy relied on the twins for help to keep from throwing out his own back. The twins worked hard, and nothing seemed to hurt them. They took turns getting up to do morning chores before school, and they did evening chores together each day. Year-round, they fed the cows silage, feed, and hay in the shallow cement mangers. They helped with milking, fed heifers and calves, cleaned barns, and had learned to drive the tractor by the time they were twelve. Although Blaine excelled at field work and Bruce was tender with animals, each knew how to do everything if they had to.

The twins broke up their work with play every chance they got. In fact, the promise of play made them work faster. When football was no longer possible on the grass north of our clotheslines in the fall, they moved into the driveway of the old barn, where Daddy had mounted a hoop, to play basketball for the winter. The sound of the basketball hitting the north door of the new barn during milking, along with their yelps and arguments, startled the cows on the other side. Once the snow melted, Bruce and Blaine ran outside between chores to hit fly balls toward the houses. The doors of the three-car garage lost paint from serving as a backstop.

All that playing got on Uncle's nerves. He loved sports, baseball especially, but the twins were obsessed. For Uncle, *work* came first, work *had* to be first. He was constantly calling them from play to work, complaining to Daddy.

The twins were so good at sports that they started getting on town teams in grade school. They campaigned to Daddy and Mama to allow them to go out for football in the fall, basketball in the winter, baseball in the spring.

Mama was so proud of them, she couldn't say no. She wanted them to be happy and recognized as *somebody* in town.

Basketball was okay, Daddy conceded, it was a winter sport. But not baseball, which came at the same time as spring planting, or football, which conflicted with fall harvest.

"One sport," he said.

"They can't choose just one sport!" Mama argued. "They're good at all of them!"

"If there were ten sports in Rush City, they couldn't go out for all ten!"

"But there aren't ten, there are three."

"Four," he corrected her. "There's track."

"Fine! Four!" She cleared her throat. "I will not have my kids be slaves to this farm—they are not slave labor for you to exploit!"

"Slaves!" He almost laughed. "No slave grows up to own the farm."

"You should be proud of them!"

"I *am*! Just how is the field work going to get done?"

"It'll get done!" she retorted, as if it were obvious.

"Easy for you to say," he said sarcastically.

"You think I don't know what field work is?" she bristled. "I know! And I'm not going to make my kids do what I had to do!"

"Your dad had no mercy," Daddy agreed. "But we've got a lot more fields now, and you're not out there."

"I don't have to be out there," she said, which was as close as she got to mentioning her town income. "You and Gaylon are not going to deprive Bruce and Blaine of this opportunity just because you didn't have it. The world doesn't begin and end on this farm!"

They argued like that more than once, and every time, Mama won. So Bruce and Blaine played a sport every season, sometimes even summer rec. In football, Blaine became a quarterback, and Bruce a running back. In basketball, they were twin guards. In baseball, Blaine pitched and Bruce played catcher. They were co-captains, or tri-captains with somebody else, and they started getting mentions in the paper.

The farmwork was always there, acres of field work from May to November, hours of barn work every day of the year. Jonathan and Steven began to feed calves. The twins bartered to switch morning chores, competed for favorite clothes, left their room a mess, dropped duffel bags by the washer unopened. Our bathroom shower ran more and more often. Shampoo and bar soap disappeared, and damp towels piled up.

When the twins talked Mama and Daddy into letting them get a snowmobile, Uncle Gaylon thought it was not only a useless waste of money but a hazard. The twins waited impatiently for snow. One sunny snow-day when school was closed and Kathy had spent the night, the twins started up the snowmobile and made a circle around the field next to the house. We went out to try it in the yard. We didn't think about the fact that Uncle was plowing the driveways with the tractor, and we scared him—he started yelling over the roar of the tractor. Kathy and I went in the house, but Bruce and Blaine hopped right back on the snowmobile. They zoomed all over the snowy fields and in and around the buildings in the yard, up and down the snowbanks Uncle had created. Uncle kept on plowing and yelling, plowing furiously, chains clanking, brakes squealing in the cold, sun glinting off the dazzling snow.

"We want the wedding pictures," we said as soon as we'd seen all the new slides.

Whenever a box of Daddy's slides came back in the mail, Daddy and Mama and the four of us kids sat down at night to look at them. In the darkness, images flashed on the huge screen set up across the room, projected through fine particles of dust and the whir of the projector fan. We analyzed every one.

Then Mama opened a drawer in the slide case, dipped out a stack, and firmly slipped a little square into the projector—upside down and backwards—rotated the plate, pulled out the last one, and inserted the next. She loved our baby pictures. Black-haired Gayla Sue—*no clue then that you'd be so blonde;* blue-lidded Bruce and Blaine—*a miracle you survived;* fuzz-headed Steven—*you were so good-natured.*

"Wedding pictures," we begged. I wanted to stare at eighteen-year-old Mama's big white dress with the Peter Pan collar, pearly tiara in her tightly curled hair, sparkly cat-eye glasses, pink lipstick on her perfect smiling mouth. The twins and Steven wanted to admire twenty-year-old Daddy, handsome in his dark suit and silk striped tie, rose boutonniere, horn-rimmed glasses, and happy smile.

The twins and I still remembered the pink and green walls of the country church. The wedding was a candlelight service, at eight-thirty on a Friday night, after milking. On May 17, 1957, the sky was pouring rain on blooming trees, and the pastor carried Mama from the parsonage to keep her dress from getting muddy. Five, ten, fifteen years later, we still became quiet when looking at our parents before they were parents in the world before we existed, together in front of the candelabra, pink roses, pink stucco wall.

On the next slide, we saw them flanked by the wedding party— tiny, lovely Auntie Lou; grinning Uncle Gaylon, just home from the army and tan from planting corn; Mama's friend Barbara; Mama and Auntie's brother, Uncle Duane.

Next, Mama and Daddy flanked by their parents. The mothers wore hats with feathers and the farmer fathers wore suits. Fat, laughing Gramma Anderson stood next to handsome Grampa Anderson in his white-blond crew cut. Gramma Marty, moon-faced from a cortisone arthritis treatment, tilted her head up bravely, glasses glinting. Beside her, dark-skinned Grampa Marty stood in a shadow, forcing a smile beneath sad eyes, haunted by illness his whole life. We stared longest at this Grampa we never knew, the one I couldn't remember even though he knew me.

Before we were ready, Mama flipped to the next slide—everyone eating in the church basement, Mama cutting the cake, Mama and Daddy greeting relatives, Mama throwing her roses, Auntie catching them. Three Mays later, Auntie would marry Uncle Gaylon. We looked at those slides too, noticing the changes and variations.

I craved wedding pictures, scanning for clues of the future. I examined the Marty album with the gold-painted cover every time I visited Uncle and Auntie in the big house, where it had been returned after Gramma Marty died. I searched the faces of the brides, framed in white voile or beige lace next to grooms in black suits—Sam Marty and Mamie Hansen, Lizzie Marty and Ed Hagen, Anna Marty and Paul Lofgren— posing solemnly before fringed drapes and wrought-iron furniture in the Rush City photographer's studio.

I wondered what my wedding would be like. Since kindergarten, I'd had crushes on boys, and the twins had crushes on girls. My favorite boy came from a pretty farm south of town—we'd passed it once on the Government Road. Mama pointed it out and Daddy commented that they favored Republicans, as the Martys did. But I knew they were Lutheran, not Baptist.

Bruce had brought Jeri West's fourth-grade school picture home and said, "This is the girl I want to marry." He thought she was as beautiful and shy as a deer, and he loved the sound of her name. Her father was a high school teacher who lived in town, and they were Lutheran too, but that didn't matter to Bruce because he figured girls had to take boys' churches the way they took their names, except if they were Catholic — then they weren't allowed to. Blaine adored a Catholic girl, which seemed hopeless, although we noticed it was considered to be less of a problem by Mama and Auntie than by Daddy or Uncle Gaylon.

Whatever happened, the twins were so popular and cute, I was sure they'd have no problem finding wives. Mama wasn't so sure. She worried that girls wouldn't want to live on a farm and endure the mud and manure coming into their houses on clothes and boots.

Mama, who had always been beautiful, was more beautiful than ever. She was only thirty-four, the youngest mother of anyone my age, her eyes green, her lips full under a shade of lipstick that matched or contrasted perfectly with her clothing. She had narrow feet and slightly bowed legs and was thin, but she wasn't thin enough, so she lost weight. She bought new clothes and matching shoes and purses for work. People said to me in passing, "Your mother is so beautiful!" as if they couldn't help it — not just the men in church but the women also, my friends, people in school. I knew it was true. I was proud of her, but embarrassed to be hers — I didn't want her to have to claim me.

My eyebrows had turned dark, my glasses didn't fit my face, and my skin broke out. Mama and Daddy felt sorry and said it was their fault — I got her fine pores and his oily skin. Every fall I lost my tan and, as winter came, my skin bloomed with blemishes no amount of washing would cure. Like Job broken out in terrible sores, crying to God, I imagined covering myself with ashes, sitting down beside the trash burner out by the orchard, pouring the ashes over my head, and feeling relief. But I wasn't Job — that was being melodramatic and heretical. Mama took me to a dermatologist in the Cities, a privilege so extravagant it, too, was embarrassing.

What counted was inside my heart, and my heart was beautiful, Mama said. I knew she thought I was good. I had learned to work hard, I was responsible, generous, patient, a good student, and I played the piano beautifully now. She praised me for these things, but I felt she was saying them because she wanted to say *something* to console me. When I looked into her face, all I saw was her flawless skin, and I coveted it.

Auntie Lou had never had bad skin but she knew how I felt, I could tell. She had always been Mama's willful little sister with the limp and the gap between her front teeth.

"Last night I dreamed about Rodney, can you believe it?" Auntie said to Mama one Saturday while having coffee at our house.

"Rodney!" Mama exclaimed. "You've got to be kidding!"

"Who's Rodney?" I asked.

"He was this guy I had a crush on," Auntie said to me, "before Uncle came along."

"Rodney was trouble," Mama said. "And he wasn't even that good looking."

"He was all right," Auntie said defensively, grinning. "Not as good looking as Gordon, of course, but who was?" She glanced at me. "Rodney had a fast car."

"You're lucky you didn't get killed," Mama said.

"Yeah, I s'pose, but it was fun at the time," said Auntie. She giggled and then wrinkled up her nose toward Mama. "*You* were so well behaved. At least it *looked* that way."

"Oh shut up!" Mama retorted. "Just because I didn't go *dancing* like you and Rodney and Doris and Bob and Duane and Judy down at the river, you got this chip on your shoulder. . . ."

Dancing was something Baptists didn't do, but saying *shut up* was not allowed in our house either.

"Who had the chip?" Auntie said to Mama, and then to me: "You should've seen your mother when I came over and told her I got engaged to Uncle Gaylon."

Mama said she was hanging laundry on the line when Auntie told her. Auntie, the little rebel, and Uncle, Mr. Straight-and-Narrow, married to each other? Mama collapsed laughing and rolled on the grass under the clothesline. But Auntie didn't care. She got her own wedding picture, just as pretty as Mama's, with Mama and Daddy standing on the outside next to her and Uncle in the middle. And she was now not only fun but beautiful, with a handsome husband who loved her, a boy and a girl, and a pretty collie besides.

Auntie's love of fast cars had been transferred to tractors. As Carolyn got older and Auntie didn't go back to work in town, Auntie became Uncle's regular baling partner. She lobbied for tractors with bigger engines and cabs with comfy seats.

"Must be a wedding dance at the Eagles tonight," Mama would say sometimes when we drove through town on a Friday or Saturday night. Her feelings were mixed—she hated alcohol, but I knew she longed to dance. She got Daddy and another couple from church to go on a trip to Nashville to see the Grand Ole Opry, and she danced alone to records in the living room. King David danced, she said—Psalm 150: *Praise him with trumpet sound, praise him with lute and harp! Praise him with tambourine and dance, praise him with strings and pipe! Let everything that breathes praise the Lord!*

But, Daddy says, he danced to praise God.

"Well, that's how I feel," Mama said.

Grampa and Gramma Anderson had met on a dance floor and become the best dancers anywhere around. When Mama was little, her parents sometimes took the kids along when they went dancing, and Mama and Auntie fell asleep to the music in a back room full of coats.

Pastor McElheran had to leave town because his daughter was a cheerleader, which some church members considered dancing in the streets.

In sixth grade, a classmate taunted me, *Can't dance, can't drink, can't smoke, can't play cards—what can you do? Are you better than everybody else?* I said nothing but I knew the answer was Romans 12:2: *Be not conformed to this world, but be ye transformed by the renewing of your mind, that ye may prove what is that good, and acceptable, and perfect will of God.*

In ninth grade, our class held a dance in the auditorium. Kathy was going, Heidi was going, Valerie was going. *All the girls are going,* I told Mama, and to my amazement, she argued with Daddy to allow me to go.

"They're too young to be dancing," Daddy said flatly.

"It's just a sock hop," Mama argued, quoting me. She made *sock hop* sound like grade school, like Pippi Longstocking.

The auditorium wasn't very full. Our class was spread out all over the gym floor, most of the boys against the wall beneath the stage by the record player, most of the girls on the other side by the seats. I stood with Kathy, realizing I had never really danced in my life. I hadn't the faintest idea what to do and the music was awful. The lights went down for a slow song and a boy with green eyes walked across the floor, straight to a girl next to me, asked her to dance, and she didn't even nod, they just danced. They were perfect together, as if they had done this for years, because they probably had.

I was anxious about boys calling me. Anybody looking me up in the phone book would guess because of my name that my father was Gaylon, not Gordon, and would call the wrong house.

Fall, winter, spring, summer. Fall was football in town and motorbikes in the country; winter was basketball in town and snowmobiles in the country; spring was baseball and more motorbikes; summer was waiting for phone calls, distracting myself with work, and listening to the sounds of the world—crickets and frogs, birds and cows, tractors and cars, motorbikes, trains. From early spring until late fall, Kathy and I rode our bicycles everywhere we could, mostly to get away from our housework for awhile, but also as distraction from the phone not ringing, to console ourselves about the boys we loved, boys who loved us in some way we couldn't understand. It was good to feel cold wind in our faces in the grayness of those March or November days, under the clarity of intermittent blue sky, and among birds departing and arriving.

Kathy and I shopped for fabric and patterns and sewed dresses and tops that fit us. We learned to use makeup and curling irons. After a long campaign against our old-fashioned parents, we got our ears pierced at the doctor's office and started to buy earrings.

We volunteered as candy-stripers at the hospital. Then I got a paying job, washing dishes at the Grant House hotel and café with kids in my class who knew everybody in town well enough to wait tables and make tips.

The housework was increasingly mine. Mama told me what to do and I did it. The twins went through more food and clean clothes than we could imagine, and Steven was right behind them. I also sat with Gramma Anderson, who was recovering from a stroke, and played the piano—*Play that one I like so much,* she would say, watching Carolyn. Alone, I listened to the radio, to stations Mama and Daddy didn't allow, stations playing George Harrison, Taj Mahal, and the Rolling Stones. I'd seen the Beatles on the Ed Sullivan show when I was five, just for a few seconds before Gramma Marty turned off the TV. Now I listened for hours to records I bought with my own money—Carole King, Cat Stevens, Elton John—keyboard artists whose value I could defend.

I had learned to type, so I typed the manuscripts of my stories on Mama's typewriter. Sometimes I stayed up at night writing until one or two in the morning, hours after everyone else had gone to bed.

If Mama and Uncle agreed on one thing, it was that my future lay in college—Bible college, if we could afford it.

When I was little, looking through the mission literature that Daddy got in the mail because he was a deacon, the single women I saw were mostly nurses, along with a few teachers. I was so distressed by the need for medicine that I announced I would be a missionary nurse.

Uncle Gaylon had wanted to help my dream come true, to make travel exciting instead of frightening. He and Auntie Lou took me along to the international airport in the Cities to see the planes take off and land. They loved the thunder of the engines, and Uncle loved to keep up on Northwest's fleet, which he'd come to know during his years in the army. He held me up to get a better view above the railing.

"Riding inside the jet, you'll see mountaintops covered with snow," he said, "and the ocean. You'll ride right through the clouds." His voice was filled with wonder, his face beaming.

After that, when I saw the tailing cloud of a jet in the sky, I thought about the airport and Uncle's excitement.

But candy-striping changed my plans. Day after day, I came home feeling despondent and tearful for no apparent reason, and I told Mama that I would never be a nurse. She was disappointed—she had dreamed of me all in white with a folded cap since I was three and dressed in a nursing smock and hat sewed by Gramma Anderson. But she was relieved I might not have to fly away.

When Uncle Gaylon found out I had a boyfriend and he was Lutheran, he erupted. Were Daddy and Mama crazy or what? How could they allow me to see him? Didn't they have any control over their children?

He said nothing directly to me, but Daddy delivered the message.

"Do you know whether he's a Christian?" Daddy asked. "Has he accepted Jesus as his personal savior? You *know* it says in II Corinthians, 'Be ye not unequally yoked together with unbelievers.'"

"He's a Lutheran!" I said. "He's confirmed! Your own dad was a Lutheran!"

"That was a mess," Daddy replied. I knew he meant it was hard for one family to go to two churches, every other Sunday.

"Why did the Hendricksons let Gramma marry Grampa Marty, anyway?" I demanded.

He hesitated and then avoided the question.

"I know that by the end of his life, Mom believed Dad was saved," he said.

"But he never stopped being a *Lutheran,* did he?"

"He was *German* Lutheran," Dad said, "which is a lot closer to Baptist belief."

I was exasperated. Even though I was already baptized, I was expected to attend pastor's instruction class on Saturday mornings in the office of our new, modern church by the freeway, with small groups of mostly girls. Our class worked through *Why I Am a Baptist.* I believed I was a Baptist—I didn't want to be any other religion—but I refused to believe that God would choose between sects at the judgment. That made him sound ridiculous, like a Pharisee. And I resisted the idea of a Bible without error.

We believe that the Bible is the Word of God, fully inspired and without error in the original manuscripts, written under the inspiration of the Holy Spirit, and that it has supreme authority in all matters of life and conduct.

Without error? What was an error anyway? How could we know that? Why did my dad have a Bible in four translations? And why did the Bible have to be inerrant or worthless?—that was a false dilemma.

"Isn't it idolatry?" I pressed.

The pastor took off his glasses and squeezed the bridge of his nose.

"This is a matter of faith," he said.

I wasn't going to Bethel now, I knew that. Nobody that mattered would recommend me.

�֍

In History 10, the standard assignment for the year was a research paper on our family history, and it took months.

Mine was the only Swiss name in a class full of mostly German and Scandinavian immigrants' descendents. Switzerland sounded exotic— Swiss chocolate, clocks, banks, Alps, brown Swiss cows, dotted Swiss fabric—all deliciousness and precision and beauty. Why would any-body want to leave Switzerland to come to America?

Kathy got her driver's license, so she drove us to cemeteries all over the countryside and we chipped ice from granite grave markers to find our ancestors, copying down names and dates. Daddy found the Marty family copy of a book of early settlers in Minnesota that included a biography of Jacob. He was the son of a miner, it said; he worked in a factory as a young boy, and he trained to be a tailor before he came to America. In Minnesota, he learned dairy.

I wanted to know about Susanna—Suzannah Trümpler before she came to America, before she married Jacob. I interviewed Uncle Gaylon and Daddy, but their grandparents had died before they were born. Everything they knew about Switzerland came from Sam, their story-telling uncle, who'd never been there himself. They'd grown up with-out sisters and barely knew their aunts because they'd left the farm so long ago. I grilled them about photos in the old Marty album, looking for dates.

"We have to go visit Aunt Anna," Daddy said.

Aunt Anna was the youngest daughter of Jacob and Susanna, now seventy-five years old, their only child still living, the little sister of Sam and Grampa. On a Sunday afternoon, Daddy drove me to the Lofgren farm southwest of town and we sat around the big kitchen table with tiny Anna, her enormous husband Paul, and their son and daughter-in-law.

Anna had the trademark dark Marty skin and hair, brown eyes that sparkled, and a perpetual smile. Her voice was soft and she laughed shyly.

"Please tell me about Susanna," I said. "How did she meet Jacob?"

"They knew each other from the time they were children," Anna said, then hesitated. "I think they were cousins."

She told me her mother's stories about working for a rich mistress in Zürich, learning to sew and write, waiting for Jacob's letter, sailing to New York, mistaking tomatoes for apples at a street grocer's, evad-ing an interested policeman, taking the train to Minnesota, finding Jacob, raising children in the cold cabin, going to work at a store in Rock Creek and learning English. As the afternoon light shifted across the room, Anna showed me letters and keepsakes inscribed with Susanna's ornate handwriting, all in German, unreadable to any of us. When Anna became a teacher, sometimes Susanna visited her classroom, and her very presence made the children sit up straight and speak out clearly.

Anna brought to the table a gold-painted album of photos, identical to the one at our farm.

"My mother made one of these for each of us as a wedding gift," she explained. "The only one not married when she died was your grampa."

"What about you and your sisters?" I asked, opening the fat covers to the familiar photos inside. "How did Lizzie and Minnie end up in Cannon Falls?"

"Ha!" Paul laughed suddenly and shifted in his seat. "We used to joke that they *simply didn't* want to marry any of the Hansen boys!"

This made Daddy and his cousin Arvid laugh and Anna chuckle and nod.

"Sam Marty was in *love* with the whole Hansen family—one farm over, you know," Paul went on. "Who ever knew *why*. Five sons and five daughters, with old C. N. for a father. . . . Well, Sam had this plan of who was going to marry whom, Hansens and Martys. His big sisters, Lizzie and Minnie, wouldn't have any of it! When the crew came to build the Marty barn—what year was that, I wonder?"

"1902," I replied.

"That sounds right," Paul nodded. "Ed Hagen on the crew caught Lizzie's eye, and vice versa. The next year she was gone—*escaped* the Hansens!—down to Ed Hagen's farm in Cannon Falls! Not long after that, Minnie followed, and she married Jim Magee."

"What about you?" I asked Anna. "When did you leave the farm?"

She appraised me with a smile of recognition.

"I must've been about your age," Anna said. "I was fifteen when Sam got married to Mamie, in 1912. Mama and Papa and I moved to town."

"How did *you* two meet?" I gestured toward Paul.

"Oh, at church, I s'pose." Anna laughed with a flirty glance. "He liked my pie."

I couldn't stop looking at Sam and Mamie's wedding picture. He was dark like Daddy, and dashing, sitting jauntily on the arm of her chair, and she was fair like Mama, but wistful, roses tossed across her lap.

In the back of a scrapbook, I found another portrait from their wedding. This one included Grampa and someone who had to be a sister of Mamie's. Sam and Mamie were both seated, and their siblings stood behind them, a perfect couple, a perfect quartet — two brothers and two sisters.

Sam Marty was in love with the whole Hansen family . . . who ever knew why . . . Sam had this plan of who was going to marry whom, Hansens and Martys. . . .

Was this the sister Sam wanted his brother to marry? What was her name? Why didn't Grampa do it?

In the archives of *The Rush City Post,* May 3, 1912, a week after the sinking Titanic appeared on the front page, came twelve inches of good news: "Married at Bride's Home."

C. N. Hansen's beautiful farm residence Rte 2 was the scene of a very pretty ceremony on Wednesday afternoon, Apr 24, when his daughter, Miss Mamie Hansen was united in marriage with Mr. Samuel Marty, Rev. Luebtker of Pine City officiating. At the appointed hour, 1 p.m., the bridal party approached an evergreen arch which had been erected in the parlor with a white wedding bell suspended in the center, under which the vows were spoken. Pink roses were used in the decorations. The bridal pair were supported by Miss Tillie Hansen as bridesmaid and John Marty as groomsman. The bride was attired in a dainty robe of white voile over an embroidery slip, she carried bride's roses. . . . The groom and groomsman wore conventional black. Following the ceremony which was witnessed by the immediate families and friends of the bridal pair, a sumptuous wedding dinner was served to the guests . . . The tables were decorated in red and white carnations with streamers of white ribbon brought to the center of the ceiling from which hung a wedding bell. The bridal party took an auto trip to Rush City during the afternoon to visit the photographer. An informal reception was followed by dancing in the evening in which a large company of guests participated. The usual wedding gifts were both elaborate and practical.

The young couple start to housekeeping at once, on a farm the groom being skilled in agricultural lines for which he has had excellent training under his father, Mr. J. Marty. The bride is a young lady of excellent qualifications and amiable disposition, their journey through life together, will surely be as happy and prosperous as their numerous friends earnestly hope. . . .

But we all knew, now, that Sam and Mamie's journey through life together had been marked by misery, not happiness.

Next to the wedding picture, I lined up other pictures I found of Sam and Mamie and their only child, Harold, born the next year. I studied the stunning alteration of Mamie's face, from exquisite bride to limp new mother to pained, bespectacled crone, barely recognizable in a span of eighteen years. Beside her, Sam's face aged gently, handsomely.

Next to the wedding story, I placed another *Post* article, a clipping.

Funeral services, in charge of Director F. W. Hanson were conducted on Saturday, April 26, 1930 for the late Mrs. Samuel Marty, who passed away at the Swedish Hospital in Minneapolis on April 24. A short service was conducted at the farm house at one p.m., followed by services at the First Lutheran church in Rush City at two o'clock. The church was packed to capacity by sorrowing relatives and friends who had gathered to pay their last sad respects to the loved one who had been called to her eternal rest. Rev. Moebius of the German Lutheran Church, of which deceased was a member, officiated and paid a glowing tribute to the departed one. . . .

Mamie Marty (nee Hansen) was born April 25, 1887, at Bloomington on the Minnesota, the daughter of Mr. C. N. Hansen and his deceased wife. In the year 1887, she came with her parents to Rush City, where she lived on the farm, three miles north of Rush City, with her parents, until her marriage to Mr. Samuel Marty, on April 24, 1912. She joined the St. John's Lutheran congregation at Rush City, by confirmation on December 16, 1915, and was a loyal worker in the church activities. Deceased had been a patient sufferer for several years, which made at last imperative an operation, which was performed at the Swedish Hospital in Minneapolis on April 19, and she was wedded to her heavenly bride-groom, with the dawn of her earthly eighteenth wedding anniversary, April 24, at the age of 42 years, 11 months and 29 days. Remains were brought to her home at Rush City by Director F. W. Hanson, where funeral services were held . . .

Deceased was a loving wife and mother and her memory will be blessed by her sorrowing husband, Mr. Samuel Marty and her only son, Harold S., her father, Charles N. Hansen, and his wife, of Rock Creek; five brothers and four sisters, Louise Pepin of Pine City, William and Henry of

Rock Creek, Charles of Kansas City, Mrs. Tillie Carlos, Fred and Rudolph of Duluth; Emma Brodt, of Henderson and Margaret at home; also other relatives and hosts of friends.

The clipping came from Gramma Marty's scrapbook, near the beginning, because it was Mamie's illness that brought Gramma to work at the farm, to become the mother of sons who would stay long after Sam and Mamie's son had gone away.

I lined up the clippings of obituaries: Jacob, 1918; Susanna, 1929; Mamie, 1930; Sam, 1951; John, 1959. The three before Sam's were long, detailed, descriptive, romantic, like his wedding story. *Sam must have been the writer.* I could see him sitting at the desk where I now sat, tabulating the years and months and days of their lives, writing with a full heart the biographies of his farm for the public record. Next to them, his own unexpected obituary was short, not even the pallbearers named — no one left to give the storyteller a worthy tribute.

I stared again into the four faces of the 1912 bridal party — Sam and John, Mamie and Tillie.

Sam and Mamie had made our farm what it is. But Grampa — the one who twice escaped deathly illness — the quiet one who refused to marry the match his older brother picked out, the only unmarried one when Susanna died — he and the wife God brought him had preserved and passed on the farm.

❧

It's hard to know whether the idea to go to Switzerland started forming during the history project or French class. Researching Switzerland, I'd learned it had four official languages — not only the German my great-grandparents had spoken, but also French, Italian, and Romansch. And I longed for some justification for learning French — who would ever use French? — the only foreign language offered in Rush City.

But the one I had to thank for making it so easy was Sam Marty, my great-uncle, dead twenty-two years but, in Uncle and Daddy's minds, still very much alive. After Mamie died, Sam's dream of visiting Switzerland, reconnecting with cousins, seeing with his own eyes the valley of his parents Jacob and Susanna, had so impressed Uncle and Daddy during their childhood that, when I explained my idea to go on a student exchange, the greatest challenge was keeping their expectations low. I would have to go to the *French-speaking* part of Switzerland. And who knew whether there would be any way to get to Engi, the village where Jacob lived when his last name was still spelled Marti.

The school counselor was stumped by my inquiry, doubtful I could get help from any organization like the American Field Service. But with the French teacher's help, I wrote letters addressed to directors of schools in Swiss towns she helped me pick off a map. I specified my goal of learning French, my preference for three months, and my desire to visit Engi.

Miraculously, replies began to arrive: one *no,* one request for an *au pair* that I declined, and a *yes* from a farm family whose eighteen-year-old son, Claude, wanted to visit the United States before starting university. Photos were exchanged and details worked out: Claude would come to us first, and after a week I would leave for three months in his village near Lake Geneva. Mama contacted a travel agent who found the lowest-fare flight — through Winnipeg and London — and took out a loan to pay for it.

"If she's going through Winnipeg, Auntie Lou and I will drive her that far instead," Uncle Gaylon said. "It would not be right for a Minnesota girl to leave America without seeing the headwaters of the Mississippi!"

I felt the relief of something important to do. Claude and I exchanged letters, and so did our mothers. I worked on French with the suddenly clear realization that I knew practically nothing. In speech competition, I went to regionals in the spring. And I made arrangements with next year's teachers to be gone for the first six weeks of classes, working on chemistry exercises all during the month of June to make up for it.

From Great-aunt Anna, I got a photocopy of Jacob's record of citizenship to carry along.

Uncle Gaylon came to me with a book and a map of Switzerland. He wanted me to know about a place called L'Abri, north of Lake Geneva, in case I had a chance to visit. The theologian Francis Schaeffer had created a Christian refuge there, where people could freely come to talk and work through questions of purpose and faith in modern life.

Claude Etierre arrived in the middle of July and couldn't believe how hot Minnesota was or how beautiful and big our farm was.

"It's a park!" he exclaimed, snapping pictures of our yard. He took a picture of me on our new tractor, the 766, because he said his mother would never believe it otherwise. We showed him the new pipeline milking system and automatic silage unloader, and I drove him around Rush City and Pine City to drive-in restaurants and movie theaters.

He rode along when Uncle and Auntie drove me to Winnipeg. There was nothing that didn't interest him—he was an observer of land-scapes, a conversationalist, learning English names for familiar things I had never called by name. He kept a notebook and wanted to know what all the Indian words meant, most of which Uncle Gaylon could tell him. He shot a whole roll of film as we walked on the stones across the little Mississippi as it flowed out of Lake Itasca.

On my transatlantic flight, I sat next to a boy from New York City who was a year older than me and couldn't believe he was sitting next to someone who came from a farm.

"You mean, your father is a *farmer*?" he asked.

I heard Mama's emphatic voice, *Your father is a dairy farm owner and operator.*

"Yes," I said. "He's a farmer."

He shook his head.

"Does he—does your father wear jeans to work?"

"What else would he wear?"

Monsieur Etierre, Claude's father, also wore denim—because it was *practical though expensive,* said his wife in French words I could understand perfectly. Madame could wash jeans in boiling water and they still seemed to last forever.

I arrived the day before the wheat harvest began and learned the family also had cherry and apple trees, hay, and grapes—a little bit of many things, meaning that a bad year couldn't wipe them out. One of Monsieur's five brothers produced wine, and the rest of them con-tributed grapes to the family press.

It was a thoroughly modern farm from what I could see, despite the age of the house and the barn, which were attached. It was smaller than our farm, but more organized and at least as prosperous. The stone house with real shutters stood on the edge of a village, the back terrace facing their fields, which rolled toward Lake Geneva two miles away and the French Alps beyond.

While Mama and Daddy took Claude, Steven, and Kathy on a trip to the Rocky Mountains, and dropped off Claude for a West Coast tour by bus, the Etierres took me along on their camping vacation in a circular route around Switzerland. Monsieur loved to scare Madame — he was an expert from years of army driving — so I laughed with Claude's brother and sister in the back seat as we wound up and down cold mountain passes, around hairpin turns, to sunny southern valleys near Italy with palm trees on blue lakes, to the green valleys where German is spoken. We stopped to visit castles and glaciers.

In the canton Glarus, we drove into Engi. We parked the car and walked among brown wooden houses clinging to the side of the mountain, just up from the base of the valley and surrounded by steep, emerald fields.

Monsieur got directions with difficulty. He spoke French with a rural accent and the locals spoke Switzer-Deutsch, a kind of German that made Pascal and Nicole laugh — it wasn't what they learned in school and it sounded to them like German baby talk. But we made it to the courthouse, a square, yellow stucco building three stories high, with one clerk on duty.

The Etierres pointed to me, showed the clerk the paper I'd prepared with Jacob and Susanna's names and the dates we knew. He thoughtfully led us upstairs, pulled forward books several feet long and inches thick, and turned pages that made dust rise in the sunlight falling through the window. The books were full of Martis — Martis and Blumers and Knobals — with a limited number of first names. It was hard to keep them straight, but after some time we found Jacob by the date of his birth: he was the seventh child and third son of Samuel and Elisabeth, who married at twenty, five months before the birth of their first child, and who lived to be eighty. We found no Trümplers, no Suzannah.

The clerk carried the book down the steps, photocopied the pages we wanted, and then beckoned us to follow.

"I think he takes us to a lady who knows the stories, the *histoires*, of the town," Pascal translated as we walked across the street and down a path through a hayfield, where women were cutting hay by hand, tying it in bundles, and stacking the bundles to dry as we used to shock oats.

At the door of a brown house with red geraniums in a window box, we stopped. The clerk knocked, and a tiny but stout black-eyed woman came to the door.

He spoke to her quickly and pointed to me. She nodded, went back inside for a few minutes, returned with her glasses, and peered at the photocopies he showed her. She glanced up at me, then down at the papers, asked some questions, pointed. The clerk spoke to Pascal, and Pascal followed his finger on the paper.

"He says—*she* says—that Ursula Marti is her grandmother," Pascal said.

"Who is Ursula Marti?" I asked.

Madame Etierre nudged me forward. The tiny woman placed her fingers on the column of names containing Jacob's. Ursula was third, and Jacob was seventh of eleven children.

The woman pointed at me and then at herself.

"You are cousins," Pascal said. The woman covered her mouth and started to shake with laughter. Madame grinned in disbelief, examined the paper and nodded, then explained to Monsieur, whose chin dropped.

"*Non!*" he exclaimed. "*Quel jour!*" and we all laughed. What a day! The tiny woman seized me as I hadn't been seized since Mama hugged me good-bye—she wouldn't let go, and tears squeezed from her eyes. The clerk smiled and formally introduced us—her name was Vreni Gerschwiler-Blumer, and when she finally let me go, she invited us in— grabbed us by the arms and pulled us into her house. The ceilings were so low that the Etierres had to be careful of door jambs and ceiling lights, but I thought my family would fit here perfectly. Pascal and Nicole kept breaking into laughter over the Switzer-Deutsch. Vreni had to call her daughter.

The clerk returned to his office, and the rest of us drank Citro as we waited for Vreni's husband, daughter, and granddaughter to arrive. They took us to supper at a public house in the next town up the valley, where the wooden chairs were so heavy we needed both hands to move them. The sun dipped behind the mountain long before the sky darkened, and I began to understand why immigrants could love the flatness of Minnesota. In the shade of the mountain, we talked in a con-fused mix of French, German, and English—Vreni's granddaughter Ruth spoke fluent French, and Ruth's fiancé spoke fair English—while we ate three kinds of bread and five kinds of cheese, drank beer, and toasted our families in every language. On the way back to Engi, we stopped at a linen mill by the stream and they weighed us down with beautiful towels and washcloths as a gift from the valley.

I wrote about all of it in long letters to home. I had accomplished what Sam Marty never had in his too-short life, what Daddy and Uncle dreamed of only remotely. I couldn't believe it myself—it seemed ludicrous in its simplicity.

When school started, I attended classes in an old village castle. After six weeks, the grape harvest began and Claude returned to join us. Alongside Spanish migrant workers, we clipped clusters of green grapes from the vineyard rows wearing yellow rain slickers. I departed weighed down not only with linens from Engi but bottles of Etierre wine and kirsch. In the airport in Minneapolis, the bottles clinked as everyone hugged me. Daddy thought they would last forever, but they were gone in a month.

As little as I knew about L'Abri, there had been no opportunity to inquire about it. The closest I got to theology in Switzerland was reading the Bible in French in the village church, arguing with Pascal, who claimed to be an atheist, and visiting Geneva's Reformation Wall, where Calvin was flanked by Farel, Beza, and Knox.

꙳♣

Everybody in our class was driving. We drove around the streets of Rush City, north to Pine City, west to Rush Lake, south to the Cities, east to the river, and across it to Wisconsin. We were juniors, and we learned the night geography of the ten miles between Rush Lake and the St. Croix River. Whatever road we took heading east, we crossed the Government Road and came to a hill that dropped sixty feet to the flats and then sloped through wetlands and woods to the St. Croix, remnant of an ancient torrent that once ran like a sea out of melting glaciers. Ten thousand years ago, the hill was the river's edge.

I fought with my boyfriend. We had been a match, hard-working oldest children, readers, planners, college-bound. He was a new boy, his presence in class had filled me with relief, and since I'd rested my head against his beating heart at a dance, we'd been flames, brushing against each other at our side-by-side lockers, competing in math. He had taken me by motorbike and snowmobile to his favorite places at the lake, and I'd taken him walking through our woods on the old paths. While I was abroad, we'd written letters to each other that I read and reread. Now he had a car and new friends and worked an after-school shift at Plastech. He didn't have time for me, and I was too confident in our future together to believe we would separate, but not confident enough to imagine myself alone.

I took as many shifts as I could at the Grant House, where Kathy cooked and her comedian boyfriend waited tables. After we closed at eight, all four or five of us on duty washed the sweat off our faces and necks and drove around the gravel roads listening to Grand Funk Railroad, Foghat, Led Zeppelin, and Deep Purple as the sky darkened and stars came out.

The truth was, whether Switzerland was an idea I got in history or in French, it had been an attempt to inoculate myself against the disease of unhappiness that had seized my mother. "I've never been anywhere," she'd say. "I've never lived *anywhere* but Route 2, Rush City, Minnesota, 55069. When I got married, I moved *one mile.*"

I knew her story like a familiar hymn: She'd moved from the rundown house of her alcoholic father to the established house of a faithful and religious husband, who gave up his Heavenly Father's calling to seminary for his earthly father's calling to farm. But it had always been clear that the ending was happy—until I fell in love. *You're too young.* My simple assumption that I would go to college and marry and make a family ran into the river of Mama's sorrow about her own life, punctuated by the gunshot suicide of a boy in our sophomore class after his girlfriend got pregnant. Study abroad had been a way to put off danger a little longer because it was less complicated than getting birth control or even discussing it.

Now unhappiness descended anyway, deeper than I had ever felt, sharper and more painful, like stones tied to arms, legs, and neck. Depression gripped me in its gray hand like it gripped Uncle and Mama, maybe Daddy and Auntie too, all of us, together, alone.

The legal drinking age had dropped to eighteen in Minnesota, and somebody always managed to get a keg for a party out by the ghostly posts of the railroad bridge sticking out of the river east of town. It wasn't that hard to get served in a bar either, and after closing time in Minnesota, we took Highway 70 seventeen miles east—past the empty spot where Auntie Lou and Rodney went dancing twenty years ago—to Grantsburg, Wisconsin, where the bars stayed open until two o'clock and it was always easy to get served.

It was one night in the wee lost hours after bar closing, long before sunrise, when I stood in the Hansen house on Highway 61 for the first time. Standing in the living room where Sam Marty and Mamie Hansen said their vows — *At the appointed hour... the bridal party approached an evergreen arch erected in the parlor with a white wedding bell suspended in the center* — I saw our farm west across the highway, across the railroad and snowy fields.

The Hansens were almost thirty years gone from that house, the family after them was gone, and the house had passed to bachelor grandsons who didn't keep up the yard or the house. On that night, the living room was a mess of bodies, glasses full of every kind of alcohol, ashtrays full of cigarettes. I stood in the half-lit living room full of outlines of people and looked out the window.

Our farm, three-quarters of a mile away, made a dark silhouette with three dots of light — the yard light and two windows of our house — the house built by Sam for his second wife, another Hansen daughter. In the twilight, the fields lay like a piece-quilt draped over the earth's frame, from the head at the woods down to the foot at the county line.

Mamie, Tillie, Margaret, and their other Hansen sisters and brothers had stood where I stood. The Marty farm was what the Hansens saw. I tried to imagine it, erase our house and imagine the farm's lights coming instead from the big house beyond it, before electricity and yard light, just kerosene lamps from twilight glowing in the night. I imagined the fields covered with snow reflecting moonlight.

Sam was in love with the whole Hansen family. Who knew why!

It was obvious why. Sam had dreamed of the Marty and Hansen farms merged into one glorious farm, spanning east and west of Highway 61. Sam built the Marty farm *for* the Hansens — all the barns along the angle of the ridge at a pretty angle, perfectly viewed from this window. But his dream didn't come true, not until 1971, fifty years after his wedding to Mamie, twenty years after his death, more than ten years after weddings of the next generation of Marty brothers to the Anderson sisters . . . and the added farm was a mile farther east.

I was the displaced daughter of our farm, our farm that didn't know what to do with daughters except teach them to work hard and recognize beauty.

The sky tipped. The world was strange, and the light and color had changed. In the eighteen months after I returned from Switzerland, I felt as though I were still caught in a narrow mountain valley, talking or driving or writing late into the night although the sky above me indicated day—the sun was somewhere outside this crevice in the earth. The seasons were mixed up, out of order, and I was listening to the sounds of the world, vibrations of the earth and sky, crickets, bird calls, choruses of frogs, the lowing of cows, the twins' new low voices calling *C'm baaaaaaas!* and trucks rumbling on the freeway, tones of the tractors and jets passing overhead, thunder, electric guitars over the radio, motors, Mama's car coming home, Auntie and Uncle's car, Grampa Anderson's car, the twins' motorbikes, and then, near the end, their car too. Only the trains were constant—morning, afternoon, middle of the night.

Spring. The snow melted, ditches filled, the swamp flooded south of the road. At the end of March the redwings came and I walked and watched them. Males came first, entirely black except for a triangle on each wing that emerged when they sang, blood red with a yellow border. In the swollen ditches along our road, across the swamp on Kathy's place, they marked off their tiny territories, dividing the bog into patches ten or twelve feet square, betting on places the females would favor. Females came, the color of marsh water, brown with a blush on their wings that brightened as they grew older. They chose their homes for the season, mated, and constructed their nests, deep hanging hammocks anchored firmly to the marsh grass but able to move gently in the wind. Through the weeks of May, as Uncle and Blaine planted corn in the fields, the females built nests and laid eggs, and the bright-winged males sang warning songs to keep their feeding grounds secure. On a prom night, Uncle and Auntie took me along with them to Orchestra Hall in Minneapolis, where we drank in music like medicine of the universe—Van Cliburn playing Brahms, Schumann, Beethoven, Chopin, and Ravel.

Summer. I picked up a weekend night shift at Plastech running presses, pulling out rubbery snow flaps for snowmobiles and trimming the flash, dispensers sixteen at a crack, Tonka truck wheels, spindles for furniture in colonial and Mediterranean styles. Driving up to the white expanse of the plant at ten minutes to eleven, opening the door to the din and smell of hot plastic, monster machines dwarfing the crew, automatic doors, manual doors, flash bins, pellets, break room, the smell of heated lunches from cans and from home, the smell of cigarettes, the fizz of cola, clocks crawling, the night crawling, watching for light in the small window on the door, driving home just after dawn in deafening quietness. The sound of the gravel under the tires was precious. I came home to sleep in the humid, restless day while Mama worked at the Plastech office downtown in nice dresses and matching shoes, while the boys and men worked outside, while the boys played.

Fall. The twins were always stars. As sophomores they got a car, they dated girls, they got in trouble, but just enough to make people love them more. Bruce dated Jeri West, the girl he'd loved forever, and he learned to laugh at himself. Blaine held himself back with a harder edge, funny in a cutting way, but I admired him. My class shrunk from sixty-six to fifty-seven to fifty, and I walked through school like a shadow. I wished I were a shadow, never sure whether I was ostracized or paranoid, steadied by Kathy's friendship, by books, by competing in speech and taking parts in plays where I escaped myself. I was saved by theater, by the vision of Dionysus and a troupe of flute-playing creatures coming out of the cow paths, out of the woods at dusk, prancing across the fields and marshes toward town. We put on our masks and played on the stage to make the people laugh and cry. Standing backstage, waiting for cues, I looked up at the oldest canvas backdrop, high above the stage, painted with a scene of a sunny field viewed from the edge of a forest, as if by a faun.

Winter. Mama fought with Daddy, trying to make him take charge, but he wasn't made like that—she was. She wanted Daddy to strive and to be the head of the house the way Ephesians said he should be, the way it was in companies. I thought Daddy wanted to be the head of the house but believed too much in free will, *the priesthood of the believer.* "I can't make you do anything—I won't even try," he would say to her. "*You* choose." And he was right, but I think she wanted him to resist her, to give her a rest from thinking so much. She was moving, turbulent water, changing and grasping, always planning, worrying. I loved her but was afraid of her anger and disappointment. I deceived and defied her. Daddy said I treated God like a big friend and forgot he was a judge, but I just said, "How do you know God's a he?" Actually, I thought God was like Daddy—I always had—I thought God cried over us.

Once, the sight of the farm saved my life.

Driving home from a party, I dropped people off, then lost heart and stopped the car on the railroad tracks by the highway, on purpose.

I came conscious for some reason, maybe the distant sound of the train or the light of a half-moon falling on the fields of our farm. Across the fields I saw the familiar silhouette of the pines and spruce and bare oaks and elms and the old barn, set at that angle on the rise, two tall silos now and all the outbuildings, just a glint of the white eastern face of our house with its black, always-open shutters. I felt my heart break open. I loved our farm. The yard light was on, sending out the steady yellow glow of rural electrification my mother never had. Inside that house, above my mother, above the rooms of my mother, was my room under an old oak tree and a young basswood, my pale yellow room with the magenta floor, the desk of Sam Marty, and the mended brass bed of Daddy and Uncle, of Grampa and Sam before them, the place for my head.

I started the car, drove down the railroad grade past the field that would be hay next summer. Behind me, the train went past, and I followed the light from the tall pole in the yard home, entered the house quietly, before Daddy woke for chores, and slept as the moon set.

The future is veiled. Is it spring or fall? I am walking alone on the road in early morning fog. I can see only a few feet ahead of me — there a bird appears and then disappears — it calls — the yodel of the redwing. What is my gift, my calling?

I can hear birds, water trickling, a motor somewhere, the minor horn of the train, but a cloud has fallen to earth. This is like crossing a mountain pass, but we are less than a thousand feet above sea level.

In my room, I set the full-length wedding picture of Grampa and Gramma Marty — John and Viola — on the table beside my bed. It was not the formal portrait Gramma had chosen to stand in the heavy, antique frame, but a snapshot taken on the lawn of her family's rented farm. She wore a lacy Sunday dress, her wavy hair uncovered. She and Grampa were smiling, even though it was 1932.

I am looking back off the tractor at Uncle's forehead under the sun as we hay, as he waits for a bale to emerge from the baler, strikes out with the hook and

*hauls the sage-green bale onto the wagon, hoists it in the way he has learned
in order to protect his back, carries it by its two strands of twine to the back of
the swaying wagon, stacks it against the back of the rack, returns to retrieve the
next bale. He lifts a gloved hand and makes a circle with his forefinger, faster,
and I move the throttle three teeth to the right, look back to catch his nod and
his grin. We are haying on the field south of the woods and the sun is moving
across the afternoon sky, there is a slight breeze that turns the oak leaves over
to show their silver undersides as we approach the woods each round, and the
sound of the motor echoes off the surface of their trunks, off the leafy wall of
green. The sound of the motor of the tractor and the rhythmic ker-ker-ker-
chunk, ker-ker-ker-chunk of the baler. He has tucked his hat in his back
pocket, wipes the sweat off his forehead with the inside of his forearm, wipes his
forearm on the hip of his jeans.*

*Uncle and I can no longer speak to each other about anything that matters,
but we can work together. We can put up hay. Work is our refuge from thinking, from making meaning. This is our language.*

*The sky turns from blue to white in the heat, then the sun glares and
glances off the treetops as we finish the last tight turn of the windrow and head
the tractor home, two high heavy wagons hitched behind, their shadows like
swaying towers on the field, on the road.*

The day after graduation, Kathy and I moved to St. Paul to take jobs
we'd already found and live in an apartment we rented. We kept our
jobs at the Grant House, driving up every other weekend, visiting our
families, marking the progress of the corn. Steven moved into my room,
so I slept on the couch in the living room near the piano and my agate—
the same space that had been my bedroom as a child, windows facing
south and east to the sounds of the night swamp and the train across
the fields.

I wasn't home on the Saturday that Uncle threw Mama out of his
house. She was having coffee with Auntie Lou when he came into the
house distressed about a broken machine part—he needed Auntie to
drive somewhere *right now* and get a new one. She had been planning
to paint. He made a sarcastic remark about it and Mama said, "Oh shut
up, don't talk to her like that." It just slipped out. Uncle Gaylon told
her to get out of his house, but she said no, so he picked her up and she
yelled as he carried her out. Daddy heard the yelling from the machine
shed and ran up there so fast Uncle didn't know what hit him. Uncle

and Mama didn't stop yelling at each other even after Daddy got her inside our house.

In the heat, the corn grew. In late July, it tasseled, and the smell of it covered the fields, permeating the night. I drove on the road east of town, past the farm by Rush Creek where Jacob worked as an immigrant, turned my headlights into the driveway of the cemetery, flipped them off, turned off the car.

The moon, not quite full, glowed above hazy cornfields. Between the long cedars, it showed the way to our family's place under the maple, the gray-brown granite marker almost as tall as me, and small squares of smooth granite in the earth. I kneeled and touched the stones, ran my fingers in the outlines of the names, passed my hands across the graves of husbands and wives side by side, Jacob and Susanna, Sam and Mamie, John and Viola.

Apple

In the late 1800s, like millions of settlers, Susanna and Jacob Marty planted an orchard on their new American farm. Apple trees—immigrants like them—grew in the shelter of a windbreak west of the rise, with a walnut and a cherry tree. After the house was finished on the highest spot, they planted a butternut to the east. A native crab apple tree sprouted up south, in a sunny spot between the pines and oaks.

When their son Sam built his bungalow across the yard in 1940, he planted three Minnesota varieties of apple along the path between the houses. They bloomed white with just a blush of pink every spring, and dropped red fruit. In August, the Beacons; every other September, the Haralsons; in October, the Prairie Spies. My great-aunt Margaret, my grandmother, and then my mother and aunt made pies and crisps and applesauce with the good ones.

Gramma Marty's father, Charlie Hendrickson, grafted another variety onto the tree closest to her house.

It was apple blossoms that Effie Hendrickson cut to decorate the country church at East Rock Creek when Daddy and Mama were married on May 17, 1957. They had no money for flowers beyond the bouquets carried by Mama and her two bridesmaids and the boutonnieres worn by the men . . . and besides, Effie was an artist with flowers, not only in her gardens, which produced the nectar for Hendrickson honey, but in our little sanctuary across the fields from her house. The whole church smelled like that perfect perfume, and the candlelight made the blossoms glow.

Before I was old enough for school, Gramma Marty took me to our old orchard west of the house to pick apples, to climb up on a step-ladder and catch them with a wire basket attached to a stick. But I was small and not very strong, and the ground was uneven and overgrown with weeds, and I knew Gramma was frustrated because arthritis kept her from doing it herself.

"Orchards take work," she said. She couldn't do it anymore, and nobody else really knew how. By that time, the cherry and nut trees had already perished. For a while, the men put the heifers in the orchard to pasture, but after that it grew shut with weeds and bees.

For a few more years, Gramma focused on the crab apple tree by the road. She could pick many of the little sour apples herself and turn them into tart jam and apple pickles.

Mama sent me out to pick apples off the trees between the houses before they fell to the ground and got wormy, but after a few years many got worms while still on the tree and we gave up on them.

"Fruit trees take work," she said. She was so annoyed by nothing but rotten apples falling on the lawn that she got Daddy to cut down the apple tree closest to our house. Only Auntie was patient enough to sort through the two varieties on the tree closest to her house, toss the bad ones, and use the good ones for fat, juicy pies.

After Mama stopped keeping a garden, she longed for something beautiful on that big triangle of grass north of her clotheslines. She and Daddy picked out a flowering crab apple tree that bloomed deep pink every spring and produced hundreds of tiny red apples that fed the birds and didn't ruin the lawn.

Whatever kind and quality, every fruit tree on the farm bloomed every spring. And every May 17, Daddy cut a big bunch of apple blossoms and brought them into our house. Mama arranged them in a tall, old-fashioned, four-sided white vase and set them on the piano, where their perfume filled the house.

Daughters have been like apple trees, transient, adaptable, wandering the earth with their sweetness and tartness and promise, bending to the will of men in exchange for roots.

7

Memory of Trees

Joshua answered them, If thou be a great people, then get thee up
to the wood country, and cut down for thyself. The outgoings of it
shall be thine, for thou shalt drive out the Canaanites, though they
be strong.

—Joshua 17:15, 17

The Mississippi River curls out of Minnesota north woods and
bogs, heading southeast. The St. Croix River gathers off a Wisconsin watershed and heads southwest. One hundred fifty miles
south they meet. In the triangle of farms and woods between the two
rivers, the Marty farm lies near the eastern edge, a few miles from the
St. Croix. The twin cities of Minneapolis and St. Paul sit on the western edge, farther south. From the farm, heading down sixty miles and
bearing west on the interstate highway, the lakey, glacier-scarred land
comes to a jagged edge in towns called Columbia Heights, Falcon
Heights, and Vadnais Heights, then descends to the Mississippi.

Minneapolis fans out from a battered Mississippi waterfall that
powered mills for more than a century, lumber then grain, and now
power plants. It's a flat city with a modern skyline laid out on a grid
mostly on the west side of the river—once the Louisiana Purchase—a
cluster of glass and steel on streets named after French and Belgian
explorers like Hennepin, LaSalle, Marquette, and Nicollet, and British-
blooded industrialists like Pillsbury and Washburn. The slice of Minneapolis east of the river is the old town of St. Anthony on the falls,
an annexed mass of rail yards and the huge, plain clapboard houses
of immigrants—Swedish, Norwegian, and German, then Italian, East
European, and Lebanese.

Five miles downstream from the falls, joined by the Minnesota
River from the west, the Mississippi turns east through St. Paul and
heads toward its meeting place with the St. Croix. "Suzannah Trümpler, Zürich–St. Paul," said my great-grandmother's trunk in 1881
when she came to marry Jacob Marty. From St. Paul, they headed north

by train and cart to the land God showed them. As the forests fell and lumber floated south, down the St. Croix and Mississippi, farms and railroads appeared in the clearings. A century later, on a scholarship endowed by a lumber baron for the sons and daughters of Pine, Kanabec, and Washington counties, I, too, came south. In 1976 I left the farm and crossed the triangle from the St. Croix to the Mississippi side.

In the year I was born, 1958, the number on the 220-acre farm rose to six, with Grampa and Gramma Marty, their two sons, and my mother. There had not been so many on the farm for more than fifty years, before Jacob and Susanna's five children began to marry and depart.

Before I left in 1976, there were twelve of us on 460 acres, the most our farm had ever supported and ever would. In the big white house with the screen porch under the pine trees were Uncle Gaylon, 42; Auntie Lou, 36; Jonathan, almost 12; and Carolyn, 5. Across the yard, in the modified white bungalow with black trim and spruce trees were Daddy, 39; Mama, almost 37; Bruce and Blaine, 16; and Steven, 9. Grampa and Gramma Marty had been replaced by Grampa and Gramma Anderson, 72 and 73, who now lived in the trailer house next to the old orchard.

I was the first Marty daughter to leave home alone, without a wedding. Unfettered by obligation to the farm, I set out to find a calling and a mate. I was the first in the family admitted to college, and it was not nursing school or Bible college, but a public land-grant university, the University of Minnesota. It was not the university's farm campus, either—500 acres of flat farmland on the heights northwest of St. Paul—but its urban campus, 350 acres flanking the Mississippi River just south of St. Anthony Falls, seat of industry.

On a broad, shady curve in the river, I lived in the last women-only residence. Sirens woke me for the first few weeks—ambulances bursting from the university hospitals a block away, fire trucks screaming out of Station 19 to cross the river. Sometimes I heard the calm foghorn of a barge. Cool mornings in the dining room, wearing robes and slippers, we ate toast and scrambled eggs and watched the sun light up trees turning gold and red on the opposite bank and the city skyline beyond it. When the wind was right or the morning warm enough for an open window, we heard the crew-team leader call the rhythm on the river. I shared a room with a stranger from the suburbs. None of us had private bathrooms or showers, but I felt as though I lived in a spa. I was a scholarship girl and I didn't have to clean or cook, just study, go to class, keep my things neat. My work was to read and write and discern my calling.

"Latin," I said when my first adviser asked what language I would like to take.

He paused. I had been assigned to humanities as a default, and he was a graduate student. He cleared his throat and pushed up his glasses.

"Are you interested in linguistics?" he asked.

"I don't know," I said.

"Teaching languages?"

"No." I shook my head. Now I felt uncertain, unable to explain this conviction.

"Did you take a foreign language in high school?"

I told him about French, the only option I'd had, and about living in Switzerland three months. I said I wanted to be able to learn more languages if I needed them.

"Why don't you stick with French," he said gently. "Master that. If you want to learn other languages, knowing one well will help you."

I did as he said. I also signed up for classes in creative writing and theater, two things I knew I could do, and a lab class, astronomy.

In the mornings I walked out to class, across the river or up the dewy mall under gnarly oaks and the familiar fountain-shapes of old elms. The curve in the river held the heart of the campus, a rectangle of four-story brick halls in the classical style facing each other across a shady lawn, with an auditorium on the north end and the student union on the south. At each portico, tall trunks of elms and oaks gave way to columns. Entering Walter Library was like stepping into a cool grove; listening to a lecture in Smith or Vincent or Ford Hall was like sitting on a Mediterranean hillside in deep shade, listening to men and women taught by Socrates or Pliny or Jesus.

On the farm, the third crop of hay was baled, corn was picked and chopped, cows were milked, and the twins entered their junior year and glory days of high school as quarterback and running back on the football team. On the bend in the river in Minneapolis, I worked to read and write French as well as I could speak it, and traced connections between Greek and Roman drama, Shakespeare and Voltaire. One frosty night in October, I climbed with classmates up a narrow stairwell to the green dome on a roof among the bare treetops and aimed the old telescope there at Mars and Orion and the moon, then tipped it down and turned it on a prism-like office tower across the river and watched office people working late. I went out for beer with women on my floor and talked about classes, majors, gender roles, and politics. I listened to women like me debating about candidates, and stayed up on election night at a peanut party, when the farmer Jimmy Carter took the White House.

All winter as the snow flew and prices for gas and everything else went up, as Daddy and Uncle kept water lines from freezing and cows healthy and the twins' basketball exploits made the local paper every week, my French improved and I practiced writing short stories instead of novels. I resisted proofs as the way to teach introductory philosophy. When the quarter ended, I drove to Florida in a Ford with five other women, and came back tan and blonder for Grampa and Gramma's fiftieth wedding anniversary.

In the spring, as fields were plowed, corn and hay and oats seeded, and the twins tore up the Rush City diamond, I took accelerated French, psychology, and a humanities class that spanned the globe, from art in China to the novels of Virginia Woolf.

That summer I got a job at a teacher placement agency downtown, and waited for the bus twice a day as, on the farm, hay was cut, raked, baled, and put up in the mow. Sometimes I caught a ride home with Kathy. I drove the baler some Saturdays, and one weekend when Mama was gone, Gramma Anderson taught me how to can tomatoes. It was the last time I saw her. On a Sunday night a few weeks later in church, she had a stroke and died before Mama could think to call me.

The second year, I declared journalism as my major. I had run out of creative writing classes, and I reasoned that journalism would let me keep writing. Journalism was an easier major than English to explain, and the requirements made me branch out. I took history, political science, economics, mass communications, and visual communications. In reporting class, we took assignments due in two hours, ran across the campus and city, and returned to the classroom to type shallow, urgent stories with perfect leads. As students trickled back into the room, the single pecking of an electric typewriter became pounding and then a solid hum. I could write and type fast, but I felt compressed, too undisciplined and artistic for this form. Still, the hum was comforting; my fingers vibrated on the keys.

That winter I took a train out of the Great Northern depot downtown to Bismarck, North Dakota. There a weathered representative of Coal Creek Power took me to the roof of the new plant, the dazzling white land stretching north and west to meet an ice-blue sky on the flawless horizon. To the southeast, pylons marched off toward Minneapolis and St. Paul like enormous insects. I recognized the power plant rep's pitch as an argument against the power-line protests in Minnesota, though he didn't mention them—that was my job. He was spending time with me with hopes of a sympathetic story from a journalism student. My ballpoint was frozen, but I held my notebook in front of me anyway. I did not know how I would ever be a journalist.

In the spring I worked on Molière's *The Miser* for a class. As a dresser backstage, I buttoned endless rows of buttons, laced corsets, kept track of makeup, called cues, hung costumes, cleaned up, heard conversations about spouses and babies left at home, and observed mood swings and shifting relationships. The energy in the room and the lack of windows exhausted me.

I faltered. My grades were strong—every class was an adventure—but I knew I was unmoored. To my surprise, I had made friends easily, but I dated haphazardly. I found a church and taught Sunday school to unruly teenagers. I got a car and moved to northeast Minneapolis, past the falls near Boom Island, the one-time gathering place for logs headed into the mills. The riverfront there was ugly and industrial, full of small factories and sprawling warehouses. I lived alone along a tree-shaded bus route in a run-down fourplex, the only house for blocks without a tree in front or back, and the rent was cheap. On the bus you could hear Polish, Ukrainian, and Arabic in one ride home. I worked day jobs downtown, and a night job at the university hospital.

I bought different kinds of music: jazz piano and electric blues, Gato Barbieri and the Atlanta Rhythm Section. I didn't know how to cook for just one person, so I took refuge in 24-hour restaurants, where I dozed off while attempting to write plays. Minneapolis didn't feel like home but a stopping place.

During school breaks I drove with friends to Cape Hatteras and Santa Fe and flew to Seattle. I applied for a scholarship to study abroad in Tunisia, because it was the only site that required French. I was chosen as the alternate.

In my third year, I took speech and sociobiology, physiology and

mass communications law. Now the twins were in college too, and they
had separated. Blaine missed Rush City. Bruce missed the farm and his
girlfriend Jeri, who attended a Lutheran school, so he dropped out of
community college and took a job in Minneapolis to be closer to her.

During those years, Mama drove to Minneapolis once a month
and picked me up for dinner at places I couldn't afford and plays at the
Guthrie. Over dinner she told me news from the farm: the latest about
the twins and Steven; updates on Grampa's health and habits; conflicts
between Daddy and Uncle or between Uncle and her. Afterward, we
watched plays by O'Neill and Williams, Shakespeare, Voltaire, Stop-
pard, Sophocles, Euripides, Mama's beautiful face intense in the light
from the stage, flanked by multicolored seats filled with multicolored
people, rich and poor. Tennessee Williams's Maggie stepped across the
stage in a slip, taunting her drunk husband. Candide lifted his chin.
Rosencrantz and Guildenstern were missing and dead. Angels dropped
from the ceiling, chairs appeared and disappeared, a throne rose from
hell out of a swirl of smoke, a mother-in-law's shrill voice entered from
stage left, a gigantic backdrop descended—a pastoral scene, with a path
leading away toward a sunny horizon. We sat together in the dark,
laughing or silently crying, and then parted without time to talk enough
about any of it, reconvening in a month with news from our separate
worlds, hers she felt so confined, mine wide open as a wilderness.

I visited the farm mostly on holidays, and sometimes in the summer.
Jonathan and Steven were tall now—Jon shy and dark, Steve outgoing
and blond. Bruce and Blaine came home most weekends to spend time
with their girlfriends, play loud music and cards, and generally light
everybody up. They had caught up with me easily, and no one was talking about their return to the farm to stay. For the role of Marty brothers,
Jon and Steve were next in line, though they were cousins and so un-
alike it seemed impossible. Daddy and Uncle suffered back problems,
and Mama and Auntie Lou worked long hours in town. Uncle's temper had become worse. Only Carolyn seemed to make him happy and
proud. She was a pretty grade-school girl with smart comebacks as
funny and fast as Auntie Lou's or Bruce and Blaine's.

Not only the twins but our families had separated. Daddy and
Uncle still milked side by side and divided the rest of the work, and
Mama and Auntie still had coffee and cared for Grampa, but the ease

between the houses was gone. Bruce and Blaine and I were wild — that was the word used to describe children like us: we listened to loud music, swore easily, drank, and went to R-rated movies. The twins played cards and the three of us smoked at least occasionally. Mama and Daddy *let* us play that music on the living room stereo, *let* the twins have people over to play cards, *let* us stay out late, and Steven was on his way to becoming just like us. Daddy didn't approve, but he permitted it. Uncle wanted to protect his children from becoming like us. While I read Dostoevsky and Camus, Uncle kept up with every new book of Christian philosophy by Francis Schaeffer and fought terrible dark moods that seized him in rages. Uncle and I wanted to tell each other about the books we'd read, but it was difficult and we eventually stopped trying. Only Bruce could sometimes talk to Uncle in a way that made him laugh and seem familiar.

I was working nights and sleeping days in my hot upstairs apartment, with the curtains closed to keep out the light, when a letter arrived at the farm offering me the scholarship to Tunisia. The selected student could not go, and I should leave as soon as possible to arrive by October, when classes would begin. It was the summer before what should have been my senior year, and everyone on the farm was shocked. They looked up Tunisia in the encyclopedia, as I had when I applied.

Pascal Etierre had come to the United States for physics research that summer, and we arranged to meet. It had been five years since we'd seen each other, since I'd left his family's house near Lake Geneva, and now he fell in love with me at once. I was expecting someone like a brother, but he had become a man and far better looking at twenty-one than at sixteen. I was flattered and a little confused and unbelieving, but we talked for hours and he made me use every bit of my education in every conversation we had. He not only knew where Tunisia was but had always wanted to visit. Now he would.

In my memory of that August there is a bridge of sound: the sound of Minneapolis around me as I sleep with the curtains closed to the sun, the rush and vibration of traffic that becomes the sound of St. Anthony Falls and then the sound of a train — the train on the farm, the train to North Dakota, a train blaring through the rail yards of northeast Minneapolis, and the train taking me south from Luxembourg to Switzerland

and Italy, forests and patchwork fields in deep greens gradually turning to yellow, the forests receding. South of Rome, I am the only blonde
woman on the train. The trees moving past the window have changed
from familiar hardwoods and pines to those I recognize as biblical,
cedars and cypress. At the tip of Italy's boot, the train separates into sections, loads onto a ferry, and arrives among the palm trees in Catania. I
hear the names Syracuse, where Greeks and Romans waged war for a
century, and Mount Etna, still burning in the earth, as the train passes
along bare hills and mountains. The sound of the train becomes the
vibration and foghorn of the ferry to Tunis, crowded with migrant
workers returning home at midnight to a port down the coast from
Carthage. The sound of Minneapolis as I sleep becomes the sound of
Tunis as I wake. Tunis, the vibration of a city a thousand years old, the
shudder of traffic in the stone of the white building where I sleep above
a wide, tree-lined street.

C'm baaaaaaaaas!

A street vendor cries Arabic words that sound like Daddy or Uncle
Gaylon calling the cows.

I wake in warm Mediterranean air on a narrow bed against the
wall and open my eyes to a calm, darkened room. Light filters through
louvered shutters outside and sheer white curtains inside. I get up,
cross the cool tile floor, unhook the tall balcony doors, swing them
open. The street noise rushes in, and I push open the heavy blue-gray
louvers and squint in the bright daylight. The sun is high and brilliant,
the light I recognize as how Camus described it — *éclater*, crashing, glaring — but I was unprepared for white swirls of French-colonial cornices,
wrought-iron balconies, and sky-blue shutters.

On the street below, people pass through fernlike screens of foli-
age — the leaves of trees lining Avenue de la Liberté, brushing against
the lowest balconies. The leaves remind me of the honey locust on the
farm, with tiny rows of opposing green ovals on each stem, branches
off trunks that sprung from elaborate circular grates in the stone sidewalk below, the streets and sidewalks all paved in a diamond pattern.
Through the leaves I read the names of shops: *Brasserie Danielle. Tabac.
Chaussures. Patisserie Noura.* A small vegetable stand. Men and women
pass, some of the men in flat-topped, maroon *chéchia* hats, a few women

in white or cream-colored *sefsaris*. I watch the passersby, the yellow and white buses, the darting, small white cabs. Above the din of the street comes the call to prayer, a tremulous loud cry. It is midday.

Tunis al-Khadhra – Tunis the Green. Conquering Arabs named the city on the north coast of Africa for the forests and fields they found far from their desert home. The oldest university in Tunis had convened under an olive tree on the highest point of the old walled city in the year 690, *Jamaa Azzituna*, now the great mosque. The modern University of Tunis exists in faculties scattered across the modern city, which sprawl dazzling white with light blue and green shutters, up hills and down along the sea in winding back streets and wide avenues.

My French and Arabic classes began immediately at the language institute down the street, but I had to wait for bureaucratic wheels to turn to take classes at the press institute. I stayed with an American linguistics teacher named Jennifer, who welcomed my ability to cook and type. On the first holiday, she took me to the Mediterranean shore at Carthage. She made me stand at the remains of the Punic ports, no bigger than a marina, and imagine we were Phoenician women waiting for the trading ships and warships to return. On the slope above the port, Jennifer pointed out the Byrsa hill made famous by Dido—here called Elyssa, legendary refugee princess of Tyre in ancient Lebanon—who cut a sheepskin into threads to mark out the whole hill and claim it. Jennifer walked me through a grove lined with funeral urns said to once hold bones of children sacrificed to the god Baal in pleas for victory. I recognized Baal as an enemy god described in Hebrew scriptures, and told her the stories I remembered.

In Tunis, I felt at home. I could walk outside to gather groceries from nearby street vendors and markets, like picking from Mama's garden. In fact, most of what I found in Marché Palestine had come by donkey cart from gardens outside Tunis that very morning, or from farmers' flatbeds from truck gardens in the Cap Bon the night before. At Jennifer's apartment, I cooked. The family around our kitchen table or coffee table was made up of Jennifer's faculty friends, their friends, and friends I gradually made myself. It was a community I had been missing, a cross-section of disciplines and ideas and backgrounds in which mine were relevant.

I was mistaken by strangers as Swedish because of my hair, or Belgian or Swiss because of my accent when speaking French, but to me, the people all around me looked like relatives, like Martys come to life from family portraits going back a century. Olive-skinned men with black hair and brown eyes, men in dark red hats, and merchants accepting my dinars, nodding, invoking God's blessing, *Barak-allahufik,* reminded me of Daddy and Uncle, especially Uncle with his high forehead. At every call to prayer, I thought I heard Uncle's and Daddy's clear voices.

I learned my directions at once to help predict the weather by the wind coming from the desert or the mountains or the sea. On unfamiliar streets, I navigated by the shadows we cast. I escaped a week of stomach ills all the other Americans and Europeans seemed to get and chalked it up to the benefits of drinking raw milk for years on the farm.

The call to prayer gave structure to days, like mealtime prayer at home. Dawn, midday, midafternoon, sunset, nightfall. *Allahu akhbar! Allahu akhbar! La ilaha illa Allah!* (God is most great, God is most great, there is no god but God) became the prayer we said at home all together: *God is great, God is good, let us thank him for our food, by his hand we must be fed, give us Lord our daily bread. Bless us, amen.*

The first call came at dawn and the city roared to life, traffic streaming in, street vendors crying. As the sun rose above the apartments across the street and heated up our east-facing balcony and bedrooms, I made coffee and drank it in a little room on the back of the apartment, beneath a map of the Mediterranean, typing letters to Mama and Daddy, Auntie and Uncle, Grampa and brothers and cousins, my friends, and Pascal. Then errands, to the post office, to the market for vegetables and fruit, to the laundry, to the *bibliothèque* for books or supplies, to the bank, moving quickly and ignoring the ubiquitous comments and questions from men aiming to distract young women. When the call to prayer came at midday, I was making salads for whatever friends Jennifer might bring home to eat with us.

As the sun passed overhead and fell onto the back of the apartment, I drank water and ate dates and studied in my room on the cooler but still noisy side as traffic began to leave the city. At what I knew as suppertime, I walked up the shady side of the street, crossed to the language institute, stepped into its cool atrium, and climbed the steps. The young Tunisian day-students had left and the night students gathered, faces from Gambia, Mali, Senegal, South Africa, Hungary, Russia, India, Korea, Argentina. With some I studied French, with others the Tunisian dialect of Arabic. We lowered the wooden blinds and conjugated verbs. Sweat beaded on our lips while we listened and spoke, and the sun fell, loosening its grip. We walked back into the street as light glared off the flat roofs and made a silhouette of the old city in the honey-colored air.

The call to prayer came again when the sun set behind the medina, marking noon in Minnesota as the Tunis sky ignited into orange and salmon and violet. The thunder of traffic had receded like a tide on the street, now in deep shadow. The air cooled. Jennifer and I talked about the day and laughed as we made our late suppers, rice and vegetables, simple and fast, sometimes with leftover rotisserie chicken or something from the *boucherie.* Under the handheld shower, the soap lathered gray with the Sahara dust that flowed off our bodies. We rinsed out our clothes—I my long-sleeved white blouse and underclothes, sometimes my black skirt—and hung them on the balcony clothesline. We sat on the balcony in our bathrobes, read and talked in the cool, dry breeze. The sky darkened and then the color was gone.

When the call to prayer came at nightfall, the street calmed to an occasional taxi or bus. The last shops closed at eleven and, in our separate rooms, we closed the shutters and slept, the moon passing overhead, marking the months.

All along the coast of Tunisia, birds arrived from Europe, crossing the Mediterranean from France and Italy to the African promontory reaching into the sea. At dusk in Tunis, they gathered by the thousands to roost in the hundred-year-old ficus grove on Avenue Habib Bourguiba, the east-west axis of the city that connected the old, walled medina to the port. Above the strands of tiny lights and flower stands packed with roses and lilies, the branches came alive every night with shrieking choruses of birds.

I was invited to the homes of Tunisian friends in the Cap Bon—the good cape—source of the capital's fresh food and flowers, greenest and richest in winter. From the northernmost point on a clear day, it was said you might see Sicily.

I was greeted with curiosity. Arriving, we stood outside the house briefly, where the family met me, the father of the house speaking in French, the mother listening but unable to join in (*My mother can speak only Arabic,* my friend would explain), and then I was invited inside and given something to drink, thick sweet mint tea or mineral water.

Inevitably the question came: *What does your father do?*

The customary reply was businessman, doctor, lawyer, professor. I replied: *My father is a farmer.*

There would be a pause and then a wide smile, a look of recognition or even laughter, and then a string of questions: *What kind of farm does he have? Where? How big? How many tractors? Do you have brothers? Do you work on the farm too?*

I worked out the answers: *A dairy farm in Minnesota (that's on the border of Canada, west of Chicago, where the Mississippi River begins). One hundred fifty head of cattle on four hundred sixty acres (one hundred eighty hectares), five tractors, three brothers, and one boy cousin—my father and his brother farm together. Yes, I drive a tractor.*

Ah, he is a rich man!

"No, not really," I said, "not in America."

But in the world, mademoiselle, he is a rich man.

Tunisia, once the breadbasket of Rome, granary of the empire. Almost every travel brochure said it, to transcend the image of Africa as only desert and jungle, to prepare the visitor for the good bread and olives, figs and pomegranates and artichokes, wine from colonial vineyards. But centuries and conquerors had come and gone and the band of fertile soil between the desert and sea had narrowed.

In museums, I memorized the layers of inhabitants and occupants: Berber, Phoenician, Carthaginian, Roman, Vandal, Byzantine, Arab, Ottoman, French, Tunisian.

I learned the story of Virgil's Aeneas, founder of Rome and lover of Dido of Carthage before that, a confusing doppelgänger to Homer's Odysseus for someone like me, unschooled in the classics. *Exhausted, Aeneas and his men made efforts to run for the nearest land within reach. They set forth for the coast of Africa. There is a haven there, at the end of a long sound . . . beyond the water a curtain of trees with quivering leaves reaches downwards.*

I learned the true tale of Hannibal, the Carthaginian who crossed the Alps with his elephants and incredibly attacked Rome from the north—*Hannibal is at the gates!* One night, eating figs after dinner, someone told the story of the giant African figs that launched the last Punic

War. I sat in the theater at Carthage, where sixteen-year-old Augustine sat when he arrived in the romanized city from a country town in 370. He watched bawdy comedies, satires, and spectacles against elaborate backdrops years before the Christian canon was set. But Augustine would go on to become the North African bishop and saint who helped change all that.

At the Bardo museum, I wandered through rooms full of mosaics — Neptunes and Poseidons from pool bottoms of lavish but lost Roman houses, scenes of hunting and fishing and games, wild-eyed leopards and lions, crocodiles and elephants, tropical fauna and flora long vanished from Tunisia.

Jennifer and I were visiting friends the night the U.S. embassy was seized in Tehran, 2,000 miles east of Tunis. Ali, the economics professor, had been hovering over a little radio all evening, holding it close to his ear, turning it slightly, oblivious to conversation. Finally, Sonia asked, "What are you listening to?"

"You might want to listen too, but the reception is bad and some of it is in Farsi," he said, turning up the volume. "Some students in Tehran have taken American hostages."

It would be the topic of conversation in all the classes the next day. The media called the instigators fundamentalists. We talked about the shah and the ayatollah and the U.S. president.

Through November, unease rippled through capitals. In front of the U.S. embassy in Tunis, a tank rolled onto the lawn and parked, gun facing the street. For the University of Tunis, foreign admissions were halted.

There would be no journalism classes for me, but I was not disappointed. I was free to keep studying languages and reading and writing letters. The city became my classroom, dinner tables my study groups. I learned about history, politics, social science, religion, and introductory architecture, the significance of 1492 and 1948, the *Muqqadimah* of Ibn Khaldûn, the Camp David Accords.

I studied French side by side with a woman from the Soviet Union. We looked curiously alike, both blond with dark eyes, both in leather boots, hers fashionable white, mine cowgirl brown. Our nations were the superpowers now. When her government moved into Afghanistan on Christmas Eve to protect Soviet interests, mine retaliated within days by stopping sales of U.S. grain. My home was the Midwest, called the *breadbasket of the world.*

When the weather turned cold and humidity ran down the walls of apartments with no central heating, I slept soundly under wool blankets and a sheepskin.

I received more letters than anyone—sometimes three or four a day stuffed into Jennifer's mailbox in the marble hallway downstairs. Our friends recognized it as proof of the kind of family I had, extended and agricultural, and as a net they were casting to bring me safely home. I knew it was also a measure of how much I wrote to them. Without journalism classes, I studied by becoming their journalist. Between classes and meals and the work I'd found as an editor and typist, I wrote letters describing the city, the sea, current events—an Arab summit in Tunis, a visit by Palestinian leaders—and holidays, weddings, food, day trips, and travels. I wrote that I was safe but cold.

Mama wrote every weekend, telling me the rhythm of her days and weeks. Plastech was growing, business systems were changing, her boss was stressed out, she worked long hours and went home to cook supper and clean, attend school events, and help with church functions. She didn't sleep well. On weekends, the twins came home from their colleges with girlfriends and laundry and appetites.

Daddy and Auntie wrote news of the farm. After weeks of rain in the fall, the corn crop was good but didn't get in the sheds until the ground froze, December tenth. They reported inches of snow.

Uncle Gaylon didn't write, but in letters from Auntie, Mama, and Daddy, I read about him. He took Auntie to hear Francis Schaeffer speak, and he took all of them to see films. He joined people from community churches to open a crisis pregnancy center.

Steven wrote about junior high sports and jazz band—he was a running back in football, a guard in basketball, first chair in percussion. Carolyn wrote in large, third-grade printing. My friends wrote about love and work, buying a house, law school, and politics.

Blaine covered both sides of every letter in small script. Bruce wrote one page in a loose scrawl. At the University of Wisconsin, Blaine had declared a major—agriculture business—and kept going home on weekends to work at the Plastech plant. At Bible college, Bruce couldn't find a major but wanted to get married anyway—he and Jeri wrote about wondering and waiting and trying to set a date.

Pascal and I wrote back and forth, he in French, I in English. We wrote about philosophy and the possibility of our future life together, but mostly about his coming to Tunis.

He arrived from Geneva with a duffle bag, physics books, and an ardor that overwhelmed me. Friends stopped by to meet him and he impressed them all. It was his school break but not mine, so we stayed close to Tunis. We took short walks, to the pretty gated garden at Avenue Habib Thameur, to the flower sellers on Avenue Habib Bourguiba, to the souks in the medina where he bought gifts to take home. We took the commuter train to Carthage and Sidi Bou Saïd, and a bus to the Bardo. Even in bad weather, everything was more magnificent and interesting and beautiful than he'd imagined.

We talked about our careers and the lives we hoped for. He wanted to keep studying physics, to apply at universities in the United States, to escape his parents' house and leave Switzerland. I had no clear path. I still loved theater and journalism but I was too shy, all I could do was watch and write. We talked about our families and getting married. My mother dreaded losing me but put it in God's hands. His mother was against it: it was too fast, we were too young, and she knew me— I was not the right match. In my heart I agreed with her, but Pascal was adamant.

Jennifer and Sonia decided that Pascal's visit called for a trip to a truly great Roman site. They picked Dougga because none of us had been there and it was close enough for a day trip.

At six on Saturday morning, eight of us met in the bus terminal. The sky was overcast and the wind sharp. Ali warned that it was a bad idea to go on such a cold day—it would be worse on the plain. We reconsidered, but then Pascal made a joke about seeing Roman ruins on the Ides of March and there was no stopping either Sonia or Jennifer. Sonia was determined that Pascal see the best of Tunisia, and Jennifer had wanted to see Dougga since last summer, when the Comédie-Française played there in the theater.

Traveling south out of Tunis on a tar road, we pressed ourselves together into seats among children and women in cream-colored *sefsaris* carrying boxes and bags and parcels, three old men, and two younger men. I sat crammed against the window. Moving shafts of sunlight crossed our path, lighting up bands of tiny white and yellow flowers on the dark brown and green landscape. It was the fourth month of winter rain, my sixth month in Tunisia, and my first trip inland. The bus entered the hills, the eastern tail of the mountains that ranged across Morocco and Algeria.

I thought of Pascal's farm with its clear view of Lake Geneva, the French mountains, and the Jura where he trained for bicycle racing. His thigh was hard against mine as he began to apply his physicist mind to my liberal arts heart. I was pressed against the window and the view, and the idea of my father, whose birthday would be tomorrow.

"Where do you want to live," Pascal asked me gently.

"I don't know," I said. "I don't even know what I will do."

He said something else that was lost in the din of the bus and I didn't reply.

He repeated, "Do you want to stay in Minnesota?"

In the window I could see a ghost of his reflection, his pale face and pale blue eyes and brown hair, his straight nose and sharp chin. He was giving me his neutral look rather than his earnest or interested one. No one had asked me before *Do you want to stay in Minnesota?*—as if it were a reasonable choice.

"What do you mean, *stay*?" I asked. "I'm not there now."

"I mean do you want to live there, have children there, be close to your family," he explained patiently. It was a matter of fact.

The bus was passing through a field completely yellow, dense gold on a dark green border. "Look," I said, nodding toward the color.

"What?" he asked. He didn't see it, and I couldn't explain.

I wondered if it would rain. I heard Jennifer ask Pascal a question, and after awhile his weight shifted away from me.

In Minnesota, snow still covered the 460 acres of our farm and everything on it. In the house about this time of day, nine-thirty, Daddy would be alone eating breakfast—a bowl of cereal with cream, two fried eggs, three slices of buttered toast, at least two glasses of milk. Mama would be in town at the office, Steven at school, the twins at college. Daddy ate in quietness, glancing out the window toward Uncle's house, the house where they were born, the house Jacob and Susanna built. I knew the view over his flanneled shoulder: the straight white farm house, just north of it the red woodshed and bare lilac bush, the green arched-roof brooder house, the red gas tank on an eight-foot frame. Snow-covered trees, white pines and spruce, bare oaks and maples, butternut and apple trees. This was the picture in the window he faced.

Standing at the stove he could see farther north: the silos and two barns; the snow-covered barnyard and fields off to the northwest; and Clyde's red barn a quarter-mile up on the hill.

Sitting at the table Daddy would be thinking of me, I knew. He could not figure me out, but he was proud of me anyway.

He rinsed out his dishes and then lay down on the linoleum floor. He pulled one knee at a time to his chest and held it for a count, then both knees, then repeated. He was young, he would be forty-three tomorrow. He and Uncle would be planning for planting by now. They knew what crop would go in every field that waited under the snow.

Daddy was really still asleep, eight hours behind me in the middle of a twelve-hour night, snoring beside my lovely restless mother who often woke from strange and disturbing dreams.

The bus hurtled south, disgorging and taking in rural people and cold air in every whitewashed town. Tunis and the sea receded behind us over the slightest curve of the earth. Here was a landscape more familiar: broad, dark green fields interspersed with the dark brown of tilled fields. Above us, clouds flew in the wind, opening patches of sunlight that sped across the fields, fading in and out. I wanted to cover these fields with snow, protect them from the wind.

We got off the bus in a small town and rented a louage out to Dougga. Rounding a hill with six broken columns, a ghost town appeared. The car pulled up beside the remains of a theater carved into the hillside. Limestone rubble cascaded down a slope from the foot of a still-perfect capital—a streak of sunlight ran across it, briefly turning the blocks creamy yellow.

Inside the car, none of us spoke. We scanned the ruined town that ran to a broad, green plain with rectangles of orchards and crops in the distance. Dougga, in Berber *Thugga* for pastures, was an agricultural town, the center of the region, not more than 5,000 citizens. The Berbers had built it on an outcropping of limestone, the Carthaginians built it up, and the Romans seized it when Julius Caesar defeated Juba I in 46 B.C. It was no Roman town on a grid, but the Romans had made it great, complete with forum and hippodrome. Two centuries after Caesar's murder, in the age of empire, a family of landowners, shipping wheat and olive oil to Rome, had built the theater to seat more than 3,500.

Someone opened a door and the wind seemed to cut us out of the car like a knife. Two hours, Mounir told the driver. Immediately we regretted it. Together we hunched our shoulders, standing on the exposed hillside and covering our ears as the car disappeared and left us in silence, except for the whine of the wind.

We dispersed in twos and threes, drawn to different things. Pascal and I walked together through the town to the forum, to the place of twelve winds—a circle carved like an unmarked compass in the pavement at the corner of the capital. High on the capital I made out a carved eagle lifting a man to heaven in its claws—apotheosis, divine transformation of the emperor. We wandered through residential streets, archways of public baths, to the Punic monument near the bottom of the rubble. Ali stood in a sheltered place, smoking his pipe, studying a block wall, and Sonia and Jennifer traced Latin inscriptions on a doorway. Norah and Lilly ventured down another ruined path with Mounir. I wanted to be alone. I told Pascal to go on with them, and I walked back to the theater.

I developed a passion for stage plays, with the mirror they held up to my own miseries and the fuel they poured on my flame, wrote Augustine.

Through a gap in a stone wall, I walked onto the proscenium, a white marble floor facing the crescent of seats in the hillside. I crossed the stage, felt the size and scale of it, heard the sound of my boot steps echo up the stone caveau. I wandered down a short flight of steps from the stage to the orchestra and then up into one of the aisles, turned, sat down, and caught my breath. The back wall of the theater was gone and the farms of the ancient town formed the backdrop.

Dotted with flowers, olive trees, and pomegranates in small gridded patches, the fields were as green in the month of March as they would ever be. Before Carthage and Rome, they'd been grazed by moving flocks and herds, the soil held intact by the grasses' roots. But in Dougga's day, they were plowed and planted with wheat.

Cracks in the racing clouds cast bars of sunlight like searchlights across the town, warming the skin for a few moments, making the remnants of columns form shadows like a fan on the stage. From the shadows, I knew the theater faced south . . . the entire town had been built on a south-facing slope. I cupped a hand over my right ear against the west wind from the mountains, picking up particles of earth as it blew. These were the fields that flew to Tunis on the wind, lodged in our hair and the folds of our clothes, made the soap lather gray as it flowed down the drains into the sea.

Rome seized on plantation agriculture, commodity agriculture, as it defeated Carthage. At the end of the Third Punic War in 146 B.C., twenty-eight volumes of a treatise on North African agriculture by Mago were translated into Latin, according to Pliny—the only books salvaged from the library at Carthage. Rome forsook the small Italian farms whose yeoman had been recruited for the legions.

We leave the sweet boundaries and ploughlands of home, said Meliboeus in Virgil's *Eclogues,* beginning during a civil war in the wake of Julius Caesar's death. *We flee our homeland . . . the countryside's all in such turmoil . . . I keep remembering how the oak trees touched of heaven.*

And it came to pass in those days, that there went out a decree from Caesar Augustus that all the world should be counted, wrote the author of the Gospel of Luke a little more than a century later.

Conquest yielded up slaves to till enormous fields across the empire, to cut more forests and build more ships and power them, to lay not only roads and cities but erect aqueducts and waterworks to irrigate the fertile but fragile fields—aqueducts and waterworks that began to fall when Rome fell. Designed to irrigate, they eroded.

After Pascal flew home, Jennifer and I took the train south for a weekend. We stopped to see the coliseum at Al-Jem, a rival to Rome's, dwarfing the village that was once a sprawling city on the plains. We went on to the desert and walked in the salt flats and sand. In the shadow of a dune, a tan mound poised northward, we entered the shade of a palm oasis with water trickling through a network of channels.

The Arabs who came three hundred years after Rome fell chose the inlet lake south of Carthage for a market and mosque. They were desert people who knew the worth of small gardens and nourished them. For eight hundred years, they salvaged what they could.

From temples and theaters at Dougga and Carthage, from the lion-colored coliseum at Al-Jem, seats were stripped, dungeons revealed, stones quarried and redeemed to build human dwellings on a modest scale. Columns from deserted temples in every Roman town were reclaimed to build mosques. Tilled fields were returned to pastures. The damage had been great and progress was slow.

On trains, I thought of Susanna, the same age as me, heading west on a train from New York to St. Paul. She had come alone across the heaving Atlantic and through immigration, felt unsteadying hunger as she walked from ship to train. From the window, her brown eyes had recorded the flat and rolling farms of Pennsylvania, Ohio, and Indiana, and glimmers of Lake Erie and Lake Michigan. She would see the bend of the Mississippi in St. Paul, where she changed trains.

In 1881 the railroad from St. Paul to Duluth was like a scar. Rush City—*rushes in a lake, rushes in a creek, lumber rush, grain rush*—was a raw, eight-year-old town where the railroad crossed Rush Creek. Susanna would have stepped off the train at the depot, a block from the newest of four hotels.

The same year Susanna immigrated to the United States, a French general rode victorious into Tunis, established a protectorate, and expanded colonial control of North Africa. The first clearing of the forests in the Americas was well under way, but in Tunisia the first clearing was forgotten. The forests had been cut by Phoenicians, Carthaginians, and Romans more than two thousand years before, in the classical age of mercantile and military shipbuilding.

With ancient heroes, the erosion had begun, but the French blamed the creeping desert on the Arabs.

"The great Roman people of whom we are the heirs conquered this region well before the Arabs," a colonist wrote. "Like Rome, we will again expand the cultivable area . . . and transform it into fertile plains."

They set out to create a new Rome, and with a renewed appetite the desert once again gnawed toward the sea.

After the winter rain, Tunis gave a glimpse of its ancient green. Trees still rose out of stone sidewalks everywhere, lining the wide streets built by the French. Leaves in the grove on Avenue Habib Bourguiba turned glossy, and maples and jacarandas that had lost their leaves regained them. The palm trees and hedges and grass at the little park on Avenue Habib Thameur thickened and darkened. Islands of green that remained inside courtyards of banks and other businesses turned lush. On the hill north of the city, the fountains at Parc Belvédère overflowed and the grass and zoo animals revived.

Tunis al-Khadhra—Tunis the green. Tunis was a memory of trees, the green margin of forests and high plains between desert and sea.

Tunis al-Khadhra was a memory of trees and a call to preserve and protect them.

On Avenue Habib Bourguiba, I studied the gold-black metal statue of Ibn Khaldûn, historian, *father of modern sociology*, robes flowing, book in his arm.

"Agriculture is the oldest of all crafts," wrote Ibn Khaldûn. Next he named architecture, then carpentry. "God made all created things useful for man, to supply his necessities and needs. Trees belong among these things."

History repeats itself in cycles, he said.

Near the south side of the medina, I found 33 rue Tourbet el Bey, where Ibn Khaldûn was born in 1332, and the mosque nearby, where he taught before moving to Cairo.

I walked up to the great mosque at the medina's heart, the one-time university of Tunis, *Jamaa Azzituna*. Like dry grass in a marble forest, woven mats lay on the floor beneath the vaulted ceilings, arches that lifted like the branches of trees. I imagined students crowding around teachers seated column by column. Chandeliers and lanterns—Roman, Arab, Andalousian, Turkish—illuminated the shadows for reading.

"It's 7:15 now," Mama wrote to me. "Bruce has left for Jeri's and Gordon has gone out to the barn and Blaine left for a night out with the boys. Today Bruce told me that he doesn't want to go back to school next fall, but that he's coming home to work on the farm and that the men are going to pay him $5 per hour. And that he and Jeri will probably get married toward fall, maybe October, and get an apartment in town, and she will get a full-time job. Gordon and I are going to discuss this at length tonight. Bruce further went on to state that he wants to buy Gaylon out in a couple of years—Gayla, with what? And what is to say that in a couple of years he won't be tired of the farm. . . . He should at least get a degree and maybe someday after he's been out on his own for several years he could come back to the farm if that's where his heart really lies. No way can the farm even afford to pay him $5 an hour now."

There is an Arabic word, *maktoob*, which means *It is written on your forehead*. God knows your life when you are born. What is written on my brothers'? What is written on mine?

As the rains ended and the days grew warmer, I worked, studied, fed my family of friends, and found music—the Berlin Orchestra and Mingus Dynasty at Theâtre Municipale, Tunisian musicians home from Europe to play for engagements and weddings. I tried to speak Arabic with older women and asked the names of spices and flowers and trees: fig, sycamore, olive, eucalyptus, varieties of palm. I loved the light and the lay of the land, the spacing of borders, enclosed gardens, children, cattle, able-bodied old people working on farms and in shops.

In the swirl of international events, Tunisia was a country called *third-world*, but it was also like the rural places in America. My Tunisian friends and I had been lured and pushed from home, away to the big universities of Europe and the United States, adapting until it was impossible to return. City people sought vacations on our former terrain—cheap sunny beaches in warm climates, countryside and wilderness in moderate ones.

It was *Shabaan*, the eighth month on the Islamic calendar, as the moon waxed and then waned and the city prepared to fast the month of *Ramadhan*. Fresh figs were in the market. In the evenings, the streets were full of cars honking for weddings. Exams were completed and corrected.

I left Tunis on a hot July morning just before *Ramadhan* began. Mama and Daddy, anxious to see me after ten months, came with Steven to Europe, and Pascal drove us in a circle around Switzerland so Daddy could see Engi and the Matterhorn, Lake Lucerne and Lake Geneva.

What I saw was a vanishing forest, open valleys, erosion that had turned fragile places into the bare hills of Sicily, Ireland, Greece, Lebanon, and Iran and the creeping dunes of Iraq and Tunisia. I felt the movement of ghosts, wandering peoples and languages scavenging for places to plant, graze animals, satisfy hunger, build a shelter and hearth—sending legions ahead in clanking metal, enslaving each other to dig and build, like dunes devouring the green since a time before we began to measure time by moon and sun and stars.

I, too, was a memory of trees—a scholarship girl sponsored by a lumberman's fortune gained in a county named Pine.

Pascal and I parted forever, in tears, and I flew home with Mama and Daddy and Steven. As the plane descended in Minneapolis, the grid appeared beneath us—Jeffersonian, Roman—square mile by square mile of dirt roads and blacktops laid over the weblike ridges and rivers of watersheds. Now I saw not only fields but outlines of the forests cut away to create them.

On the farm, the corn was higher than my head. In Minneapolis, I took an apartment in the same house I'd left the year before. I spread a rag rug from Tunisia on the hardwood floor of the front room and then registered for classes to finish a degree in journalism. For awhile Bruce was my roommate. He had transferred to the University of Minnesota and declared the same major that Blaine had discovered—agribusiness—and neither one of them looked back.

I dressed up and caught a bus downtown, got off at 8th and Nicollet, and walked into the tallest building in Minneapolis. I rode the elevator to the personnel office and got a part-time job. IDS had just opened a new department, telemarketing, and was hiring college students to answer calls to toll-free numbers published nationwide in ads for money-market funds. As I answered phones on the twenty-second floor, I looked north-northeast, from the downtown grid across the glittering ribbon of the Mississippi to old St. Anthony, the urban landscape threaded with parks and trees to the horizon. The enormous sky over that flat line dazzled clear blue or filled with towers of cumulus clouds. Some days, clouds fell to earth, engulfing the glass tower, turning the city into the bottom of a murky sea.

As the leaves turned colors and then blew into dry drifts, I worked downtown and went to classes, Ronald Reagan was elected, and in snowy January, a few minutes after his inauguration, the hostages were released from Iran.

Interest rates were eighteen percent and, if you could muster a thousand dollars, there was money to be made. There was money to be made almost everywhere except on the farm, which lay over the horizon, sixty miles northeast of the ribbon of river.

Fig

The first tree named in the Bible is the fig, whose leaves formed the first human clothing. In the Hebrew scriptures, the fig tree is mentioned many times as shelter and a source of sustenance. In the Christian gospels and Revelation of John, it's a metaphor for signs of apocalypse.

I came to know real fig trees when I lived in Tunisia, ancient Carthage. With olive trees and pomegranate, they dotted the country-side and filled market bins with dark fruit, among the best figs any-where. The common fig thrives in rocky places, but the hundreds of ficus species in the world range from the edible fig to huge old groves of rubber trees, like the double row down the central boulevard of Tunisia's capital. I admire their dark glossy leaves, smooth gray skin, and deep shade under spreading branches.

Across the street from the apartment where I lived in Tunis in 1979 and 1980, a new mosque was under slow construction—so slow that its progress was hard to discern over the course of the year. A huge hole had been dug carefully around an old ficus tree. When I returned four-teen years later, that same old tree shaded a beautiful courtyard and made the new mosque look as though it had been there for centuries. It was a tender sign of veneration of the old and beautiful, I thought, and a subtle rebuke to ancient Rome.

In the days of the Roman republic, more than a century before Jesus and seven centuries before the Arabs brought Islam to North Africa, Carthage was at the peak of its power across the Mediterranean. The Roman senator Cato saw Carthage as a threat and a barrier to Rome's future glory, and he relentlessly sought support for a war to vanquish the city and possess its land. He ended every speech, no matter what the subject, by declaring "Carthago dalenda est!"—Carthage must be destroyed!

To prove what power and riches Carthage had and how close they lay, Cato brought to the Senate an armful of North African figs, still fresh after a three-day voyage. At the end of his speech that day, he shook the giant figs out of the folds of his toga onto the floor to gasps of disbelief and roared, "Carthago dalenda est!" With this, Cato secured the vote to wage the third Punic War.

Two hundred years later, three of the gospel writers recorded a cryptic story of a fig tree in Palestine that bore no fruit. When Jesus cursed it, the tree withered. Some call it a miracle that showed his power over nature. Some call it a parable of what will happen to those who don't do what God creates them to do.

But I wonder if Jesus cursed the tree at all. Maybe he simply observed that the fig tree was already cursed, unable to flee as animals and humans could. Maybe the Roman occupiers had picked its figs and left none for the local people. Maybe, as in the Gospel of Mark, figs weren't even in season, but Jesus had heard the story of Cato and lamented that the valuable tree attracted builders of empire.

8

The Way Out

Jesus said to him, "The foxes have holes, and the birds of the air have nests, but the human one has nowhere to lay his head."

—Matthew 8:20 and Luke 9:58

Elm trees were dying everywhere. The first sign was a yellow patch like a flag in the canopy, then a browning of leaves by midsummer, the cascades of almond-shaped, jagged-edged leaves tarnished. The next spring, the leaves never came out. The tree seemed to remain in a state of prolonged spring, as if the buds had frozen, and then the tree dropped them to the earth. The tenderest branches became brittle. Swaying through the summer and the next turn of seasons, the graceful fingers of the tree fell away.

In Minneapolis and St. Paul, the city councils were aggressive. Foresters combed each block to identify disease and mark trunks with a blaze-orange circle or slash, and within days a mammoth tree was gone, root extracted like a tooth, disposed of carefully to extinguish the predators. One by one the elms on the university mall were removed, stumps exhumed, until only twelve out of thirty remained with a stand of oaks at the southwest corner. The mall became sunny. Whole city streets were stripped of shade to save those trees not yet stricken.

On the farm, the elm that draped over our driveway was the first to go. Then the elm at the entrance to the lane behind the barns. Then the lone elm in the Eifflers' pasture, south of the road, the one Uncle said had been a council elm since Indian times. The Eifflers' elm stood alone through all the stages of decay. Branches larger and larger broke and fell until only the insect-infested gray trunk and six or seven large arms remained, so awful they begged to be cut.

A logger approached Uncle Gaylon and Daddy about the Marty farm woods and made an offer to harvest the mature trees — fifty hardwoods, elm as well as maple, oak, and basswood — before disease and old age wasted them. The cows no longer pastured, they ate monitored portions of corn and hay in the bunk feeder by the barn, so the cow paths through the sixty acres of woods were closing up with brush anyway. Best to get some cash value before access disappeared. Working from the middle to the edges, the logger took the trunks and left a diminished profile of trees on the rise north of the fields. He left the old tops too, an impassable tangle of dying branches that sealed it all shut.

One by one, the sons left the farm. The twins finished college degrees and got married — Bruce and Jeri in a big Christmas wedding at First Lutheran in Rush City; Blaine and Sandy in an even bigger summer wedding at Our Redeemer Lutheran in Pine City, followed by a dance. Blaine and Bruce both got good agriculture jobs, Blaine in Wisconsin and Bruce in Iowa. With such good prospects, it didn't seem likely they would return.

Jonathan started Bible college in 1983. Steven got accepted at the University of Minnesota in 1985, but he hated it. He didn't want to farm either, so he settled into factory work in town for a regular paycheck — anything was preferable to manure, he said with a laugh, and a town job left evenings free to play softball and socialize.

Carolyn was the last one home, scheduled to graduate with the class of '89, a top student in jazz band and choir, an athlete in the world of Title IX that opened sports to girls.

I was the second to marry, first to have a baby. Patrick was another student renter in the house where I lived the winter after I returned from Tunis. He played his guitar unplugged in the basement when he got home from his night job. I woke on dark mornings to his soft, bending, sliding notes resonating in the floorboards, straight-ahead rhythm and chords like gospel.

When I brought him to the farm, everybody was shocked. They hadn't expected a red-blond, long-haired city boy. But he played hard basketball with the twins, entertained Steven's cat, spoke respectfully to Daddy, and was kind to my cousins. He was accepted by Uncle Gaylon because he preferred tea to coffee and could talk about history, from glaciers to Guam; by Grampa Anderson because he listened with interest to talk about politics, labor, and the history of Rock Creek. He talked with Mom and Auntie Lou about Emmylou Harris and Hank Williams, and asked Mom if she would please play her guitar — but it had gone missing. She'd lent it to someone and never got it back.

Patrick was a Minneapolis southsider for whom crossing the Mississippi to the east side meant leaving the Louisiana Purchase for the Old World. But we stayed by the river in northeast Minneapolis because of the low rent. We walked and biked and bused to jobs until we had a baby girl we named Susanna Claire and got a car. In the winter, we moved to a bigger apartment nearby, upstairs and full of light, with a long porch along the front where Patrick could practice guitar.

We soon learned that the apartment was full of light because the landlord of the apartments next door had cut down the grove of trees that once shaded our building. He was tired, he said, of cleaning up the mess the trees made in his parking lot. In truth, he and our landlord had a falling out, and he knew the summer sun on the southwest side of our old house would turn it into a furnace. The woman downstairs who had thrown pots in the shady driveway gave her notice and moved.

I worked in a university office, and Patrick worked in a warehouse. Every morning, Claire woke easily with us, ate cheerfully, allowed me to strap her into her car seat, and accompanied me across the Mississippi, down Bloomington Avenue, past Powderhorn Park to Shari's daycare house before I headed to campus. At four-thirty, I drove back through the streets full of kids of all colors to pick her up, and we rode home together, naming the cars and trucks, the downtown skyline, and the colors of the sky. On the dark winter drives, she found the moon — old moon in the mornings in the east, new moon in the evenings in the west.

I started going back to the farm because of Claire. At first, I went because I was nursing, and the presence of the cows was comforting. None of my friends or coworkers had young children, and neither Mom nor Auntie Lou had nursed their babies — they thought it was old-fashioned — but I could ask Daddy questions about dairy that indirectly informed me and made me feel normal. Claire reminded me of a headstrong little heifer calf.

I kept going back because I was exhausted from office work, hot and desperate for shade trees when summer came, and I didn't know how to be a mother without a bigger family around me, without space to let my girl run.

Claire rode behind me in her car seat, on the side opposite the sun. In the rearview mirror, I could see the wind blowing her blond hair as she squinted into the landscape—Minneapolis, St. Anthony, Roseville, Arden Hills, Lino Lakes . . . then fields began to appear . . . hay, corn, soybeans, a sod farm, tree farms, a dairy pasture, red barns of metal then wood, silos of gray cement and blue metal.

"Horse," Claire said, and a few minutes later, "Cows."

"Water," she called a lake.

We would drive for an hour north on I-35, and she wouldn't nap. The sky was pale blue with clouds like clots of pulled cotton. Our legs stuck to the seats. At the Rush City exit, Claire became animated, looking for the giant walleye by the gas station.

"Fish," she said, pointing.

I turned east, parallel to the creek, past Kinger's mall and the still-new Baptist church, the fairgrounds, and the hospital, through the old downtown to old Highway 61, the Grant House hotel and café on the corner. Then north, three miles to the Pine County line. To the left across the fields we could see the Marty farm between fence lines of trees before we reached our next turn. Then west, over the tracks— hardly a train anymore—down the gravel road, past cornfields and hayfields to the oasis of barns, cement silos, houses, and trees. A cloud of dust rose behind the car, nudged north by a breeze carrying the whir and warble of a redwing, the piercing cry of a killdeer.

Claire craned to see the farm. When we pulled into the driveway, strange without the welcoming elm, I felt the familiar reverberation of the engine sound against the house and smelled the faint reflected odor of gasoline before we rounded the house and entered the space of the yard. I stopped the car, sat back for a few seconds to absorb the silence, then began to hear the birds.

"Mama," said Claire, "Mama, out, please."

I unbuckled her and set her down on the grassy triangle north of the house. She toddled away on her baby legs, a distance she thought dangerously far, turning to see my expression, waiting for me to follow. My mother came out of the house and pulled deadheads off impatiens as Claire worked her way back to us, let her gramma scoop her up, and sighed happily.

Coming out of the house behind Mom, Daddy brightened to see us. Even Uncle's anxious face eased a little, coming out of his house, heading to the field.

"Hi!" Claire called to one and then the other.

"Hi there!" they called back.

She pointed to the sky, arched her back, grinned foolishly, and yelled, "Kye!" then fell down on the grass.

Daddy and Uncle laughed, as she wanted them to.

"Sky," Daddy said.

"That's right, that's the sky," Uncle repeated. "Big sky with clouds!"

"Clouds," she said carefully, getting up and throwing her head back again. Suddenly she pointed toward the barns. "Cows in there?"

"No, the cows are outside," Uncle said, enunciating clearly.

There was a lot to do and not many hands to do it, so they didn't pause too long. Uncle's smile faded and creases returned to his forehead as he walked, gaze lowered, toward the barn.

On a blanket from the car, I lay down in the shade of the basswood tree that had grown up outside the dining room window, now shading my old bedroom window. Claire lay down beside me, looking at clouds.

The farm was more than a hundred years old, waiting for the next generation. It was quieter just because the twins were gone. Sometimes I heard Carolyn's sax or piano. In the early afternoon, Auntie came home from her job at the nursing home; Mom came home from work by five-thirty. Grampa lived alone in the trailer house, but the sawmill at his home place kept him busy during the day and he ate at Mom's table almost every night.

Daddy and Uncle's aggravation and exhaustion far surpassed anything I experienced—I saw it with my own eyes now. A lifetime of twice-a-day milking and field work had worn them down, body and spirit. Daddy walked more slowly, and Uncle's temper was shorter, his moods more despairing. The Marty brothers had followed expert advice for feeding and breeding. They'd built a third silo for corn. But no matter what they tried, the herd started by Jacob, built up by Sam and John and Daddy and Uncle, couldn't seem to reach the production level of other farmers' herds. Our big black and white Holsteins stood in the barn, ate hay, drank water, avoided the shock of the electric trainers above their backs, lay down, stood still for a pipeline milker to be attached twice a day, and yielded an average of sixty pounds of milk a day.

The demands of dairy were too great. A young son with energy and patience could probably do better, but the work wasn't the only thing crushing them. The farm had debt too, and they dreaded passing it on.

One day that September, when Uncle Gaylon saw my car in the driveway, he walked over carrying a parchment-colored flyer from the state fair.

"You have a degree in journalism, isn't that right?" he asked. I smiled. "Then you should be able to help me with this." He laid the flyer on the picnic table. "They're publishing a book of century farms in Minnesota, and since our farm was a hundred years old in 1981, I thought you could help figure out what to write."

"Sure," I said. I scanned for a word count. "What picture would you like?"

"I'm not sure. What do you think?" he asked. "We've got those aerial pictures of the farm, of course."

"Something historic, I think," I said.

"Well, you could come take a look at a picture I found in the attic," he said. "It was in a frame, but covered up by another picture from a calendar or something."

I followed him across the yard to the front of the big house and inside the porch, where he pointed to it, hanging high on the wall.

There was the big house when it was new, the whole family arranged in a loose line in front of it: thin Jacob standing feet apart with hat in one hand; little Anna the size of Claire pressed shyly against Susanna's long skirt; pretty Lizzie and Minnie with hands on their slim hips; young Sam and John posing like their father.

"What year do you think that was?" Uncle asked me, and I could tell it was a quiz, like when he tested me about bird calls.

"Nineteen-hundred," I said. "It has to be. Anna was born in 1897, and they took the picture for the turn of the century."

"That's exactly what I was thinking," Uncle grinned. "Exactly."

"What's the building over there behind it," I asked, "where our house is now?"

"I don't know!" he exclaimed. "The only thing I can think of is the cabin."

"That sure isn't where you and Dad thought it was!" I said. He let out a peel of laughter as I peered at the ghostly structure.

Together, we drafted a history of essential events, pared it to three hundred words, and sent it in by the deadline.

The summer Claire turned two, I took my week of vacation at the farm. She ran in the clover field east of the house until she could barely see me over a crest, then waited. Daddy flew a kite with her in the same field. Where the old sandbox used to be next to the little white pump house, he made a new one from a tractor tire. Claire gathered sticks and small stones, asked questions, walked with him in her corduroys to the barn to pet the cows and cats, walked before the mangers and counted black and white heads, asked for the cows' names and then repeated them—Dixie, Dana, Denise, Chloe, Chris, Colleen—lifted feed to their mouths, walked in rhythm to their milking, squatted down by the milk bowl to pat cats' heads as they drank.

"Grampa, I need a swing out here," she said, standing outside the kitchen door. He made her one on the basswood, which had grown as thick as she was.

Every night after Mom came home from work, she and Claire had long conversations. Mom measured her to sew new dresses, and they did projects in the kitchen.

I walked to the barn to visit, to wash a cow's udder with grown-up tenderness and feel her warm flank with my forehead. The new barn was no longer white; it was twenty-two years old, dented and marred, full of cobwebs in corners.

Daddy told me the day was cool enough that the cows would stay in the barn all night after milking rather than going through the work of letting them out and back in again. Uncle Gaylon had broken more than one cow's tail in frustration, trying to get them into and out of the barn, into the right stanchion, holding them still for treatment of some malady. They left the barn now only to stand in the barnyard and eat from the bunk feeder. Youngstock grazed in the near pasture. The painstaking work and cost of fencing around the woods and fields wasn't worthwhile.

"Show me the feeder," I said.

Daddy walked with me to the west doors of the barn and pointed out the machinery in the all-dirt barnyard, described how the cows ate carefully measured portions from a trough beside the water tank. A machine extracted contents of the silos and distributed it into that narrow trough.

"These cows probably couldn't find their way back from the woods anymore, anyway," Daddy said. "We've bred the brains right out of them, that's my theory."

He pointed across the fields. Clyde, their neighbor to the north, had expanded his farm. A new wing extended south of his red barn on the hill, more silos for more corn and hay. Despite his age, Clyde seemed to have more energy than Uncle and Daddy combined. He'd installed a carousel parlor, everything difficult was automated, and he was buying and renting more land than ever.

In our old barn, I opened the door to the stanchion room, empty of youngstock, dusty with the smell of old hay and old wood. Late-afternoon sunlight filtered through the quarter-pane windows and cobwebs.

Behind the barn that night, after milking was over, I drove the truck for the hay rope as the men put bales in the mow. Bugs swarmed in the headlights as we emptied racks they had filled all day.

The nights were not quiet. They had never seemed so loud to me as they were now on the farm. The traffic noise of the freeway a mile west seemed like nothing, only a thin backdrop of sound. It was the crickets in the neighbor's wetland that were loud, and the night birds squawking unexpectedly in our ditches and grass, the bats sending clicks that echoed above the lawn, and the insects whirring against the screen.

One afternoon, I hayed with Uncle Gaylon. The smell and color and weight of the hay still affected him, gave him peace as it acquiesced to machinery and the hay mow of the old barn, safe from the elements. He was happy because I hadn't lost the hang of it—I still started and stopped smoothly, turned corners perfectly, and cleaned the field of every precious remnant.

That was the summer Jonathan gave the farm his best shot for a month, while Uncle Gaylon and Auntie Lou went on vacation for their twenty-fifth wedding anniversary. Twice, cows kicked him in the back, but the real kick was financial. The farm credit association told him he could not buy out even half of the Marty brothers because interest rates were so high and farm economics so bad everywhere.

Even with all those sons, the Marty brothers were stuck. Neither partner could risk trying to buy out the other—they had been in debt since building the last silo, and the value of the land had plummeted from just a few years ago. None of the sons had the equity to buy out a partner either, and interest rates were still in the double digits. Uncle and Daddy didn't want to saddle a son with debt, and they wanted all their sons to get the college education they didn't have.

No one had the optimism or drive to think of something out of the mainstream. Daddy had lost heart and had no vision for the farm. Uncle Gaylon had a vision, but it didn't include milking. The number of dairy cows in the United States had peaked during World War II at more than 25 million, when each cow gave less than 5,000 pounds of milk a year. Forty years later, each cow's yearly output had more than doubled. From far fewer cows and far fewer farms, more milk than ever flowed from plantation-sized farms. The market was glutted with dairy, and small farmers couldn't compete with newer and bigger farms milking hundreds of cows.

When a federal program was announced—*government dairy buyout*—it seemed like an answer to prayer. It was a chance to sell the cows for a fair price, to get out of dairy and out of debt.

Uncle Gaylon and Auntie Lou went to a meeting where they submitted the farm's numbers for analysis, and the outlook was as grim as they'd expected. They discussed options with Daddy and Mom and talked to their sons. If they made a bid and it was accepted, they would receive installment payments spread over five years for the value of the herd. For five years, the barn and other outbuildings could not be used for dairy by anyone. For five years, they would make a transition—Daddy and Uncle would retrain themselves for the rest of their working lives.

The sons were unanimous—none of them wanted to milk cows. Bruce and Blaine had advanced in their jobs, selling chemicals and perfectly balanced livestock feeds to farmers who were staying competitive. Bruce and Jeri had a new son, and Blaine and his wife were expecting a baby in the spring. Jonathan was finishing school at Northwestern College in Roseville and had a job in medical supplies. Steven said he'd do anything but shovel shit.

"What about the land?" I asked when, in February, Mom explained this to me.

"We're getting out of debt," she said, "we're not selling the land."

"We're not selling the land," Daddy repeated when I visited. "We're not thinking of that."

It was an easy decision. Nearly 40,000 farms submitted bids, and nearly 14,000 were accepted, ours among them. A government representative came to the farm, branded every head of cattle with a red chemical X, and set the shipping date for Memorial Day 1986, the last Monday in May.

I drove up with Claire to watch the cows go. She was not yet three, and I explained to her in the simplest terms what would happen and why it must. I didn't know what to expect myself, but felt compelled to see it with my own eyes. My family's dairy was a century old, this was a federal program, and I was trained as a journalist.

We had 130 head of cattle, a little more than a third of them milking, the rest heifers and calves. At midafternoon, the metal double trailer backed up to a door on the south side of the white barn—a door the cows had never used—and all the other doors were closed. The trucker, his hired man, and a half-grown son dropped slatted ramps in place. Claire and I sat on a hay bale pushed against the door at the east end. Uncle Gaylon smiled and waved at us. It was the last time he would drive cows in or out of this barn. I had worried about his emotions, but saw now that they could be only happiness and relief. Daddy came down to make sure we were okay and showed us the door we should use in case cows started running toward our end.

The cows shifted in their stanchions while the trucker surveyed the barn and made a strategy with Daddy and Uncle, the hired man, and the boy. The cows must back out of their stanchions into the central walk, be guided up the aisle to the milk house, turn past the milk house door, then go out and up the slatted ramp single file into the truck.

The cows near the open door went first. They were gentle anyway, easily led, responsive to the cattle prods the trucker and his hired man used. But the herd was tense, and when one cow hesitated—she looked confused and began to turn around—the trucker yelled *Haaah!* and slapped her on the hip bone, and then the next cow and the next began to bolt. There was a snarl of cows on the walk, some slipped and stood stunned with one or two legs in the gutter until shocked by the prod to bolt out again.

"Poor cows," Claire said. She couldn't distinguish a stick from a cattle prod, but it didn't matter.

"We used to have a good dog who helped do this. That was a lot easier, but it was a long time ago."

A few cows bellowed, some lowed anxiously. I was long past nursing but my breasts ached. If I'd been the type to admit this to Daddy, he would have smiled, shaken his head, and told me that's why he loved me—because I felt so deeply, because everything to me was physical. But he or Uncle would also quote to me from Genesis: *And God said, Let us make man in our image, after our likeness: and let them have dominion over the fish of the sea, and over the fowl of the air, and over the cattle, and over all the earth, and over every creeping thing that creepeth upon the earth.*

The trucker's son stood in front of the cows, opened stanchions one at a time, and scared each bewildered cow so she backed out, and turned, sometimes so nervous she slipped a hind leg into the gutter. One by one the stalls emptied beneath the bent and uneven name plaques and trainers, covered with dust and fly specks like everything else.

"Where will the cows go, Mama?" Claire asked for the third time.

"They'll go to town."

"Why?"

"Because there's too much milk." I looked at her smooth round face, her white-blond hair and clear blue eyes. She looked at me for a moment, unconvinced, then turned back to the cows.

Another cow slipped and both back legs went in the gutter. She stopped as though stunned, reason enough for Uncle to whoop and whack her on the head. Dazed, she lurched and turned, a front leg slipped down, then she heaved herself out, scuttling on the now slippery walk.

"Why are they hitting the cows?"

"I don't agree with it, I think it's wrong and unnecessary," I said. "But I'm sure they think it makes the cows go faster."

The next cow, shaken by the commotion of the cow beside her, also slipped into the gutter, leaped out as Uncle yelled, and careened off into the aisle toward the old barn, which was blocked. She found herself stuck in front of the manger, facing the boy.

"You dumb sucker!" Uncle cursed, cutting between two stanchions to emerge in front of her and beat her broad nose with an old rubber teat cup. In a cartoon, it could be funny and I felt the urge to laugh except

I was aching and recognized that it must really be an urge to cry, seeing the side of Uncle I had only glimpsed, had never wanted to know.

After a few seconds, the cow managed to back out of the dead-end walkway and lurch off in another direction.

Uncle and Daddy were both anxious to be done with this — they had lived with the rhythm of milking since they were born, oriented toward the barn under the north star, toward that pulsating sound, the cycle of seasons eclipsed by the monotony of two milkings a day, five-thirty in the morning, five-thirty in the afternoon, day after day after day, an iron framework to which all other things in their lives must conform: sleeping, waking, eating, public lives, family lives, and the private lives of making love and marriage. Those twin moorings, milking morning and evening, once a framework for communities, had become an anachronism, an aberration, an alienation from community, children, wives. The lines on their faces were deeper than ever, their joints not as supple, their movements not as smooth.

A cow that wouldn't budge out of her stanchion took a shock to her nose from the trucker's prod and bolted backward into the gutter. She scrambled to lift her heavy black body out, and slipped again.

"Come on," Daddy urged her. Even frustrated, he was rarely loud, never hysterical. The cow paused, heaved herself out, and turned around, away from the door.

"The cows don't want to go, do they, Mom?" Claire said.

"No . . . they've never been out that door before, or in a truck."

"And they're nervous?" It was a big word for her. I nodded.

The barn was still about a third full of cows in the late afternoon light, which fell in a shaft from the windows on the west end.

I was sure there was a better way to do this, faster and quieter, but maybe they had to do it this way, yell and exert themselves, release some of those years of their own tension and resentment and guilt — guilt for being the ones who didn't continue.

"D'you want to go outside?" I asked Claire.

"Yeah," she said immediately, the anxiety leaving her face as she slid off the hay bale. I stood by the door on the east end while she went around to pet the cow in the last stanchion one more time, the black and white face with large, liquid eyes. But the cow flinched and banged the stanchion loudly. Claire looked at me startled, as if she might cry.

"She's just nervous, it's not you," I said. "Come on."

She ran back to my side and we slipped out the east door as Uncle bellowed again.

"He shouldn't yell like that," Claire said.

"You're right," I agreed.

The truck didn't leave until after the sun set and the sky streaked with orange. It contained by then all the calves and heifers from the old barn and the barnyard as well. Claire and I stood by the house that was once mine, Auntie came out of hers, and we watched the truck move out slowly from Uncle's driveway in the widest turn it could manage.

Daddy and Uncle emerged from the barn smiling. Daddy looked tired, Uncle shook his head. He held up his arms and broke into a smile.

"It's over," he said, "it's over."

The truck moved down the road away from the farm, shifting and shifting again, crawled up the grade of the railroad crossing, paused, then turned south on Highway 61.

Claire and I walked to the barn to see it empty, but we didn't walk through because it was too much of a mess, manure all over the walks and aisles from all that slipping in the gutter.

We stood outside, on the hill between the old barn and the milk house where the log barn used to stand, under the darkening sky as the first stars appeared.

"This is where the first barn was," I said. "The log barn. And where Grampa and Gramma's house is now," I pointed, "there was the log cabin where Susanna lived."

Claire looked skeptical, but took my hand.

"Susanna, who my first name is after?"

"Yes."

"Susanna," she repeated. "Did she have cows?"

"Yes, she did."

"Was she kind to them?"

"I am sure of it."

There was a lull that summer, a respite, time to think and regain balance and health. A decision had been made and carried out.

Daddy and Uncle bought thirty head of low-maintenance beef cattle, although beef prices dropped and cattlemen complained because dairymen across the country were doing the same thing. The Marty brothers kept growing hay and corn and filling the silos to feed their beef instead of dairy cattle, splitting the work along new lines that didn't include milking. Field work was released from the bounds of twice-a-day milking.

Five years, three payments, and they had to find a way to support themselves.

Mom got information about classes and Daddy took them—basic electrical, and an exam for a boiler's license. He found jobs in janitorial and then maintenance, evenings and weekend hours, changing when he was laid off or better hours became available somewhere else, at the nursing home and technical school in Pine City, then at the nursing home in Rush City.

Uncle Gaylon took care of the beef cattle and got a rural paper route. He drove the gravel roads at night, watching the moon, navigating patches of fog, counting deer, skunk, and raccoon. When school started, he became a full-time fan of Carolyn at volleyball and basketball games and concerts.

In the afternoons, driving through the Powderhorn neighborhood on my way to pick up Claire, I watched carefully for children along Bloomington and Cedar. They were American Indian kids mostly, some not much more than a year old, many watched by kids not much older, pedaling on metal trikes and plastic tractors. Their hair was black, their eyes seemed huge and piercing when they turned to look in my direction, looked into cars, looked at the drivers. On those afternoons, I began to have flashbacks of first grade, of sitting behind a child with that hair, with that skin, and of Miss Gilbert's voice, raised as it almost never was, her face toward me but speaking to that child in front of me, who wouldn't speak—*Ozzie*. She wrote a giant Z on the board—*worse than F*—the chalk crumbled, and he disappeared forever that summer. I wondered where he was now, if he made it, if he ended up here in Minneapolis too, if these could be his children or nieces or nephews. My cheeks burned.

At the farm, Grampa Anderson was dying. He'd had all the transfusions he could stand, his bone marrow no longer made red blood cells, but no one would name what he had. He was just worn out. He made arrangements with Mom. "Let's not prolong this," he said, and she put a bed on the front porch of her house, where he lay, slipping in and out of dreams through the days and nights of July. A hospice nurse came once a day, he stopped taking food, and while Mom and Auntie worked in town, Uncle and Daddy took turns checking on him, bringing him water, turning him gently. One morning, they both came at the same time. Uncle turned him, and then they paused in the kitchen to plot the day. When Daddy went back one more time with water, Grampa had died.

Two weeks before my son was born in Minneapolis, Grampa was laid in the ground at the Lutheran cemetery next to Gramma, ten yards from the Martys, in humid heat, tree frogs buzzing like the saw of his mill.

Nearly a million cows and more than half a million heifers and calves went to slaughter in the dairy buyout authorized by the Farm Bill of 1985. The supply of milk went down and prices for the farmers who remained went up for awhile. Dairy farms were moving south and getting bigger. New barns had canvas walls that could be opened in summer. Cows were put into stanchions only to be milked, and new multilevel designs meant an end to all that human bending and stooping and lifting. Manure was stored in underground containers until it was needed, spread as fertilizer in efficient treatments. With the help of a new hormone, farmers increased cows' milk output from 12,000 pounds to 15,000 pounds a year, and it was still going up. Cows were milked three times a day instead of two, and lived four or five years. New wage jobs attracted the unskilled to around-the-clock shift work.

When I went back to work after William's birth, Patrick quit his Minneapolis warehouse job to take care of the kids during the day. He bought all the groceries—milk without hormones, produce as fresh and unprocessed as we could afford and from farms as local as possible. He told me about small farmers who were trying new things, combining traditional lives with modern methods and thinking.

The summer William turned one and Claire turned five, drought struck the Midwest—more than forty days of temperatures above ninety, and weeks without rain. Our upstairs apartment full of light was too hot to sleep in and I was filled with rage toward the landlord west of us who'd cut down our shady basswoods. I dreamed of confronting him, and then woke from nightmares of axes and chopping.

William lay awake in his crib. When I opened my eyes, he was watching me, face tan and glistening.

We looked for apartments but bought a house instead, with a loan for first-time home buyers. The house stood on a forty-foot lot a little farther upriver from St. Anthony Falls, close to the school where Claire was assigned to go in the fall. It looked to me like a two-story farmhouse in a forest of houses instead of trees. It faced east, with a white birch in front and an old elm in back that spread its shady arms over the roof and brick driveway all hours of the afternoon. On the alley, a white picket fence enclosed a small garden with irises and peonies, strawberries, raspberries, and rhubarb. We moved in October when the leaves were gold.

After twenty years at Plastech and a professional-secretary certification she had studied years to earn, Mom went to work at a printing company in St. Paul. When I stopped to pick her up one day for lunch, I heard the executive yelling on the phone as she emerged from an adjoining office in a cream-colored linen skirt, mint-green linen blouse, cream-colored heels, and matching purse. She was still a perfectionist, a fast and thorough worker, a voice of graciousness, calmness, and competency. She could tolerate his temper and the commute, having increased her income by half.

She turned fifty in September, Daddy worked evenings, her children had left home, her father departed from her supper table—his small payroll and tax computation gone from her list of things to do. She fixed her eyes on the future and worked feverishly, determined to plan and put money in the bank.

"I'm thinking about buying a condo," she told me, salad poised on her fork, "something I can sell in a few years and at least come out even. I can't stand all this money for gas, and the *time* I'm wasting on the road."

"I couldn't commute," I said.

"Anyway," she went on, "you *know* I've always wanted to live somewhere else in my life."

"Somewhere other than Route 2, Rush City, 55069," I said.

"Yes—you know I have, even if it's only a few years."

She fixed her green eyes on me. "I'm so glad I did this. I hope you understand. I'm sure the people in Rush City think I've gone completely nuts. Poor Daddy."

"He understands, though."

"Yes, he does," she said. "You know, Clyde has expressed interest in buying the land—we may not live on the farm forever."

She took another bite, but I stopped.

"Wait," I said. "It can't be used for dairy for five years. He'd use it for dairy, wouldn't he?"

"After five years it doesn't matter what it's used for. If we have an offer, we can sell it."

"You would sell it?"

She waved her fork. "He hasn't made an offer—anyway, that's two years away."

I talked with Patrick, then wrote a letter:

Dear Dad and Mom, Uncle and Auntie . . . Please don't pass me by because I am a daughter—and Carolyn is still so young . . . Before you seriously entertain an offer to buy any part of the farm, please give us the information we would need to make a competing offer. We need to know, even if it's hopelessly out of our reach.

I would like to see the maps again, to know how much you need per acre, the condition of the soil in different fields, the ideas you've had for different things to grow on it. I myself would like to declare my interests and hear my brothers' and my cousins'.

I would like to know the impact of selling it. What would the buyer do with it? If the buyer can't buy now, would you lose that offer for good? What are the benefits of selling now rather than continuing to let it for rent? What do you need from the sale and for your retirement? Please don't assume our feelings or abilities . . .

Daddy mentioned it to me once. "Gaylon couldn't bear to sell it," he said. "He says he will die in that house."

※ ※

Clyde's offer came in the winter of 1991, as the five-year anniversary of our farm's government dairy buyout contract neared. He was prepared to buy the Marty land and outbuildings—a little more than two hundred acres of fields and woods, two barns, three silos, a good pole shed, and assorted other outbuildings—all for just two-and-a-half times the price of our little city house. He would pay a little less than a quarter down in June, and the remainder in five installments.

He wasn't interested in the two narrow fields between the railroad tracks and old Highway 61, which were too small for his equipment.

Not included were the two houses on the island of lawn, or the orchard and windbreak west of them. But, he stated, he would take an option to buy Mom and Daddy's house if they decided not to retire there.

The two hundred acres of Anderson land, a mile away, would remain in our family.

I didn't know who among the partners talked to whom—whether Daddy and Mom and Uncle and Auntie all met, or whether Daddy and Uncle talked separately from Mom and Auntie Lou.

Mom called Blaine and Bruce to talk through the offer. They were experts, working successfully in agribusiness. And she talked to Steven, and Auntie and Uncle talked through it with Jonathan.

Carolyn and I were told the news by our mothers. They were relieved, Mom explained, that they could sell to a good neighbor and a good farmer. And they were lucky to be able to sell to a dairy farmer for whom the buildings had the most value.

"We'll still have the Anderson land," she said quickly. "That's better land anyway."

"By whose standard?" I asked.

"It's better farmland—my Dad always said so, and Gaylon and Daddy and the boys agree," she said. "And for hunting, the boys can still hunt in Grampa's woods. They say that's all they really care about."

"Can't we meet? Can't we all talk about this?"

"I don't know what there is to talk about," she said. "We've agreed, unless you and Patrick want to make an offer."

"Mom, this is our family's farm, can't we *meet*?"

"I am not meeting with Gaylon and Lorraine and their children," she said flatly. "I consider our decisions private."

Patrick and I talked in our city kitchen at night, and later I lay awake, looking at the winter sky through the bare branches of our elm in the light from the alley. Patrick admitted he was scared of farm machinery. Patrick, who grew up on Minnehaha Creek and the Mississippi River, who as a boy rode his bicycle thirty miles to the St. Croix just to feel the watersheds, who spent summers in northern Arkansas with his grandparents, who was elated by shoveling snow, exhilarated by labor. Fifty years ago, he would have been a farmer, I was sure of it. He was as strong as any of the men in my family, and I was durable.

"Isn't it too open?" he pressed me. "Between the freeway and the highway, with the railroad going through it . . . wouldn't we want something more private, more out of the way?"

"No," I said. "There's plenty of gravel road between that farm and the highway. And I love it because it *is* public — it's a public farm, it's visible, it's beautiful. From the highway you see the spread of land, those stripes and blocks of color. As you drive past, you can see across those fields — you can see a white house, a red barn built at an angle, just so. They built that barn so you could *see it from the tracks,* from the *road.* Jacob chose that place because of *public access* and because it had *everything:* wood, pasture, wetland, and land high enough to clear into fields. Everyone knows where we live. Our farm is easy to see, easy to find. I am proud of it, proud that I come from that place."

"Gayla," he said, "it's too big for us. Think. What would we do with those barns?"

The barns — *the old barn.*

I felt panic in my chest.

Bruce and Blaine were good at sales and had won raises, promotions, and prizes. Three years earlier, Bruce negotiated with his company for a transfer from Iowa to Minnesota, but then a competitor hired him into Wisconsin, twenty miles from Blaine. Now they drove across the countryside calling on the same farmers, who could tell them apart by their styles. Bruce, who loved animals with tenderness and skill, sold seed corn for rolling farmland, made friendships with his dealers, and hosted milk-can suppers. Blaine, who loved field work, sold feed for cattle, hogs, and poultry, and was all business, closing sales, no time wasted.

Steven had landed a union job at the flour mill in Rush City.

Although they had already made up their minds about the Marty farm, they consented to meet for my sake. Bruce called me back to find out my goals for the meeting. He took notes of our conversation and sent me a copy. The week of Daddy's birthday in March, we gathered in the cold fireplace room in the basement of Rush City Baptist Church. Blaine brought his flip chart, and Mom brought copies of a typed list:

annual costs
Real estate taxes on our house and all the home farmland: $1600
Taxes, house alone: $400
Insurance (fire, windstorm, liability): $1400

monthly costs
Heating fuel, our house: $150
Electricity: $100

necessary improvements
New well: $2500 (1/2 of $5000)
Sewer changeover (to mound type): $3500
Electrical changeover: $500
New roof 1963 barn: _____

She also brought a breakdown of Clyde's offer—the total over five years, the down payment, the five years of interest. The Marty brothers would ask for rights to cut firewood.

Steven wanted to make it clear: He had a job at the mill in town now, and two sons. He didn't want the Marty farm. All he wanted was five acres on the Anderson land, north and east of the creek, to build his own house. Whatever Mom and Dad wanted to do was fine with him.

Blaine agreed, that it was Mom and Dad's prerogative to do whatever they wanted to ensure their retirement, and he would not interfere with that. He thought the offer was great and they should take it.

Bruce said he felt bad. He'd loved the Marty farm, he'd thought seriously about farming it, but farming was probably unrealistic. He had a good job now and would be crazy to leave it. And he loved the Anderson land more; it was probably better land, and he just liked how it looked, with the woods and the creek.

"What about Jon?" I asked.

"He's already decided he's not going to farm," Bruce said. "I've talked to him too."

"What about you and Patrick?" Mom asked.

"I thought . . . I expected," I began. "I thought you and Dad might depend on me in your last years, as your parents depended on you."

But as I said it, I realized that I was the one who had fallen short of what was expected — the child with no better income or aspirations than a farm might provide. Raised in the comfort that the farm had provided me, I was unmotivated by material things and now had nothing they needed.

"Honestly," Patrick said, his eyes grave, apologetic, "for me, for us, it's too big."

"Would you just want to live in our house?" Daddy asked.

"No," I said, emphatically, "it is a *whole farm* — the lines of it, the woods, the fields, the tracks, the road, the pastures, the orchard, the barns and houses together — they make a whole. It's the scale of it, and it can't be taken apart."

Did I really want the whole farm or nothing? I couldn't imagine living in the house cut off from the fields, a torn corner of a quilt, a head separated from its body, a tiny domestic island in a sea of a single crop. I imagined the nine fields made into one, assaulted by ever bigger and louder machinery, ever more sprays to treat weeds and pests, watching what I was sure would be a monotonous decline over the rest of my life.

It was not just a month or a year too late. It was too late in 1963 when the new barn was built and we gave up everything but dairy. I loved an old farm, a farm that no longer existed.

Riding home, I cried with rage and grief. For many nights, I woke up in the darkness, crying, exhausted, looking down on my own bowed head in a bed on the second floor of a house that was not my home in the middle of Minneapolis. I felt unmoored, wandering, and found no consolation in my husband's arms. The farm was my home, the place I'd always counted on, my refuge and comfort, the anchor I'd needed to raise children. I was angry at myself for taking it for granted and marrying a man my family didn't have the confidence could farm. I was angry at the sons for evading the responsibility of their birthright, angry at our parents for discounting Carolyn and me, ignoring us, requiring less of us and pretending it was equal, telling us we were lucky, we had no obligation to stay. We daughters stood on the sidelines of this playing field, unqualified, ineligible, as a century of our forefathers' and foremothers' intention and labor and care went for five hundred dollars an acre.

I didn't know that Uncle Gaylon cried too, that he went to the old barn night after night, climbed into the haymow, and cried out loud, hot salty tears in the sweet-smelling cool darkness, asking God for an answer. *If the decision affected only him, he could say no, but it didn't. This could be the only offer, and he couldn't deny this chance to his brother.*

He grieved, and he asked forgiveness — from his father and mother, his uncle, his grandfather and grandmother, from God — for every way he felt he'd failed.

I sat in church, gripping the seat of the oak pew, leaning forward. I imagined I could see through the stone floor, down through the basement beneath the sanctuary, into that earth beside the river where the forest grew, into the branches of possibility.

If only I'd known. I shouldn't have married Patrick. His father's Missouri family left the land in the 1920s after cholera wiped out their hogs twice. His mother's family left northwestern Minnesota in the Great Depression. I should have married a farmer — I should have married a farm.

But I love this farm and no other—

Bruce and Blaine and Jonathan and Steven should have been helped. They should have been encouraged to farm, not just expected to work.

If we could change the past—

Uncle Gaylon and Daddy never should have continued the partnership. They should have learned more from the harrowing experience of Sam's death and Aunt Margaret's departure than the value of life insurance. They should have seen how vulnerable a partnership made the farm. When Uncle got back from the army in 1957, he should have used his training to leave the farm, or he should have taken over the farm and let Daddy leave for seminary — except Grampa was sick—

Grampa shouldn't have been sick, Sam shouldn't have died, and Mamie shouldn't have died. Sam's only son shouldn't have left—

If we could change the past—

Thomas Jefferson, envisioning the new American republic, fastened his eye on the Roman republic made immortal by Virgil, first poet of the empire. Virgil, looking back as Rome took the road to empire, saw clearly the farmers and herders upon whose backs the senators and emperors were carried. He saw Tiberius and Gaius Gracchus and all the other vilified agricultural reformers sent off to fight for Rome while their little farms were seized by landowning senators and their friends. He paid tribute in poems that read like elegies, *Eclogues* for the shepherds and migrant labor, *Georgics* for the planters.

But, Jefferson thought, what if Rome had *not* gone the route of empire — the route that paved the way for Vandals and Vikings, Anglo-Saxons and Arabs and Ottomans, Spain and Portugal, France and Britain? How could a republic be created that would remain a *republic*, the raw but real realm of the common people to which Virgil sang?

In his idealist eye, Jefferson saw the land distributed to men, created equal, in plots requiring just the labor of an owner and family to feed and support itself — no slaves necessary. The Federal Land Ordinance of 1785, based on his dream, created a grid, each square mile divided four by four into sixteen plots of forty acres each. It would be another century before the end of the slavery that supported American plantations modeled on the big farms of the Roman Empire. Forty acres and a mule, the slaves were promised at the end of the Civil War, but those few who received land in Georgia and Carolina saw it revoked within months.

In Jefferson's eye, some things were taken for granted — settlement and attachment as corollaries of ownership, the ability to be satisfied, and the ability of the land. On the grid he imagined, a mountain and plain were equal, and land that stretched beyond the forests was barely known. The nomads and indigenous were invisible, unaccounted for. Love and restlessness in the human heart were unacknowledged.

In the two hundred years since Jefferson, the number of farmers in the workforce has shrunk from more than 90 percent to less than 2 percent, while small farms grew to the size of plantations.

If we could undo the past . . .

Jacob died on a Saturday in October 1918. His obituary, "Prominent Retired Farmer Passes Away," ran on page one of the *Rush City Post*. "Deceased was a native of Switzerland," it said. It gave his date of birth, 1855, and immigration, 1880, and marriage to Susanna — *his childhood sweetheart, who had left her people and come across the ocean deep alone.*

The young couple took wild land on the site of the beautiful farm home north of Rush City in Pine County, where they both labored industriously for many years, Mr. Marty clearing the forest away and reducing the 120 acres into one of the most productive and successful farms in this section.

It was the verb *reducing* that told the story. On the eighty acres added along the tracks, where the railroad company had taken a swath of trees, Sam and John continued what their father had started and made it tillable. Yet from the severe valleys of Switzerland, they knew the value of trees. Clearing fields, they left pastures with oaks and elms. Around the house, they planted an orchard of apples and plums, nut trees and evergreens. Only half the farm was put to the plow, and the wetland preserved.

One day in May I walked with Claire around the farm that Jacob and Susanna made.

We walked up the lane, along the border of the fields, along the fence, barbed wire falling down, past the plum tree. We couldn't walk into the woods because the brush was so thick among huge treetops felled by the logger, but we followed the fence line the length of the woods, then around the bay of the field we called "east of the woods" to Applegate's—the rock pile, the Ojibwe camp where Jacob Marty traded for a horsehair blanket. On Applegate's, with its lovely, slender white trunks of a thousand birch trees growing from mossy earth, I showed Claire faded cow paths where she could disappear, step into a crease among trees like an optical illusion. We crossed a wet place and wove our way to the railroad tracks, then followed the tracks south to the road. We walked the road back to the house, looking for agates, counting birds in ditches, calling their names.

The weekend before the sale, Carolyn came home from college and accidentally burned the deed and title to the farm. She did it in a fit of cleaning while Uncle and Auntie were gone to town—the important papers were sitting in a paper bag among other paper bags, piles that looked to her like junk mail. She swept them all up, carted them out to the trash burner by the orchard, and lit it. Auntie Lou came home and grinned at the magic Carolyn had committed over the entire first floor. The mistake was not discovered until that evening, when Uncle went to take out the deed and . . . *Where was it?*

"In a flat paper bag right here," Auntie said, and looked at Carolyn, wide eyed.

"I thought that was all junk," Carolyn said.

Uncle's breath accelerated.

"No, no!" he cried.

The deed and title were redrawn, and somewhere the papers were signed. They were all in the same room, Martys and Moultons, old neighbors, though the Martys had been neighbors to others on that farm before Clyde Moulton bought it.

Forty-acre plots in the southern half of Minnesota's Range 21, Township 38, Section 33 — plots of land claimed by the United States in a treaty with the Ojibwe in 1837; plots purchased by railroad barons, prospectors named Eglehart and Rockhold and Ryan and later owned by men named Jenni, Grant, Applegate, Bergfalk, Kiley, and Monster; plots gathered by Martys over a hundred years and held together for another decade were subsumed by Clyde Moulton with strokes of pens on a day in June 1991.

The land changed hands, from the partnership of Marty Brothers — Gaylon, Gordon, Lorraine, and Margaret Marty — to Clyde Moulton.

The Anderson land got its name back. The Marty farm became an island of ten acres, two houses with garages, and the overgrown orchard. Somewhere between the houses and barns, an imaginary line had been drawn, cutting off the houses from pastures and fields and woods, joining the rest to Moultons' estate.

"The wild animals that range over Italy have their holes," Tiberius Gracchus said to the senators of the Roman republic, "and each of them has its lair and its nest, but the men who fight and die for Italy have no part in anything but the air and the sunlight."

Tiberius Gracchus had been a farmer. He was a veteran, home from fighting for Rome in Africa. His speeches, remembered and passed down, must have haunted Virgil.

"Without home or domicile, they wander over the face of the Earth with their children and their wives. When, in action, their generals exhorted them to fight for the sake of their cemeteries and sanctuaries, they were cheating them. Of all these thousands of Romans, not one has an ancestral altar or a family tomb. It is for the sake of other men's wealth and luxury that these go to wars and give their lives. They are called the lords of the World, but they have not a single clod to call their own."

Uncle Gaylon was lucky. He came home from the army, saw the farm of his family with new eyes, knew how lucky he was, how blessed, and he stayed.

In the people Rome subjugated and enslaved, it gained the labor force to work the giant farms it found in conquered Carthage, and to press into service on the expanding farms of wealthy senators at home. The small farms of Italy were seized and added to larger ones, their tillers and herders conscripted or displaced.

Tiberius proposed laws to keep land in the hands of those who planted and grazed it, and he was ridiculed and then killed for it. But he was not forgotten. For eighty years, agricultural reformers would rise up to follow him. His brother Gaius and half a dozen more would be vilified, called threats to the Roman order, and assassinated. Last was Caesar, whose popularity his enemies attributed to ego and pandering instead of the land policies he sought to change, whose murder ended the republic and launched the empire. In Plutarch's masterwork on Greek and Roman lives, he would include Tiberius Gracchus and frag-ments of his speeches.

An itinerant rabbi in another nation occupied by Rome could have heard the speeches of Tiberius. He was not a Roman soldier but recog-nized their humanity. Jesus was a witness to the reign of a god revealed to him as giver of life, transcendent of temple and place, present to the exiled and dispossessed.

I sat on the edge of the bed looking out the west-facing windows down at the garden under the elm tree — our elm tree that had not died — at the alley and crowded houses on forty-foot lots. The windows were open to the screens, there was the caw of a crow, the acceleration of a train in the rail yards by the mill two blocks east. My throat constricted, burn-ing, and my body ached. I looked over the rooftops toward the river, crying in the night surrounded by city sounds along with sounds I'd known all my life, my strong husband sleeping beside me, my daugh-ter and son in nearby rooms of this small farmhouse in Minneapolis, my space reduced.

By the rivers of Babylon, there we sat down, yea, we wept, when we remembered Zion.

These are the trees I have loved: The apple and plum trees, the butternut, the evergreens that made whishing sounds and private, good-smelling places to play, summer and winter; the elm at the head of the lane that made an arch like a green port of entry; the woods where the cows spent hot summer days, grazing down the brush and making powdery fairy-tale paths, perfect for children's feet; and the brilliant white birches on Applegate's forty, where we found hornets nests and looked for arrowheads. These are the trees that I know, that I love.

There are trees, also, whose bodies, whose trunks, form the frame of the old red barn, virgin timber from the St. Croix River valley, three miles east, cut for the summer of 1902. The builders come, and with Jacob and his sons lay a foundation along the rise running northwest to southeast, seventy feet long, thirty feet wide. The timbers are fifteen and twenty feet long, two are thirty feet, all as thick as a strong man's thigh. The peak of the barn stands thirty feet above a generous hayloft. On the ground floor, the dairy barn faces east, the horse barn faces west, and a driveway runs through the middle with sliding doors made for giants, north and south, stone floor for threshing, big enough for dancing.

The barn is painted red, and the oldest son carves his name and the date in the wood: Sam Marty, 1902. The two oldest daughters marry two of the builders and move away.

Patrick wakes, groans with sympathy, and says my name, caresses my arm.

Why do I feel pain like this and the rest of them do not? What is wrong with me?

Gaylon has felt this. Now that it's done, Daddy has told me that Uncle climbed up in the haymow and wept, raged and wept. As Daddy walked to the house in the snow, he could hear the sound of his brother crying.

We hanged our harps upon the willows in the midst thereof, For there they that carried us away captive required of us a song; and they that wasted us required of us mirth, saying, Sing us one of the songs of Zion.

How shall we sing the Lord's song in a strange land?

I join the streams and rivers of displaced souls, transient since the beginning of the world, gathering ripening things, fleeing predators, stalking prey, evading glaciers and then tracking their retreat, following trees and forests, learning to plant as we're cast out of Eden, grazing flocks, fleeing famine or slavery, dreaming of fame or wealth, seized in war, taking refuge from enemies and conquerors, seeking shelter or water or opportunity, seeking love.

Why do we love places at all when we must continually leave them? Why do we trouble to make homes and farms with the illusion that they will endure and be holy? Or is every place holy, drawing us to itself, to care for creation?

Patrick's acoustic guitar, made in St. Paul, has a rosewood body with a spruce top and mahogany neck. It looks and sounds like honey. His solid-body electric is made of mahogany from a South American rain forest.

I am waking, hearing music beneath me — the sound of Mom's guitar — but in Minneapolis, the sound of crying.

I had been looking for a place, a habitat, to raise my children. There were times I came close to saying yes, one time I said yes and then quickly *No, I can't wait for you* — some part of me knew it was a *place*, not just a mate, that I sought. Patrick offered it, Patrick who loved and knew Minneapolis, a place adjacent to my birthplace, which I had left, displaced as women have always been displaced. Patrick offered me a habitat, an urban one, on a river connected to the world, and a song. He sang his heart out like a red-winged blackbird, *My place, choose my place.*

As the night begins to fade, the mourning dove coos in the pine tree across the alley. I lie back in my bed under the sheltering elm tree, exhausted from crying and half-sleep.

If I forget thee, O Jerusalem, let my right hand forget her cunning.

The sun lights up the back of the white house across the alley, reflects brilliant white, as Uncle and Auntie and Gramma's house reflected on my bedroom window at the farm. I wake from the bright light, my eyes hurt, my mouth is dry.

If I do not remember thee, let my tongue cleave to the roof of my mouth.

Pine

Our farm lay at the southern edge of Pine County. Five white pines stood on the front lawn, shading the big house. They were the only pines on the Marty farm, but there they were, announcing the county border.

In spring, the soft-looking sprays of four-inch needles sprouted with yellow candles, and by fall, reddish brown cones fell like fat cigars on the floor of rust-colored needles beneath the broad branches. The younger pines had smooth, purplish gray bark, but the oldest one had furrowed gray bark and a trunk so big it required two or three of us to circle it with our arms.

Pine—strong and light and perfect for the ship masts of Europe's navies—was one of the golds Columbus discovered. Defiant, the first flag of the American revolutionary forces contained the silhouette of a white pine. Fifty years later, the St. Croix watershed became synonymous with pine, and the first Minnesota land secured after Fort Snelling by U.S. government treaties with the original people was the triangle between the St. Croix and Mississippi rivers in 1837. White pine built not only ships but houses and barns, roofs and floors, furniture and fences, from the Atlantic seaboard to the Pacific cities of Seattle and San Francisco. In Minnesota, four miles west of the St. Croix River, pine built the Marty house in 1897 and the Marty barn in 1902.

Farmers followed in the path of fallen pine forests by about twenty-five years, from New England to Minnesota, where the prairies and plains began. Where slash was left behind, fires followed too. In 1894,

Lizzie, Minnie, Sam, and John Marty were eleven, nine, six, and two when the Hinckley fire swept like a fireball twenty miles north of the Marty farm. Trains rushed from Rush City and Pine City to save fleeing people, and the sky turned dark with smoke.

A mile east of the Marty farm, even closer to the St. Croix River, white pines towered over hardwoods on the Anderson land that became part of our farm in 1970. Just a few pines made the eighty acres of woods dark and dense as a forest, full of deer and bears that made their way up Rock Creek from the St. Croix valley. Through pine shadows, Grampa Anderson's logging trail traced a wide circle.

Grampa Anderson himself was named after Clarence McKuen, a cook at a logging camp up north. It was McKuen who taught my Swedish great-grandfather the English he needed to get by as a lumber-jack in 1904—the winter before Grampa was born—felling pine and sledding it out of the forest to a frozen river, where after the thaw it would float to a St. Croix boom. A cook may have given Grampa his name, but logging gave him his nickname—Sawmill Anderson—on a landscape full of Swedes. The sawmills closed on the St. Croix River in 1914, but Grampa grew up to saw lumber as a micro-operator on his home place until he was eighty years old.

It was the pine trees in Grampa's woods that my brothers loved, that made it wild and dark, a sportsman's paradise.

It was the pine trees shading the old Marty house that I loved, that whooshed in the winds and breezes and lulled us to sleep in all sea-sons, that cooled us all summer as we lay on the swing inside the screen porch, that filled the air with sharp pungency as we slept with windows wide open on humid nights, that gave us green beauty all the bleak winter.

9

Wake

As he was leaving the temple, one of his disciples exclaimed, "Look, Master, what huge stones! What fine buildings!" Jesus said to him, "Not one stone will be left upon another. All will be thrown down. Learn a lesson from the fig tree. When its tender shoots appear and are breaking into leaf, you know that summer is near. And what I say to you, I say to everyone: Keep awake."

—Mark 13:1–2, 28, 37

There was a hard freeze on September 19, and then Indian summer. Uncle Gaylon was working on Clyde's corn harvest when the box-wagon of corn crushed him against the tractor tire on October 1. In an earlier time, he wouldn't have lived for a day, but in 1991 his trauma stretched into days and then weeks.

As the moon waxed and rose full at early nightfall, straight east from Uncle Gaylon's hospital room window, his lungs became infected and his heart began to fail. His kidneys and liver reached their limits and his skin turned yellow with jaundice. As his kidneys stopped responding to dialysis and shut down, he began to swell. He became enormous in the white bed, creases vanished from his face and neck and hands, and for the first time we saw him as if he'd been obese rather than small, thin, and muscular. Still I stroked his forehead, his black hair. Still the forehead, skin, and hair were familiar, the high bridge of his nose, the clear brown of his irises when his eyes flickered open.

The visitor rules loosened. In the halls and the waiting rooms and elevators, I met my brothers and parents, Auntie Lou, Jonathan and his wife Rachel, sometimes Carolyn. The Minnesota Twins were in the World Series, so we listened and watched on the waiting room TVs, relieved to be distracted, to have something else to think and talk about. Bruce and Mom were the ones who talked most when they came. Bruce sat by Uncle's bed and told him the scores and all the best plays.

When I visited alone, I sat by his bed and described the progression of the weather, the falling of leaves, the color of the sky, the dryness of the air. Sometimes I read psalms and he nodded. He remained bloated, toxins accumulating in his blood and tissues.

It was supernatural that he continued to live, even the medical staff began to say it.

They don't get many farmers anymore, I thought—entire lives lived without alcohol, without coffee, always in motion, tissue tough and taut.

The last Friday of October we were told he would not make it past the weekend, his liver and kidneys had stopped working entirely. It was almost a relief. The strain was showing on all of us and we didn't know how long trauma could go on before it turned us numb as well.

On Saturday, as nurses changed the feeder tube of medications on his IV, his vital signs plummeted on the electronic indicators, lines flattened, then returned, each time more faintly, like the echo of a whisper.

Sunday, medications were stopped, and only morphine dripped through the IV. A respirator breathed on his behalf, inflating his lungs each time like a sigh. Sterility was no longer required, chairs were moved into his room. We all found each other at the hospital. It would be a few hours.

For a long time Auntie sat by the bed holding his hand. A computer screen in the corner visually recorded his vital signs, which immediately dropped after the medicine stopped, but then leveled off at an impossibly low rate. Sunday night passed into Monday, then Tuesday.

Thursday, a Gulf air mass moved north and snow began to fall. It was Halloween and kids went trick-or-treating with winter jackets underneath their costumes.

In the darkness, snow thickened and accumulated, covering grass and gardens harvested and put to bed. A wind swept down from Canada in the night, and snow and wind became a blizzard. By the small hours of Friday, across the Midwest, transportation stopped. We were millions closed inside our separate houses, city and country. Only vital services continued, work shifts doubled and tripled, hospitals and homes were containers of heat and light in the half-light of day, a muffled world connected by airwaves, telephones, and prayer.

Auntie Lou and Carolyn were closed inside the hospital with staff that began second and third shifts.

In the path of the Halloween storm, life as everyone knew it stopped. All over Pine, Chisago, Hennepin, and Ramsey counties, in Minnesota homes encased in snow, in homes of relatives and friends from the Canadian border to Arizona, people thought of God. Those that knew Uncle Gaylon thought of him as they remembered him before the accident, thoughtful and serious, intense and laughing, farming and fishing and praying and singing. They thought of his beautiful tenor voice. They thought of him and prayed.

Snow beat against windows, white as the sheets in which he slept, a giant in bed for the first time in his life.

I lay at home in my own bed, facing the window and the swinging bare branches of our old tree. Day into night, I slept, hanging on to him, his image standing on the hayrack behind me in the sun.

A color slide: Autumn-colored flowers, asters and chrysanthemums in whites and golds and lavenders, and ghostly images transposed upon them. I make out Gramma first because of her glinting glasses, then me, a child in someone's arms, a man's arms — at first I think it's Uncle Gaylon because I recognize his high forehead, but then I realize it must be Grampa Marty. In this photograph, which is really two photographs, Grampa's forehead is made of flowers. Then I make out his eyes.

Then the image is gone.

"Double exposure," Mama says, "I should throw that out." She slips the next slide in, rotates the plate, returns the ghost slide to the pile. "I've got to organize these," she says.

In 1959, the year that photograph was taken, Grampa was dying. His symptoms were the same as those of his father's forty years before. Over a year, Grampa had lost his appetite, stopped eating all but the blandest foods, and to the dismay of my grandmother, had become even thinner. The doctor came out to the farm and named the thing my grandfather had known since not long after I was born. He wanted to die at home, and the doctor prepared to treat him accordingly.

On a Monday in May 1958, just before sunrise, my grandfather walked into the west end of the barn through the small door on the south side. The horses, Tom and Jerry, recognized his step. He dipped a can of feed for each of them and greeted them in German. The sounds of Daddy and Uncle milking on the other end of the barn, voices rising and falling in conversation, seemed far away across the quietness of what had been the threshing floor and the wide expanse of empty haymows above it. The broad timbers with their Y-beams stood like strong women holding wide baskets above their heads, flesh-colored in the cool darkness, waiting for the first crop of green hay.

Grampa let down the boards separating the horses from the threshing floor and tossed feed into their manger. Tom and Jerry lifted their giant heads and blew, smelling him, greeting his lined face and haunted eyes. He worked quietly, clenching his jaw against the pain in his gut, ignoring a cream-colored cat that brushed against the denim of his overalls in the dim light. He opened the door on the north corner and a shaft of pink light coming across the fields lit up the back wall behind the horses where the harnesses hung. With the metal scraper, he cleaned out the gutter, then lifted the black leather harnesses one at a time from their hooks and onto each horse. He had done this with Tom and Jerry nearly every day for ten years, with his team May and June before that, with every team on the farm since 1901, when he became tall enough to throw the straps over their huge necks. As a man, he remained small — all the Martys were small — he never got above five feet, nine inches.

Standing between the horses, he was embraced by their warmth, their quivering soft hides and flesh. He felt the hotness of tears easing out of his eyes. He cleared his throat and a needle of pain pulled him involuntarily forward. He pressed his forehead against Tom's brown belly and clutched the harness until the pain passed, then eased up. Slowly he placed the bits in their mouths and the bridles across their wide faces.

It was his favorite time of day. All his life he had risen before dawn, most of those years at four. Milking twice a day, twelve hours apart, he and Sam had done it nearly forty years, now his sons were doing it, though not quite as early. He wondered how it would go, how his sons would do left on their own at such young ages, twenty-four and twenty-one.

He led the horses one at a time out the door, down the slatted cement ramp with sharp clop-clops, and hitched their harnesses to the tongue of the hay wagon. The sun had come up and the barn cast a long shadow to the southwest, where he stood with the horses. It made the two white houses dazzle. The grass glittered. A couple of hogs squealed from the pig house and a chicken squawked outside the coop.

The dog Prince joined him, blinking in the sun. He readjusted the harnesses. The trees and lawn were just reaching their true green, the sky was a soft unearthly blue, and a pattern of clouds stretched like sheep's wool across the western sky. Beyond the pasture, Connie Muenzer's black-and-white youngstock grazed on the hillside leading up to a red barn.

Jerry patiently watched every move Grampa made, while Tom made grand gestures to get moving. *Jerry knew.* But it couldn't be helped, the horses needed to work, and the summer lay ahead. He hoisted himself onto the hayrack and flicked the reins, *Hü,* and they started out of the barnyard, under the oak tree over the driveway, up the hill past the old house, and then down again to the road. Daddy and Uncle slid open one of the big south doors of the barn, and Gramma came out of the house. She saw, under the shade of his wide-brimmed summer hat, that Grampa was crying.

In the other house, my mother held me up to the window, three months old, too little to wave bye-bye to the horses.

Grampa paused at the entrance to the road and then turned the horses right, beyond the windbreak of evergreens, west down the county line. They turned north on the next road, up the hill past Muenzers', where they could be seen again in the distance. They continued out of sight, a mile to the farm of a man named Friday, who'd agreed to buy the team and wagon for two hundred dollars.

Grampa Marty lived more than a year after the horses were gone. My mother's and father's visits with me became a welcome distraction, as I learned to smile and sit up and pronounce words and then toddle around the living room of the big house. I put my hands on the glass of the china cabinet and admired the figurines inside, and he coaxed Gramma to take them out for me.

In the heat of summer 1959, my grandfather gradually took to his chair in the northwest room of the house, where he could look out toward the barn. It was a beautiful barn, with fresh paint they put on last year, and he remembered the year it was built, a miracle in the summer he turned ten.

It had happened sooner than his father had planned — the house was built first, they'd lived in that only five years — but Jacob's cousin Fred by town had ordered a barn that he'd decided not to build. A better one for Fred's needs had become available. Could Jacob use the other? Yes, he would take it. The logs were sent to the Marty farm north of town and arrived on a hot day in July, a load of virgin timber from the St. Croix River valley, on a team of four matching Percherons, chestnut with white blazes. Four days later a team of builders descended on the farm.

It was the week of Grampa's birthday and, although birthdays were not generally celebrated in a big way, he thought of the barn as a gift.

Sam, who was fourteen, climbed up on the barn's frame and gave his mother, Susanna, fits of anxiety. Rushing around the house and preparing food with his sisters, Susanna exclaimed in German and pled with God to keep her men from harm. Sam became even more daring. One day Lizzie said, *Oh look, Mama!* Susanna glanced out from the kitchen window to see her son doing a handstand on the top beam of the sidewall, twenty feet off the ground.

It was a mighty thing, that barn, and he remembered standing inside it for the first time after the builders left, all quiet and smelling of fresh-cut wood, still like living trees, their bodies majestic above him.

Grampa remembered the barn filled with dancers and music the summer after it was built, after the wedding of his big sister Lizzie to Ed, one of the barn builders. The barn exploded with music and laughter and voices of neighbors and family. He climbed up in the haymow and looked down on all of them whirling—Lizzie laughing—

Lizzie! Elizabeth! What happened to you, dear, dear sister? You married a good man on a good farm in Cannon Falls, you were a good wife, so gentle and kind and hard working, you raised a daughter and son, became a widow, and just past fifty years old, you took your life. What could make you do it? Oh, Lizzie, Lizzie, your kind, dark eyes, closed forever—what demon led you to the garden shed and poisoned you, what kind of pain could have caused you to lift your hand against your own gentle self?

But the demon had come for him next, and, if not for Viola, he too might have succumbed. No, no — he didn't want to remember that—

He lifted his eyes again to the barn and returned to the day it was new and quiet. He was leading their four cows to their stanchions on the east end, leading the team of oxen and the buggy team into the west end. He remembered the smell of alfalfa and timothy and clover stuffed up to the rafters at the end of that first summer, bulging around the arms of the truss beams, and he remembered lying in the full mow, falling asleep in its warmth.

In his brown stuffed chair in the northwest room, he awakened from a boy's pang of hunger in the haymow — *It's suppertime!* — and cried out as much from grief as from the bite of the cancer devouring his guts.

"Oh Papa, Papa," Gramma said, trying to soothe him, wiping the sweat from the deep furrows of his forehead and the tears from his cheeks.

Through the hottest days of summer, Grampa lay in the northwest room. The doctor came. He prescribed morphine, which Uncle Gaylon administered in careful doses. The smell of food caused so much pain that my grandmother stopped cooking and ate meals prepared by my mother at our house next door.

That summer while my mother and grandmother planted and weeded and picked vegetables together in the garden west of the old house, my mother struggled to conceal morning sickness. In June, they shelled washtubs of peas, pickled little beets, and stemmed buckets of strawberries. In July, they snapped green beans, canned peaches and then pears. Then the tomatoes and sweet corn came ripe all at once and canning began in earnest.

My grandmother, distracted by my grandfather's illness and frustrated by arthritis and by working in a kitchen not her own, pushed to regain speed and quantity. My mother, standing in the steam, slipping skin after skin from beets that stained her hands purple, finally fled to the bathroom to vomit, her face burning.

After regaining her composure and returning to the kitchen, taking up the paring knife, she said to my grandmother, "I'm expecting again."

"Already!" my grandmother said, frowning, without looking up from her pot.

My mother brought me to visit Grampa and sat beside him in the room to watch me.

"I heard the news," he said to her and reached weakly for her hand, managing a smile. She put her hand on the arm of the chair and he patted it.

"It's good," he said, "it's good. This one will be a boy, I am sure of that."

My first memory is of the night Grampa Marty died. An image of night, like a dream—of night and a bright ceiling light that should not be on, things not as they should be. My mother is in the room, moving about, moving around me, circling. I am crying, but I don't know I'm crying until I stop—there is an echo off the goose-bump plaster and the hardwood floor when I stop. The room is silent as Mama pulls the heavy grey and pink drape aside and I strain to see outside. I am clutching something at chin-level, it must be the bar of the playpen, and I see past Mama's stomach.

Daddy has gone outside, and she is looking outside. She is upset. She cups her hand around her face against the window. In the glass, I see the reflection of my forehead.

My mother lets the drape fall back and I whimper. She walks across the room and turns off the light, a hard snap. Darkness. Relief.

She comes again to stand by the window, to pull back the drape. This time, I see out into the October night, across the yard, through the bare branches of trees. I see something red, bright red.

Is it Gramma's red sweater shining through the lit kitchen window of the big house?

I look at that red thing in the night and inhale with a shudder. A hiccup echoes in the room. My mother watches for a long time before she lets the drape fall back and turns to stroke my head.

When I was thirteen or fourteen I described this to Mama. Was it a dream or a memory? She looked at me strangely.

"Did Gramma tell you that?" she asked.

"No," I said.

"I had forgotten that night," she said, "but that's exactly how it was. I was upset because Daddy never came back and never called, and I didn't dare call over there, and you kept crying and crying. Then the ambulance came, but Grampa Marty had already died."

"Was *that* the red thing I saw—the light on the ambulance?"

She paused.

"Yes," she said. "The red light of the ambulance was on."

I can see now that during the years of my childhood, we were living in the wake of my grandfather, in the space he had shaped and given meaning, the youngest son of immigrants, bilingual, conservative, close to the land, the source of his life. He outlived his forward-looking older brother, raised two sons and secured the marriage of the youngest, secured a future. His whole life he farmed with horses. He loved them because they were beautiful and quiet—he could hear things while he worked in the fields, he could be close to the ground, part of the field. The sound of the horses coming—the clank of metal on wood, the rub and light slapping of leather—gave ground life and fowl time to scatter, to get out of the way.

Grampa didn't say this. He spoke very little, left the speaking to others. His humor was understated and surprising, a counterbalance to Sam's. He was the alternate, the spare son, the tiny child who recovered from pneumonia caught in the cold cabin while his mother milked cows, who survived a burst appendix as a half-grown boy. Most of his life, he followed Sam's lead. It was only after Mamie died, after Sam and Mamie's only son Harold left the farm at eighteen, that everything changed. When did they know Harold would never come back?

Grampa was thrust into the lead when Harold left, to marry and reproduce late in life, to safeguard the farm, this hard-won prize of his parents.

Cleaning the big house for Carolyn's high school graduation in 1989, Auntie had stuffed old things into Gramma Marty's tattered sewing trunk, an upholstered wood box with a matching cover and small wheels.

"I have a box for you to take back," she said to me as I drank coffee in Mom's kitchen.

"What's in it?" Mom asked.

"Junk," Auntie said, "nothing you'd want, but Gayla might." She turned to me. "Keep what you want and throw the rest."

I'd collected all the old things I could stand but I took Gramma's sewing trunk anyway. It was a month before I opened it.

Inside were Gramma's scrapbooks—news clippings, obituaries, one entire album of postcards and mementos from her winter in California after Grampa died, picture scrapbooks made by Effie for me. And there was my own first scrapbook, pasted into an old farm ledger over Gramma's handwriting. In the bottom of the trunk, I found albums of her snapshots and envelopes of family portraits.

In one album there was a photograph of Grampa sitting in a chair in a wide yard with a nurse and doctor behind him, Uncle Gaylon and

Daddy, still little boys, on either side of his chair. In ink in my grand-mother's hand is written: *July 1941 Coming home from the hospital.* It's Mounds Hospital in St. Paul.

"Daddy," I called him on the phone. "Daddy, I thought Grampa Marty was in the hospital at Moose Lake, when you were in your teens."

"He was."

"I found this picture from 1941 at Mounds Hospital."

There was a pause as he thought.

"He was there too. I hardly remember that."

"You mean, he was hospitalized twice."

"Yes . . . that's right, he was. The first time he got sick was the summer Sam built his house." He paused again. "I think that's why Mom hated the new house so much. She said it made Dad sick, because he had to do all the farmwork that summer."

In my head, I lined up dates. 1940: a second marriage and a new house for Sam, and Grampa and Gramma and their boys got the big house to themselves. 1941: Grampa was treated for a nervous break-down at Mounds Hospital, on the east side of St. Paul.

I looked at Daddy's round, four-year-old face in the photograph. Uncle Gaylon was seven and sober. Both boys were squinting, Daddy's mouth forced into a smile as if from the sun, or as if to keep from crying.

From that time on, nothing was the same. Uncle Sam's humor had departed from their house. They lived in the shadow and fear of sick-ness, that it could come again, and they followed their mother's cues. *Your father has been worrying about that. Now you mustn't make noise or you'll make Papa nervous. You better not, I can tell things are just too much right now.*

And then it came again, on that morning not long after Sam died in 1951, an October morning as Grampa walked in from milking, when halfway to the house he turned over the milk pail under the oak tree by the gas tank and sat down on its bottom, bewildered.

I wonder whether Uncle Gaylon recognized some form of Grampa's ill-ness inside himself, one of the days when he snapped and cried out. It came disguised, because his father had been silent. Maybe Uncle thought that if he cried out it wouldn't destroy him — the world, the wind, the ground, and the trees could absorb it, could drain it away from him. If he cried out to God like David or Jeremiah did, God would hear him and answer.

I wonder whether Daddy recognized it when he realized what it took inside him to bear up beneath it, to stay calm, his brother's keeper, to remain like a rock.

The silent demon that tormented Grampa burst out of Uncle Gaylon in a form none of us recognized. I had left the farm by the blazing summer day in 1977 when his rage escaped the confines of houses and barns in a way Daddy and the twins could not forget. Coming back from the field on a tractor, Jonathan had passed too close to the gas tank, clipped off the spigot, and braked to a halt as diesel fuel came pouring out on the ground. Jon scrambled down, shocked at the prospect of explosion. The twins saw it from our kitchen, where they were eating supper, and they ran out, yelling for help. Then Uncle came running out of his house in a torrent of words, fear and blame and scorn, flailing his arms and yelling words to set their ears on fire — *Unthinkable carelessness! Idiot! I can't believe it!* Daddy ran from the barn, where he was milking, imagining death or fatal injury, to see Uncle in a rage, Jonathan running with hands over his head, Auntie Lou holding open the door of her house.

Uncle ranted in circles as Daddy and the twins shut off the tractor, pulled off a shirt and stuffed it into the gap left by the broken spigot, and then ran to find barrels to store the diesel fuel. It happened in the middle of the yard, in the middle of the driveway, near the very spot where Daddy and Uncle remembered their own father sitting down helplessly on an overturned milk pail in 1951, in the glaring light of day, with witnesses from every direction. The story was told to me so vividly that I thought I had seen it myself from the kitchen window.

We thought of it as sin instead of sickness. But whatever it was, for the twins it had made the prospect of farming with Uncle Gaylon unbearable.

Sheltered from the howling blizzard inside the sealed envelope of the hospital's rhythm and ticking of monitors and the double and triple shifts through Friday, November 1, a new resident made the rounds. At Uncle's side he paused, disbelieving. He asked for charts, listened, and ordered new blood tests. One set of results showed liver function. He'd heard of a new drug at a conference in Toronto, but after more than four weeks, the chance of brain damage was overwhelming. The doctor talked to Auntie Lou, and she agreed. Dialysis was restarted, and the drug was ordered.

Maktoob: It is written on your forehead. The Arabic word I learned in Tunis haunted me.

Fatalism and free will, submission and strength.

Standing on Clyde's field that Tuesday in October under fleeting clouds, taken by surprise after years of despair, there was something inside Uncle Gaylon that would not submit to death after all, something, if not in his mind or soul, then in the rest of him, bone and muscle. Perhaps the image of a grandchild's eyes invoked it, or the red rectangle of a barn across the field, a bird's call or flash of wing, a breath of coolness from the shadow of a cloud or a warm shaft of passing sunlight. From his body, some force we called God surged and seized him, extracted him from between the teeth of rubber and metal, and propelled him up that rise of ground to call for help.

His tissue responded — that damaged tissue torn, but put back into place—quivering tissue remembered, answered, repeated a familiar pattern, cleansing, gathering, cleansing, discarding. Within hours his liver and kidneys began returning to their old ways, flushing poisons and fluids from his body.

As the storm calmed, an old moon appeared before dawn, hanging like a cup in the clear sky of black morning, east of the city, east of his room. In two days, Uncle's body returned to its own size, with no sign of stretching in his skin — it was perfectly elastic.

It was December before he regained consciousness, with Carolyn beside him. He remembered nothing of the accident, nothing of our visits. It was as if he'd slept through the falling leaves, the World Series, the blizzard, and the bitter onset of winter.

Maktoob: It is written on your forehead. What was written on my own forehead had not been visible to me, but now I knew a part of it — that I should see this, and write it down.

Cedar

The only cedar on our farm was really arborvitae — *tree of life* — the signature tree of cemeteries, one of the first American trees to be planted in Europe. It was nothing like the cedars of Lebanon mentioned in the Bible, which were used to build Solomon's temple. Ours was young and small and scrawny standing by the old pump outside the big house, with orange-brown scaly bark and flat, spiky, branching leaves. It was surrounded by a dirt patch in the grass because Auntie Lou's dogs always lay under it.

"Grampa Marty loved that tree," Mama said, "but Gramma hated it."

True cedar was known to me only in fragrant cedar chests, used to store winter clothing as well as precious mementos. Every family seemed to have one. Ours matched my parents' bedroom set, and Mama used it to keep our satin baby shoes, birth mementoes, and winter sweaters out of season.

Gramma Marty used her cedar chest to store keepsakes and Christmas ornaments, including her nativity set. There was also a cardboard blue box with a red-cross label. Because I wanted to be a nurse when I grew up, I thought one day she would let me use that box to play. But she never did.

One December when I was helping her take out the nativity set, I asked her about the blue box with the red cross.

"That's from when your grampa was sick," she said. "I'm saving that."

When she left the room, I opened the box and found plain surgical cotton. I lifted it to my face and smelled only cedar.

All my life, the smell of cedar has reminded me of the grandfather I can't remember but came to love because of how my grandmother preserved his memory in photographs, stories, and that box of cotton.

What Remains

Our auction was held in the spring, a week after Uncle came home. The auction bill was printed in green ink on cream-colored legal-sized paper.

Having sold our farm we are selling our farm equipment at a public auction located: 3 miles north of Rush City, Minnesota, on State Hwy. 361, then ¾ mile west on Chisago County Road 52 (540th Street). Watch for auction arrows.

Note: Be on time because there is very little miscellaneous items to sell. Saturday, April 4, 1992, Sale starting at 11:00 A.M. Lunch sold by Rock Creek Ramblers 4H Club. Marty Brothers Farm, Owners.

Tractors and farm machinery were listed down one column and a third of the next, followed by a section for the pickup and riding lawn mower, then a section for the corncrib, farm, and miscellaneous items.

Steve and his wife Gin and their two little boys were living on the farm, Mom was living in a condominium in Roseville near a new job with a humane boss, and Dad spent weekdays on the farm and weekends with Mom. But during the week before the auction, the rest of us appeared on various days to help prepare—to sort, clean machinery and park it in rows on the bare hayfield east of the house and the barns, and cook.

The morning of the auction was a hubbub, with Bruce and Blaine and their families in from Wisconsin, Jon and me and our families in from Minneapolis. Mom kept thinking of things to wash up and get out on the hayrack with the household items and furniture—pieces like the old orange-toned brass bed with the soldered bedposts, which had been mine, and Daddy and Uncle's bed before me, and who knows whose bed in the generation before them. Jeri and Gin tried to help Mom and watch their kids, especially Sam, who was two, and Blair and Elise, who were one, toddling around haphazardly.

The twins' boys climbed up on the machinery, pretending to drive tractors and the pickup, darting away from their dads and then back to pester them with questions. My four-year-old William followed Jeff and Nick for awhile, and then lost interest and went to the sandbox by the house to play with Sam and with Jon's boys, Jacob and Jeremy, in the yard. Rachel worked in the house with Auntie Lou. Bruce and Blaine and Steve stood around and drank coffee, talked with Jon, took over watching the little kids, and talked with Dad.

Dad talked to the auctioneer because Uncle wasn't strong enough to come outside. He kept getting nosebleeds—he'd had one that morning.

Early in the overcast morning when it was still quiet, when we heard the first robins in the yard and redwings out in the ditches and swamp, Claire and I walked around the farm. She was eight and liked old things. I showed her where things used to be.

"This foundation used to be the chicken coop, where Gramma Marty had her chickens, close to the house," I said. "It had windows on the south so the sun would shine in and keep the chickens warm.

"See that little hut with the curving roof? That's a dog house now. That used to be the brooder house, where Gramma kept the baby chicks as soon as they were hatched under a big heating lamp. But after the chickens were gone, my mom cleaned it out completely and painted it inside to be a playhouse for me. But it was way too cold in the winter, and too hot in the summer.

"This is the woodshed, here," I explained, "and back there, behind the lilac bush, that's the old outhouse they used, before they had plumbing."

Claire peered between the bushes to see, and drew her hand back from thorns.

"Wild roses," I said. "I cleared out all the weeds and planted mayflowers from the woods. I packed down the dirt and made this into my own secret garden to play in. Back there, that used to be the orchard—Susanna planted that." I went on, "We played under those pine trees. We made pretend campfires."

"Mom, Mom," Claire interrupted me finally, "this whole farm is a ruin."

I came across Claire later in Mom and Dad's metal garage. She'd found not only a bunch of brilliant-colored paints in tubes, but an easel and a huge tablet of paper. Now she intently drew pictures of houses of all sizes and colors — scarlet red like the wing of a blackbird, blue like the sky at dusk, metallic gold — all outlined in black with tall gables and black roofs. The whole garage smelled like oil paint.

"Can she do that?" I asked Mom, who hurried past carrying a plastic dish drainer.

"What?"

"Use those paints and that easel."

"Oh, sure, I guess so," she said. "If she wants that easel, we'll keep that."

"Aren't these paints something special?"

"I can't remember. I'm sure it's okay."

"It's okay, Mom," Claire assured me without looking up. She was drawing curving black lines, paths from house to house.

Pickups and cars began to arrive, parking east from the driveway along the gravel road. The gray sky separated and showed signs of blue.

"You want these?" Jon asked quietly, appearing from behind me. He held a bunch of black leather straps in his hand, cracking with age. "Harnesses from Grampa Marty's horses. Found them in the machine shed behind the barn."

I hesitated. "D'*you* want them?"

He shrugged. "Split 'em with you."

"Sure," I said. "Thanks."

I carried them to our car, and stowed them in the trunk.

Starting at ten o'clock, I was stationed by the garage to greet people I knew, direct them to the table where they registered for numbers or to coffee and lunch and the satellites. By eleven, the line of cars reached a quarter-mile toward the highway along both sides of the road. The auctioneer began with the household items at 11:05. The breeze was cool but the sun began to come out briefly, in intervals.

Most of our neighbors came and lots of people from Rock Creek — lots of old church friends and relatives and some Amish men, some people from Rush Lake, a few we didn't know. I made conversation with my friend Kathy's brothers, the husband of an old classmate recently separated, fathers of other classmates. As the afternoon wore on, Dad and Uncle's cousin Oliver told me his clearest memory of Grampa Marty and Uncle Sam—the best hog butchers around and a skillful and welcome team because Sam told such great stories and John came out with straight-faced and unexpected punch lines. Oliver was a boy then, five or six, and it was always cold when Sam and John came to butcher. Autumn nights had come to hard frost and his mother hung a cauldron on a frame in the backyard. The fire lit up the farm buildings and cast long shadows. It was like no other night. The kids stood around the fire to warm themselves and watch in morbid fascination, and then, with the first slice of side meat, ran into the house, where their mother had the skillet hot, ready to fry up that slice for all of them to taste, juicy inside and crisp outside, sweet and salty at once.

The weather held and so did the crowd. Bruce and Blaine and Jon, their boys, and Steve followed the knot of men and a few women up the rise toward the windmill as the auctioneer moved on to the big machinery. Piece by piece it went. Machinery for cutting, drying, and harvesting hay; machinery for all the stages of working with corn; machinery for tearing the ground, breaking it up, and smoothing it out; manure spreaders; and, last, the pickup and tractors.

Jeri came outside and told us Jon took Gaylon to the local hospital because his nose wouldn't stop bleeding. Later Gaylon came home and went straight to bed.

It never rained. By four o'clock, the sky was clear and most people had left, paying cash and taking their purchases: the tractors, the five-bottom plow, the drag and the twelve-foot disc, the four-row corn planter and cultivator, the hay mower, the five-bar side rake, the haybine, the Massey Ferguson hay baler, the Gehl chopper, the hay wagons, John Deere wagons, and Dakon gravity boxes. Barbed wire, wood and steel fence posts, rolls of wood-slatted snow fence, the 265-gallon fuel tank, the 1100-bushel round wire corncrib—nearly a building in itself—mounted on the back of a pickup and carried away.

The numbers looked okay, as good as Mom and Dad had hoped. Nobody could believe we got a thousand bucks for the '78 Chevy pickup. Mom and Dad sat back on the bench of the picnic table by the house and sighed in unison. Auntie Lou wrinkled her nose.

"Well I'm glad *that's* over," she said, and turned to go back to her house.

My first scrapbook was cloth and leather bound in black with a red title. On top of farm accounts, I pasted horses, birds, trees, children.

I lift the pasted cutouts and, beneath them, read the penciled columns written in Gramma Marty's hand.

> *January expenses 1945*
> *truck oil & gas .91*
> *telephone assessment 6.60*
> *overalls for John 2.41*
> *cattle tank 13.47*
> *salt & gas & feed ground 1.28*
> *bakery & ovaltine & groceries 5.36*
> *sulpher .60*
> *gas for truck .46*

These were piano lessons for Daddy, 8, and Uncle, 11, as well as galoshes, barn coats, and caps.

The next spring, I walked by the river with William on the channel side of Nicollet Island, showing him the red-winged blackbirds. The males had arrived, singing their hearts out in their hard trill, *o-konka-reeee*, claiming their territories in the high grass and reeds. I showed him how they opened their wings to expose red patches with a yellow border.

Agelaius phoeniceus — *Agelaius* for flock, *phoeniceus* for the red known in ancient times as Phoenician purple.

"There's one!" he pointed, "I see it!"

William had turned five and started kindergarten, cutting paper, painting, forming letters, unconsciously hearing rhythms, variations in pitch. In the morning when I woke, I always knew he was awake if I heard his humming. It carried from the farthest corner of the house.

"Their wings are like my jacket," he said, holding out his sleeves.

His jacket was the color of charcoal, with red shoulders and yellow bands around the sleeves. We smiled.

Every spring, I bend over the garden with Claire, teaching her to plant black-eyed Susans while I mark off rows for green beans. She waters, sprinkles dirt, tamps it down. She comes behind me, watering, pushing the row closed, tamping it down with the hoe.

She gathers green beans in August, snapping them open and eating them as she squats by the row.

On dark mornings through the months of fall and winter, I light a candle on the kitchen table, prepare cereal and milk for a daughter, son, and husband. We eat by candlelight.

Uncle Gaylon will live twelve years after his accident, with a succession of surgeries and medications, a failing heart, and a stroke that finally grips his mind, but not before he gives his testimony to all who will hear it, appears in the newspaper, and speaks with Auntie Lou for an interview on the radio.

It is another March. Uncle has been checked into the university hospitals for tests. He is familiar with hospitals now, having seen a lot of them, but nobody will visit him here because it's too hard to get to and find parking and too far to walk, Auntie thinks. He has been there two days, two blocks from my office, but overtaken by deadlines, I haven't stopped to see him.

Finally, a noon-hour half spent, I fly out the door with my coat open, jump curbs full of melted snow and chemicals, dodge icy spots and slush, stop in the gift shop for a flower, take the elevator up, worrying a little about what we will say, about the tension that always comes because of God and beliefs.

He sits in a bed by a window looking over the Mississippi River, reading his Bible, so frail, but his eyes are piercing and alive.

"Hi, Gayla!" he greets me. "Hello, hello! Hello!"

"Here you are," I reply, "with the best view in Minneapolis!"

"Yes, yes," he says, smiling, his voice raspy, "it's pretty nice."

"There's St. Mary's Hospital, or what used to be," I point across the river. "That's where Claire and William were born."

"That's right. My, my. What have you brought? A lily! Oh, you know I love lilies."

"I love lilies too, but they didn't have an orange one."

"No, not yet," he grins. "This is so nice, thank you." He takes it and places it on his rolling table, adjusting the vase. There is not a trace of the Jeremiah that once possessed him.

We talk about his tests—he is here mostly to find out why he can't gain weight. While I sit with him, a nutritionist comes in and talks to him about changes he needs to make—more carbohydrates, but no more fat.

When she leaves, he says, "The Lord has been good to me." He sits back against his pillows, tired, and closes his eyes. "I will bless the Lord at all times," he begins to recite, "his praise shall continually be in my mouth.

"My soul shall make her boast in the Lord: the humble shall hear thereof, and be glad.

"Oh magnify the Lord with me, and let us exalt his name together. I sought the Lord, and he heard me, and delivered me from all my fears."

Above the Mississippi, he recites to me a song, three-thousand years old, in an English translation three-hundred years old. Finally, the love of the Bible is what binds us closest together.

I think of that other psalm, *By the rivers of Babylon* . . . but now I know the reply. It is the reply of Jeremiah: *Thus saith the Lord of hosts unto all that are carried away, Build houses, and dwell in them, and plant gardens, and eat the fruit of them; take wives, and beget sons and daughters, that ye may be increased there, and not diminished.*

"This poor man cried," Uncle is saying, happily, "and the Lord heard him, and saved him out of all his troubles."

Sun glints on the body of the river, turning beneath us as it flows out of the forests and fields through the city.

Seek the welfare of the city where I have sent you, and pray for it, for in the peace thereof shall you have peace.

Uncle breathes deeply. His hands form fists.

"The Lord is nigh unto them . . . that are of a broken heart . . . and saveth such as be of a contrite spirit."

He opens his eyes now. He looks at me joyfully.

"Many are the afflictions of the righteous, but the Lord delivereth him out of them all. . . . He keepeth all his bones: *not one of them* is broken."

I still see him in sunlight, surrounded by a green field, fire lilies in the ditches, his face in the shade of the brim of his hat, light shirt, denim jeans, leather high-tops, gloves, swinging the hook out to catch the bale emerging from the hay baler, pulling it, dragging it back, pitching it up by the double strands of twine, off his knee, six bales high—exulting under the sky.

Then shall I fulfill my promise and bring you back to this place.

"The Lord redeemeth the soul of his servants, and none of them that trust in him shall be desolate!" he concludes with a flourish, a trembling nod.

In the silence after song — divine word — we sit together for another half-hour, as the sun tips over the zenith of the sky. It slants into his windowsill onto the waxy freckled petals of the lily, illuminating the powder of its stamens, the curve of its leaves.

He sleeps, and I walk back to my office slowly, noticing the damp, black bark of trees, the elms and oaks along the mall, looking up between the branches and bricks and glass, drinking in the blueness of the sky.

Acknowledgments

I am grateful to everyone, named and unnamed, who appears within this book. My gratitude goes especially to those connected to the Marty family history who remain in Rock Creek: you are roots that anchor the rest of us. Thank you to each one who has generously provided documents; consented to be interviewed; and heard, read, and corrected drafts — especially Margaret, Lorraine, Bruce, Blaine, Steve, Jon, Carolyn, Patrick, Claire, and William. My sawyer uncle, C. Duane Anderson, provided expertise on trees and lumber. Thanks to Duane and Judy, Doris Wolf, Arvid and Joyce Lofgren, Richard McAvoy, Oliver and Elaine Westman, Joy Bergfalk, Beverly Johnson, and the late Harold Hendrickson for their sleuthing, their fact-checking, their perspectives, and their stories.

Thanks beyond measure to my mother, who housed and fed me and set the fire every weekend through a cycle of seasons, and to my husband, Patrick Mavity, companion and challenger, who exemplifies the single-mindedness required to finish.

My father, Gordon Marty, gave me a love of history and respect for contemplation. His preparation for paradise deepened my perception of paradise around me. He was a companion for most of this journey, and I miss him every day.

The many generous friends, colleagues, teachers, and mentors who helped me include Kathleen Cleberg, Inge Steglitz, and Kathryn Swickard, whose questions and conversation sustained me; Sandra Mavity, who cheered me and backed me up at key times; Nadia Boudidah Falfoul and Esma Maamouri Ghrib in Tunisia; Hal Gold and Jon Klaverkamp; and, at the University of Minnesota, Roger Clemence, Martha Coventry, Gail Dubrow, Patricia Hampl, Imed Labidi, Josef Mestenhauser, Michael Kiesow Moore, Kathleen and Philip Sellew, Madelon Sprengnether, Charles Sugnet, Gayle Woodruff, the creative services group led by Steve Baker, and members of the Evergreen Writers group, especially Maggie and Pat, who were there from the beginning.

Thanks to Todd Orjala at the University of Minnesota Press for being a capable and dedicated champion of the trees. Thanks also to Margaret Yeakel-Twum at the Marjorie McNeely Conservatory at Como Park, and Katherine Allen at the Andersen Horticultural Library at the Minnesota Landscape Arboretum. Many staff members at the Minnesota Historical Society aided me over the years, and Jane Jewett at the Minnesota Institute for Sustainable Agriculture assisted me in researching documentation of the federal dairy buyout.

I am grateful for brief but essential residencies at Norcroft: A Writing Retreat for Women in Tofte, Minnesota, and at the Anderson Center in Red Wing, Minnesota. Bill Mavity and Jane Whiteside gave me a place to write at Lake Pepin. Mary Dobbins made possible a crucial return to Tunisia. The late Irene Steglitz gave me the woods at Eschringen.

The congregation of University Baptist Church (established as the abolitionist First Baptist Church of St. Anthony in 1850) provided the intellectual and spiritual space in which this story took shape. I am forever grateful for the preaching of the late Lee Freeman, who opened the Bible to me again; the wisdom of Pamela Carter Joern, who, as a seminary intern, counseled me through the dark night of my soul; and a community that cares about language, loves music, and testifies to the continuing revelation of God.

I have made every effort to leave an accurate record, sometimes navigating inconsistent memories. In a few cases I changed a name or details to preserve someone's privacy. I apologize for any instance in which I have mistaken details or inadvertently caused pain. This book owes its life and merits to so many; any errors or inadequacies that remain are my own.

Notes

Donald Culross Peattie's classic, *A Natural History of Trees of Eastern and Central North America*, first published in 1948 and reprinted many times before I discovered the 1991 edition, was an invaluable resource. Easton's Bible Dictionary helped to identify modern equivalents of trees in the Bible. A missing piece of the apple tree story was provided by Michael Pollan in *The Botany of Desire* (2000). Agnes Larson's seminal study *The White Pine Industry in Minnesota: A History* (1949; reprinted in 2007) was like a Rosetta stone for Pine County.

Redwings, a study by Robert W. Nero at the University of Wisconsin (1984), provided the language to describe these birds so familiar and beloved to me.

A source of information about the history of Rush City, Minnesota, was *Looking Back over One Hundred Years in Northern Chisago County* (1958) by Carl H. Sommer. The vast majority of information about the history of Rush City came from the *Rush City Post*, now archived at the Minnesota Historical Society.

Bible references come primarily from the King James Version. Some passages are adapted based on the 1974 parallel-translation Bible of World-Wide Publications.

The Carthaginian Mago's multivolume treatise on agriculture, mentioned in chapter 7, has vanished, but Arnold Toynbee explored the impact of Carthage on Rome in *Hannibal's Legacy* (1965), and there is new interest in the development of agriculture in the empires of the classical period. The ancient agricultural town of Dougga, which made a strong impression on me in 1980 and drew me back to see it again in 1994, is detailed in *Les Ruines de Dougga* by Claude Poinssot (1983). Dougga was designated a UNESCO World Heritage Site in 1997.

The statistics cited in chapter 8 are from "Participation in the Dairy Termination Program," by James J. Miller (1986), and from the paper

"What Impacts Have Past U.S.–Canadian Dairy Programs Had on Structure, Efficiency, and Trading Relationships? U.S. Analysis," by Bob Cropp and Hal Harris (1995). A comprehensive report of the federal dairy buyout of 1986, authorized by the Food Security Act of 1985, including its impact on land ownership, has not been made.

Douglas O. Wilson traced Thomas Jefferson's knowledge and esteem of Virgil in "The American 'Agricola': Jefferson's Agrarianism and the Classical Tradition," *South Atlantic Quarterly* 80, no. 3 (1981): 339–54. See also *Jefferson's Literary Commonplace Book,* edited by Douglas O. Wilson (1989). A clear description of the grid system for plotting U.S. townships and farms, and Jefferson's role in adapting it from the Roman system, appears in *America by Design,* by Spiro Kostof (1987).

Publication History

GAYLA MARTY works in communications at the University of Minnesota. She is active in the Land Stewardship Project's Farm Beginnings program and writes for liturgy and worship. She still walks the gravel roads in Pine County with her mother, who lives on a remaining portion of the family farm.